Contents

KT-116-814

Foreword: How to use this book

By the Dulnain near Carrbridge

Foreword: How to use this book

As much as possible via back-roads and on foot, this is a tour of the land about Inverness. It visits hills and moors and ancient cairns, duns, forts and castles, waterfalls and river-gorges, sea-cliffs and deserted beaches, forgotten hamlets, cloutie wells, symbol stones, drove trails and military roads. There are battle-sites and haunted places, tales of curse and kelpie, and old church settlements resonant with the names of Ninian, Columba and Duthac. *En route* we meet Macbeth, the Brahan and Petty Seers, Hugh Miller of Cromarty, Telford and Wade, Isobel Gowdie and the Witches of Auldearn, the Bonnie Earl of Moray and not-so-Bonnie Prince Charlie, also villains like the Wolf of Badenoch, the Old Fox of the '45, Aleister Crowley the 'Great Beast', and of course the world's most famous Monster.

Divided into four sections (south, west, north and east of Inverness as far as Carrbridge, Fort Augustus, Tomich, Glen Affric, Strathpeffer, Dingwall, Cromarty, Forres and Lochindorb) this itinerary doesn't have to be read consecutively, but can be taken in any order. For clarity and ease of cross-reference it is written in short chapters, each dealing with a specific route, walk, visit or subject. Frequent cross-references to related sites or subjects discussed elsewhere are inserted as bracketed numbers in **bold type** - i.e., (**45**) or (see **45**). These refer to chapter-numbers, not pages. A meeting with an old military road (as on the cover of this book) may cross-refer to the chapter on Wade's Military Roads (**15**); likewise Knockfarrel vitrified fort refers to its neighbours at Craig Phadrig (**5**) and Ord Hill (**51**), and so on.

Of 40-plus walks described or mentioned, some explore high or remote ground, but none are really strenuous, and there are no Munros. This tour is for folk who seek fresh air and discovery without risk of heart attack or broken neck. It is also for those who enjoy seeking out hidden places as well as better-known landscapes. Loch Ness and Glen Affric are here, but so too are the backlands of Strathnairn, Stratherrick, the Black Isle and Nairn.

As to access, Scotland has no law of trespass as such, but those owning or working the land may have a different view of things than folk seeking rural or wilderness recreation. Most people are reasonable, but a few can easily spoil it for others by leaving gates open, littering, failing to control their dog, and so on. So, please follow the country code and, though as far as I know walkers are welcome on all routes described, if in doubt ASK FIRST - especially during the stalking or shooting seasons. Many rely for a living on the land: it and they deserve respect.

Especially in remote areas, wear good boots, dress appropriately, take a piece to eat, and let someone know where you are going. The weather can change fast: a compass is always useful, and the $1^{1}/_{4}$ in.-1 mile (2cm-1km)

Ordnance Survey map is essential. The map references cited read from the top (eastings) first (e.g., in ref. 431405, '431' reads left-to-right from the top; '405' lower-to-higher from the side of the map).

The itinerary in this book has, since it first appeared, been expanded by the publication of two companion volumes, *Round Moray, Badenoch and Strathspey* (1999) and *Round Aberdeen, from Deeside to the Deveron* (2000).

Enough of the preamble. Now let's start, with Inverness itself.

Note: Few of the photos are captioned, as their position in the text should clearly identify their subject. However, where there's room for doubt, I have inserted at the appropriate point in the text (see photo) or (as shown opposite), etc.

As for the illustrations, the cover shows a Wade military road and bridge in use after the '45. On page 9 is a typical Highland scene; on page 45 is the ruin of Urquhart Castle, Loch Ness, as it might have been in the 18th century. The Moray Firth dolphins star on page 89; while page 127 shows folk visiting Cawdor Castle near Nairn. To round things off, on page 175 Urquhart Castle is depicted in a more modern setting. The back cover photo shows falls on the Leonach Burn near Dulsie Bridge (**96**).

Inverness & South

Inverness, Strathnairn, Strathdearn & Stratherrick

1. Introduction: The Lay of the Land *(Description)*

Long the hub and crossroads of the Highlands, strategically sited by the lowest crossing of the River Ness at the neck of the Moray Firth by the head of the Great Glen (**21**), never before did Inverness have the buzz it has now.

With its population almost doubled from 30,000 in 1961, with new housing sprouting on slopes above the old town founded on the flat east bank by the river's final run to the sea - thus the name 'Inverness' (*inbhir nis* or *nesta*, possibly 'mouth of the roaring one') - the 'Capital of the Highlands' (so Dr Johnson called it in 1773) projects a new confidence and exuberance.

Cultural, commercial and administrative centre of the Northwest, with Loch Ness and Culloden Battlefield (**7**) so close it is both a tourist magnet and transport bottleneck. Trains from London Euston terminate here, internal flights land at Dalcross Airport, and roads converge from all directions: the A9 from Perth; the A96 from Nairn and Aberdeen; the A82 from Fort William; and all routes from north and west.

Facing the Black Isle from the south side of the Kessock Narrows west of which the Moray Firth becomes the Beauly Firth, Inverness lies at the heart of a spectacular natural wilderness dominated by the Great Glen. Dividing Scotland in two, from Fort William and Loch Linnhe this vast fault runs arrow-straight 60 miles northeast, bringing with it Telford's 1822 Caledonian Canal. Linking Lochs Lochy and Oich with Fort Augustus and Loch Ness, north of the loch the canal is carried by the River Ness to weirs beyond which, for five miles, river and canal run side-by-side under wooded crags. Entering Inverness, the canal breaks north through western suburbs past Tomnahurich (**4**) and Craig Phadrig (**5**) to Muirtown Basin and the Beauly Firth. The now-broad river flows rapidly past Castle Hill, focus of the medieval burgh, under Ness Bridge then under Friars Bridge to South Kessock and the sea.

In summer this energetic burgh seethes with visitors. Along the pedestrianised chain-store High Street, where folk from Wick to Ullapool and Aviemore come to shop, fast food franchises compete with guitar-strumming buskers and tartan emporia. Men in kilts may be from Perth or Inverness, meaning Perth Australia, or Inverness California. If local, they're probably off to a wedding or in the tourist trade. For this is first and foremost a utilitarian town. Architecturally, the walk west from the Eastgate complex to the river via High Street and Bridge Street offers little to turn the head. The crenellated pink sandstone castle (rebuilt 1833-6 in the 'English Gothic Castellated' style) looms above the heavy Victorian Town House on Bridge Street. A few yards on past the Tourist Information Centre (01463-234353), either side of Ness Bridge spectacularly ugly local government concrete pill-boxes deface the otherwise lovely riverfront. The west bank, with St Andrew's Cathedral (1869) and Eden Court

Theatre, offers fine riverside walks (**3**), but the best way to see Inverness as a whole is from nearby slopes - from Upper Leachkin by Craig Phadrig to the west (as in the photo below); or from above the Old Edinburgh Road to the south, or from the B9006 above Balloch to the east.

The main road-approaches are unflattering. The A9 from Perth descends under the B9006 and over the roundabout (685456) east of town, showing little. Crossing the Kessock Bridge from the north, this trunk route offers fine views west and east up the Beauly and Moray Firths, but then encounters the new football stadium and Longman Industrial Estate's sprawl of light industries and car showrooms. The A96 from Nairn (avoid it: take the B9006 where possible) runs in past Stoneyfield's new supermarket and the A9 roundabout via filling stations, 'travel lodges' and the Cameron barracks. Car-parks under and near the Eastgate shopping centre precede town centre one-way systems cunningly designed to ensure that visitors can never escape.

The A82 approach from Loch Ness under Dunain Hill past Torvean Golf Course and over the canal is more pleasant; as is the B862 from Beauly. Leaving the firth to wriggle over a railway bridge through the old fisher village of Clachnaharry, past Muirtown Basin it crosses Muirtown swing-bridge into Inverness via Telford Street, named after the canal's builder.

Northeast of Inverness the Great Glen fault continues via the Black Isle's coastal cliffs past the neck of the Cromarty Firth 30 miles to Tarbat Ness, where the sea cuts west into the Dornoch Firth. Further north, its continued line is implied by the angle of the coast to Wick and John O'Groats, and some trace it to Spitzbergen - a bit further than this tour takes us.

2.   Inverness: Castles & Kings *(Description, History)*

Folk were here long ago. 7500 years ago mesolithic (Middle Stone Age) hunter-gatherers camped on a site now under the A96 by Stoneyfield. By 3000BC neolithic (New Stone Age) farmers were building elaborate burial-cairns of high-ground Orkney-Cromarty or low-ground Clava type (**8**) throughout the area. This megalithic ('big stone') culture prospered until *c*.1500BC the climate began to fail. For a long time thereafter few folk were about. Then, *c*.700BC, suggesting hard times and hard men, the first stone *duns* and hill-forts were built, many round Inverness. Christian missionaries were active after *c*.AD400, and in 565 St Columba visited the Pictish King Brude at his stone fort here, probably Craig Phadrig (**5**).

Macbeth (**86**), the *mormaer* (steward) of Moray, then a land from the Spey to the west coast, may also have had a fort here. Slain by Malcolm Canmore in 1057, later maligned not only by Shakespeare but by Scots chroniclers like Hector Boece, he was the last Celtic King of Scots. After he died, Moray folk kept resisting the Canmore kings, which may be why he came to be maligned. Despite local tradition that his castle was near Auldcastle Road, a more likely site is the obvious one: Castle Hill, guarding the crossing of the Ness.

Determined to impose feudalism, David I (1124-53) established Inverness as a royal burgh, planting it with lowland traders and craftsmen. He also forti-fied (or refortified) Castle Hill, probably as a motte-and-bailey with wooden buildings - the mound below the present Castle may be partly artificial. With the river below it to the west and 'Doomsdale' (the route to the town gibbet: now less-dramatically named Castle Street) below to the east, it dominated a small place that hardly grew until the 18th century. Yet Inverness had its share of trou-bles. Recaptured from the English during the Wars of Independence, the castle was destroyed by Robert the Bruce. Was it immediately rebuilt? Probably not, for in 1411, *en route* to the Battle of Harlaw to press his claim to the Earldom of Ross, Donald Lord of the Isles sacked and burned most of the town, his quar-rel being that Lord Lovat, chief of the locally-powerful Frasers (**36**) and many local folk denied his cause. His attack was resisted from the bridge, 'the famous-est and finest off oak in Brittain', which was also burned. A year later - bolting the stable door, etc. - Alexander of Mar erected stone fortifications

In 1508 King James IV (in 1513 slain at Flodden) ordered the Earl of Huntly to add to these a strong stone tower 'upon vaults of stone'. Huntly, who thought himself above the law, ignored the order; yet in time the additions were made. In 1562 another Gordon, Alexander, was in command when Mary Queen of Scots demanded entry to the castle. Denied, she took it with the help of local Frasers and Mackintoshes, and Alexander Gordon was hanged.

Amid the Civil War in April 1646 the Royalist James Graham, Marquis of Montrose, unsuccessfully besieged the burgh, setting up his guns under a hawthorn tree atop the 'old castlehill'. Meanwhile his army sacked the Fraser lands of the Aird and Strathglass so that: 'there was not left...a sheep to bleet, or a cock to crow day...' As in 1411, the quarrel was again with a Fraser refusal to co-operate. Despite Montrose's bloodily brilliant successes (as at Auldearn: see **86**) the clan supported the Covenant. But they (and Inverness) had the last laugh. Four years later the captive Montrose was marched through the town on his way to execution in Edinburgh, and: 'All the way through the streets he never lowered his aspect'.

In 1655, during the Commonwealth, 'Cromwell's Fort' was built, but its career was short-lived. After the Restoration, in 1662 it was demolished amid: 'demonstrations of joy and gladnes'. Much of its stone went into a new bridge built over the Ness in 1685. Nothing of it remains now but a reconstructed clock tower.

After the 1715 Jacobite rebellion ended in Inverness with the surrender of Glengarry and Keppoch to General Cadogan, in 1726 the military road-builder General George Wade (**15**) enlarged the castle, naming it Fort George after the king. His roads and bridges have lasted better than his castles. Fort Augustus, built in 1730 at the south end of Loch Ness, held out just two days when besieged in 1746; 'Fort George' (not to be confused with the surviving fort at Ardersier: see **75**) fared little better. The gravel hill under it nearly collapsed before it was finished, then in February 1746 one of Prince Charlie's French engineers blew it up. Killing himself in the explosion, the hapless man also managed to blow his dog across the river. Incredibly, the dog survived, though minus its tail.

Two months later, within hours of the Battle of Culloden (**7**), Cumberland's blood-crazed redcoats fell on Inverness, and a time of terror began throughout the Highlands. Yet Inverness didn't do so badly. Visiting in 1767, the Welshman Thomas Pennant found a 'large and well-built' town of some 11,000 people. His *A Tour in Scotland* (1769) suggests a local economy recovering after the Jacobite disaster. Charmed by the view from 'old Fort St. George' and climbing Tomnahurich (**4**), he notes the price of beef (2d.-4d. per 22-ounce pound-weight), eggs (7 a penny) and other commodities, and mentions the 1400 volumes in the Church Street hospital library.

Hard on his heels came Boswell and Johnson. For three days late in August 1773 they stayed in Mackenzie's inn where, Boswell writes crossly: 'Dr Johnson expatiated rather too strongly upon the benefits derived to Scotland from the Union, and the bad state of our people before it...I therefore diverted the subject.' As well he might.

The local *Statistical Account* of 1791, written by Inverness ministers, has it that: 'In the year 1746, the town began to revive, and [since] has been in a rapid progress of improvement'. Factors involved include: 'money circulated by the army after the suppression of the rebellion in the year 1746'. Detailing thriving industries including hemp manufacture, employing over a thousand people, and the employment of nearly 10,000 Highland folk in 'heckling, spinning, twisting, bleaching and dyeing' of thread from flax imported from the Baltic (average weekly wage 1s. 6d. to 2s. - 15-20p.), they also mention four whisky stills and 12 brewers of ale in the town, and some 70 'retailers of ale and spirituous liquors'.

As to the 80 folk that year held in the Inverness Tolbooth, 30 were horsethieves, 17 debtors and eight petty thieves. Five men of Campbelltown (Ardersier: see **74**) had broken the peace, and two women 'of bad fame' were guilty of 'irregularities and misdemeanours'.

Yet, with revolution first in America then France, and dissent increasing along with the price of grain, riots erupted in Inverness as elsewhere. Privileged folk were well-fed and clad; ordinary folk were not. In the 1730s, English military road-builder Captain Edmund Burt had spoken of Inverness folk: 'in the dirt or in snow...without stockings and shoes...in the hardest of the seasons...'; of: '...a man dragging along a half-starved horse little bigger than an ass...', and of children: '...whose wretched food makes them look pot-bellied; they are seldom washed...boys have nothing but a coarse kind of vest buttoned down the back...girls have a piece of blanket wrapped about their shoulders...'. For many, starvation was never far away, but the riots of the 1790s were the last serious disturbances. Conditions improved. The start of work on the Caledonian Canal in 1804 provided employment, and in 1855 the railway arrived. Soon, with Inverness the northern terminus for London trains, and with lines west to Kyle and north to Caithness, the era of popular tourism began.

As an Inverness icon, the Castle gave way to the Clachnacuddin, the 'Stone of the Tubs', where washerwomen once paused on their way to and fro the river. Now sited by the Mercat Cross outside the Town House, it gave its name to one of the town's two Highland League football teams. These are now merged into one, with a new stadium just east of the A9 and the Longman Industrial Estate. By the Kessock Bridge, the stadium is on low firthside ground where, under 200 years ago, huge crowds turned out to enjoy public executions. Maybe football is preferable.

Today, facing St Andrew's Cathedral and Eden Court Theatre over the river from its knoll above the east bank, the 19th-century castle is the Sheriff Court House.

And west of the river is the Caledonian Canal.

3.   Inverness: Riverbank & Caledonian Canal *(History, Walks)*

Short in course, but potent in spate, the river is the main focus of Inverness. North of Ness Bridge, a Victorian suspension footbridge crosses to the west bank near Balnain House folk music centre (40 Huntly Street, 01463-715757). Starting south with a fine view east of church spires and castle, cross Young Street by Ness Bridge onto Ness Walk. Past St Andrew's Cathedral, Eden Court Theatre, and a second footbridge, Edwardian footbridges link the wooded Ness Islands to Ladies Walk on the east bank. Continuing south, the west bank path passes the Boating Pond and playing fields to a near-junction with the Caledonian Canal. Here (see below) canalbank and riverside paths converge to continue south three miles to Dochgarroch Lock.

The son of a Dumfriesshire shepherd, Thomas Telford (1757-1834) built so many roads, churches, bridges and harbours it's safe to assume he never slept - or maybe there were three of him. Though never a commercial success, the canal was his greatest project. Connecting the Moray Firth via Loch Linnhe with the Inner Hebridean sea, and completed in 1822, it made unnecessary the perilous northern sea-route round Cape Wrath. Begun during the Napoleonic War, it brought the Industrial Revolution (and much-needed work) to north Scotland. Raising the level of Loch Ness nine feet, the great work - the 22 miles of actual canal connect the lochs of Dochfour, Ness, Oich and Lochy - seemingly fulfilled a prophecy attributed to the famed local prophet, the Brahan Seer (**57**):

Strange as it may seem to you, the day will come, and it is not far off, when full-rigged ships will be seen sailing eastward and west by the back of Tomnahurich Hill.

15

If rarely full-rigged, many craft still using the canal are under sail. Yachts and cabin cruisers predominate, though many fishermen prefer it to the Cape Wrath route. Described in 1958 as a 'social service', it is maintained as such, remaining in public ownership.

From Muirtown Basin, where ships enter the canal through the 1822 swing-bridge, there is a five-mile walk south, first by the canal, then between canal and river to Dochgarroch Lock (619415). Via the canal's east bank and after the first four locks (out of 28) the path runs under Tomnahurich Hill to Tomnahurich swing-bridge (carrying the A82 Loch Ness-Fort William road), south of which the canal all but joins the river. The path follows a narrow, wooded strip of land between them. Just before they do converge at weirs by Loch Dochfour, Dochgarroch Lock (619415) allows access to the canal's north bank.

Nearby at Dunaincroy in 1825 the canal sprung a massive leak. Telford stoppered it by lining almost 600 yards of the bed and sides with clay-puddled woollen cloth, then planted whin to hold this vital bandage. This imaginative solution remains sound.

The way back, via path and minor road, starts from the canalside camping-ground by the A82 under Dochgarroch House and Battlefield. Leaving the canal to cut behind Dunain Park Hotel, on rejoining the waterway it passes the site of St Bean's Church, said to be haunted by Lady Macbeth, and the remains of Torvean motehill (**23**). Returning to Inverness via Tomnahurich Bridge, where cruises (01463-233999) to Urquhart Castle (**26**) begin, for a second time it passes Tomnahurich Hill - the Hill of the Fairies.

4.　　　Tomnahurich: Fingal, Ossian & True Thomas *(History, Legend)*

In *A Tour in Scotland*, Thomas Pennant climbed this 'strange-shaped hill', describing it as 'of an oblong form, broad at the base, and sloping on all sides towards the top; so that it looks like a ship with its keep upwards'. He added: 'It is perfectly detached from any other hill; and if it was not for its great size might pass for a work of art'. Reckoning its summit as 300 yards long, and not over 20 yards wide, he was not the first to be impressed. Tomnahurich's wooded 200-foot height has long hosted supernatural legend. Looming above the Fort William road, popularly known as the Hill of the Fairies, its name means Hillock of the Yew Trees (*Tom na h-iubraich*). It's said two itinerant fiddlers, Thomas and Farquhar, were lured here by the Fairy Queen to play for a night's dancing. In the morning they found the town oddly altered, its strangely-dressed folk laughing at them. The 'night' had lasted a century. Seeking refuge in a church, they crumbled into dust - a tale reminiscent of an ancient Irish myth about Oisin (Ossian), son of the hero Finn McCumhal (Fingal).

Discovering Tir na nOg, the Land of Eternal Youth, Oisin ruled it, yet longed to see Ireland again. His fairy bride, Niav of the Golden Hair, gave him a white horse, but warned him not to dismount when back on mortal shores. Returning, he found his castle in ruins, his folk long dead and gone. In shock, he pulled away his horse so hard it threw him to the ground and he crumbled to dust - but not before St Patrick recorded his tale.

Is it coincidence that Fingal and his warriors are said to sleep under Tomnahurich, awaiting the man who blows Fingal's great hunting-horn to awake them? And a similar tale is told of Thomas the Rhymer, True Thomas. Historically a Learmont of Ercildoune in Berwickshire, born c.1220 this prophet-poet allegedly got his magic powers from 'the queen of fair Elfland'. Niav again? When he dares to kiss her, she carries him away from 'living land' through 'mirk mirk night' to the Land of Faerie. Warned that: 'if you speak word in Elfyn land/Ye'll never get back to your ain countrie', on returning to the mortal world he finds 'seven years past and gane', though to him it had seemed; 'nought but the space of days three'. He too sleeps under Tomnahurich, sometimes awakening to emerge and buy horses for his warriors. When he has them all, the great king he prophesied will rise, the great battle will be fought, and: 'The lands of the north sall a' be free/And ae king rule owre kingdoms three'.

This ancient tale of the buried, sleeping hero awaiting recall in time of need is also told of Charlemagne, Frederick Barbarossa, and others. Tomnahurich offers a fascinating example of mythic cross-reference, of a tale imported to explain a site which does not look natural.

Less fantastic, for many years a popular local event involved annual horse-races round Tomnahurich. Banned during the Commonwealth, their resumption in 1661 on 24-25 May was a great event. Lord Lovat and the Earls of Moray and Seaforth were there: Lovat took the honours the first day, and on the second dead-heated with Baillie Fraser of Inverness, 'so that they cast lots, and Balife Fraser carried the cup and sword with approbation and applause'.

A prophecy attributed to the Brahan Seer runs: *The day will come when Tomnahurich will be under lock and key, with spirits secured within*. That day came with the first recorded burial on the site in 1846. Today, the cemetery is surrounded by a wrought-iron fence which, hopefully, secures the spirits and stops them straying too far.

5.   Craig Phadrig & Dunain Hill *(Route, Walks)*

The vanished stone walls of the Iron Age fort on Craig Phadrig, a wooded crag west of and above Inverness were once vitrified, fused by immense heat. Current wisdom has it that this resulted from timber-laced walls being fired accidentally or by enemy action. Firewood stored and wooden buildings propped against these walls, it is said, and especially in high winds, would when fired create heat intense enough to make stone melt and run like molten glass. Yet, given up to 50 vitrified sites in the region, this theory assumes (a) failure to learn from past mistakes; or (b) that the conquerors of such forts destroyed them rather than retain such well-chosen defensive sites for their own use. Were our ancestors such idiots? But if vitrification was deliberate, then why? A ritual way to 'decommission' a site? A way to create smooth hard defensive walls difficult for enemies to scale? I confess I have no idea; yet I discount the *X-Files* notion that they were heat-blasted by UFOs.

So to Craig Phadrig. 260 feet long by 90 wide above its lower ramparts, now no more than a mounded site amid mature forestry blocking the view over Inverness and the Beauly Firth, it was occupied from *c*.500BC, and was again in use after the 4th century AD, this time by the Picts (**66**).

From central Inverness it's reached via the A862 Beauly road over the canal. At the roundabout after the swing-bridge turn left up King Brude Road, then right up Leachkin Road towards the hospitals over a mini-roundabout, and right again up the Upper Leachkin/Blackpark road. The first of two car-parks is up on the right, opposite a white cottage. Here, on the south slope of the craggy, forested hill, is a sign: 'Craig Phadrig Forest Blue Walk 2.7km'. The second car-park, also opposite a lone house (cream, not white), is just up the brae.

From either start, various tracks climb to circle the forested hill-fort summit. None are steep, save for the final feet to the top, then only briefly. Up the east side the path passes the Giant's Chair, a natural stone throne. At the main trail's northwest point, before a turn down to Clachnaharry, is a fine viewpoint which, given the speed of growth of conifer forest below, will soon be viewless. As of 1998, Ord Hill (another vitrified site: see **51**) over the firth above Kessock Bridge leads the eye up the Black Isle shore to Chanonry Point (**68**) and Fort George (**75**). With Inverness immediately below to the east, to the west the Beauly Firth stretches away, Ben Wyvis dominating the northern horizon.

Returning to your car from the surviving grass-mounded walls of the old fort at the top, continue up the brae past the Upper Leachkin road (left) and the fork to Blackpark, downhill on the right. For the start of the old high road south to Glen Urquhart (**39**) keep on, not far, to a scrappy site on the right, by Heath View. A track starts past an old white caravan. This looks so unpromising you may bypass it to the top of the brae, where a track on the right below a modern lodge looks more likely. But soon this woodland track meets a fenced transmitter compound. The lower track is the way to go, via the high wooded ridge above the firth. In under a mile at 629441 it passes the Leachkin Chambered Cairn (Orkney-Cromarty type: see **8**), then follows the western flanks of Dunain Hill and Craig Leach via the spine of the Aird to the minor road at Blackfold (589407: see **30**). In between, with many wide views, numerous forestry trails traverse these heights west of Inverness.

### 6.	Above the Old Edinburgh Road *(Route, Walk)*

Also worth exploring is the moorland track climbing south from the Old Edinburgh Road. Beginning life in 1729 as a Wade military road (**15**), it can be reached from the roundabout by the Inshes Co-op superstore. Take the Old Perth Road past Raigmore Hospital to the roundabout (687445) and bear right (the road ahead is the B9006 to Culloden Muir) past the Co-op onto Sir Walter Scott Drive (B8082). This runs south one mile to a roundabout. Turn left onto Stevenson Road (a new housing estate), then immediately right and uphill for a mile, past the Glen Druidh Hotel and the turn-off right to Druidtemple Farm (a Clava-type passage grave nearby: 685420; see **8**). Beyond is a sign *Unsuitable for motor vehicles*. The road, suitable for motor vehicles, continues uphill to gates barring access save to walkers. A track to the east over the wide high moor is also barred to cars by well-placed rocks. From here the view over Inverness to the Black Isle and beyond is spectacular.

Start south up the rough narrow old military road between high-banked gorse-fringed drystane dykes. These at first block any view. Soon, greedy whin on scrubby moorland either side gives way to heather and gorse heath where Scots Pine regenerates naturally.

Parallel to the A9 this track climbs into Daviot Wood, on the ridge above Strathnairn. There are forest walks here, also Dun Davie (718393), a multi-walled stone fort on the 947ft. summit above a vast quarry. Below it, at the bypassed hamlet of Daviot a minor road breaks southwest from the A9 (724397) into Strathnairn. Offering fine views high above the Nairn's west bank *en route* towards Dunlichity (**13**), this road is crossed by the public footpath where the latter leaves Daviot Wood. Descending over the river, the footpath continues to the B851 - the main route southwest through Strathnairn (**12**).

7.   Culloden: Battle & Aftermath *(Route, History)*

Southeast of and above Inverness runs the broad 800ft.-high ridge of Drumossie Muir. Above the village and wood of Culloden, that part of Drumossie called Culloden Muir is a bleak flat heath. Over it the B9006 (first turn east from the southbound A9 to Perth, or from the Inshes roundabout: see above) curls past the site of the last pitched battle fought in Britain. Here, on 16 April 1746, a dreich grey day, Stuart hopes of regaining the British throne were destroyed.

To visit the battlefield and its memorials - the Keppoch Stone, the Gravestones of the Clans, the Well of the Dead - park at the National Trust museum and visitor centre with its audio-visual displays, exhibitions, cafe and shop (01463-790607: map ref. 745451). This lies by the battlefield, behind it the Leanach Cottage, a heather-thatched stone cottage of the time.

Annually some 120,000 pilgrims visit this Jacobite graveyard - twice as many as visit Bannockburn by Stirling, where on 23-24 June 1314 Robert the Bruce defeated the English, so for 400 years deciding who ruled Scotland. True, Bannockburn, surrounded by council estates, lacks what the Scottish Tourist Board calls 'the magic of the real' - but unlike Culloden it *was* a home win.

Yet Culloden was not really an England-Scotland fight. As many Scots fought for the government as for the Jacobites. In the Hanoverian army were Lowland Scots and Irish units, also Highlanders. Some were Campbells, eyed askance ever since the 1692 Massacre of Glencoe. Others had been pressed into service. There was no unanimity of belief about the Jacobite cause. Many Highland chiefs had rejected it, sensing a disaster in the making. They were right. After a campaign which had seen the Highlanders as far south as Derby in England, at Culloden 1200 (minimum estimate) starving, exhausted, ill-clad, poorly-armed clansmen were shot to pieces or bayoneted when dying.

The worst of battles, it presaged the end of the old clan society which, destroyed, was then sentimentalised. Prince Charles Edward Stuart's fatal presumption on behalf of his father (the 'Old Pretender') was punished by the army of William Duke of Cumberland, George II's brother. Public relief in the south was vast. With the War of the Austrian Succession raging in Europe, the prince had failed to take advantage of Hanoverian concerns elsewhere. Celebrating his 25th birthday the day before the battle, Cumberland was the hero of the hour. Handel composed 'See The Conquering Hero Comes' and a flower was named after him, Sweet William. But in Scotland 'The Butcher' gave his name to a weed, Stinkin' Billy.

Not-so-Bonnie Prince Charlie, who'd denied Lord George Murray's warning that this was no place to fight, fled the field. Rejecting those who'd died for him, relying on survivors who refused to betray him (despite a £30,000 reward: worth over a million at today's prices), for five months he hid in the wilderness. For a while he was helped by the 'Seven Men of Glenmoriston' (see **28**), rebels who hid him with them in a cave, Corriedhoga. Several times he was nearly caught. Once, with government troops closing in, he swapped clothes with young Roderick Mackenzie. Shot and dying as Charlie escaped, Mackenzie shouted: 'You have killed your Prince!' This fatal bravery took the heat off the hunt. The best-known episode (romanticised in Lady Nairne's 'Skye Boat Song'), occurred one June night. Disguising the fugitive as her Irish maid 'Betty Bourke', Flora Macdonald (born 1722 in South Uist), carried him in an open boat from Benbecula to Skye. On Skye 'Betty Bourke' nearly gave the game away, exposing hairy legs by holding his skirts too high when crossing a stream.

In September 1773 Flora, now mother of seven children, received Boswell and Johnson in her home at Kingsburgh, Skye. 'She is a little woman,' wrote Boswell, 'of a genteel appearance, and uncommonly mild and well-bred.' Her name, added Johnson, 'will be mentioned in history, and if courage and fidelity be virtues mentioned with honour.'

Less so, maybe, the name of Prince Charlie. On 20 September 1746 he boarded the French frigate *L'Heureux* at Loch nan Uamh in Lochaber. Swearing to return with a French army, he never set foot in Scotland again. In 1788 he died in Venice, a drunken wife-beater. Hardly a reliable role-model, yet still some romantics sing: 'Will ye no' come back again?'

The retribution was severe. Even as Charlie fled, the oppression began. Highland dress was prohibited; armed men could be killed on the spot; children heard speaking Gaelic were flogged. Later, in many districts the hardy Cheviot sheep (*caoraich mhor*, the 'Great Sheep') replaced the people in what became known as the Clearances (**43**). How many died on 'plague-ships' during emigration (forced or otherwise) remains obscure.

Of the battle, it's said Coinneach Odhar, the legendary 'Brahan Seer' (**57**), when many years earlier crossing the future battlefield, had exclaimed: *'Oh! Drumossie, thy bleak moor shall, ere many generations have passed away, be stained with the best blood of the Highlands. Glad am I that I shall not see that* *day, for it will be a fearful period; heads will be lopped off by the score, and no mercy will be shown or quarter given on either side.'*

8.   The Clava Cairns & their Builders *(Visit, History)*

Immediately east of the battlefield is a crossroads by Cumberland's Stone (749452), a huge boulder dumped long ago by retreating ice. Here a sign indicates the way to the Clava Cairns. Turn south downhill over the B851 to cross the River Nairn by Clava Lodge Hotel near the impressive Culloden Viaduct. Carrying the Inverness-Perth railway line over the Nairn valley and built of local Leanach sandstone in 1897 by Murdo Paterson, its 700-yard span and 29 arches catch the eye - at least, from below. Cross it in a train, and you'll hardly notice.

This elegant Victorian masterpiece overlooks an ancient site nearby. At the T-junction south of the river turn right to the car-park at Balnuaran of Clava (757444). Here, on flat ground, amid a glade of tall beech trees, are the three large old rubble cairns that give all Clava-type (as opposed to Orkney-Cromarty-type) cairns their name.

With many other standing stones and cairns nearby, each is circled by smaller and larger standing stones. Of two types, the middle one is a ring-cairn, its central cavity walled in, raised stone lines emanating like spokes from its kerbed perimeter to the outer circle. The other two are passage-graves. Orientated southwest (midwinter sunset?), a narrow low passage enters a circular inner chamber, the corbelled walls once roofed by a capstone. None are complete. A better example is at Corrimony (**40**); while the largest (also incomplete) ring-cairn is at Gask in Strathnairn (**13**). Found in the straths of Nairn, Ness, Beauly, Enrick and Spey, the 35 recognised Clava cairns differ from the Orkney-Cromarty type in that the latter (like the Carn Glas complex above Essich: **13**) are usually on high ground, lack the outer ring of monoliths, and have subdivided rectangular chambers within.

Both types - which came first is unclear; maybe they co-existed - were used as long ago as *c.*3500BC for collective burials by cremation and inhumation. The beliefs of their builders, neolithic farmers, remain speculative. Skulls retrieved from such tombs, communal until *c.*3000BC, suggest an oddly child-like folk with dainty, refined features: small turned-up noses, narrow faces, and rarely taller than 5'7". Their culture, enduring from before 3500BC to *c.*1500BC, seems to have been peaceful. Folk so skilled in working stone could easily have built stone forts, but none exist. From Orkney to southern England this culture was so well integrated that pottery-designs originating in the far north appear in the far south within a generation. The first folk to domesticate

animals, break land and burn old forest for farming, their society was coopera-
tive. Different groups, it may be, each had their own collective tomb; the labour
of the building requiring inter-tribal collaboration, feasts and gifts being given
to neighbourly helpers. Their concern with precise astronomical alignment and
orientation (as with megalithic circles like Callanish and Stenness) led to their
use of Pythagorean geometry two millennia before Pythagoras. Their works suggest belief in the migration of the souls of the dead to lunar or stellar regions.
Some tombs suggest ritual preparation for the soul-journey; the bodies of the
dead being dismembered. Skulls (the soul's container, maybe carried from elsewhere to seed a new site), and ceramic vessels are usually shattered. Animal
bones indicate food-offerings. Fires might be lit, the tomb being used as a cre-
matorium.

Another Clava mystery is that several stones have 'cup-and-ring' marks.
These consist of a hollowed 'cup' within a dotted 'ring' or series of concentric
circles. Spirals, lozenges, engravings of hands, feet and axes, and other symbols
and patterns (some like 'letters') also appear. Dated as early as 3240BC, most
are late second millennium BC, being associated with Bronze Age burial sites,
though also found on single menhirs and rock outcrops throughout the
Highlands. Their purpose? Professor Alexander Thom reckoned that the marks
have diameters in multiples of a unit he termed the 'megalithic inch', related to
the 'megalithic yard' of 2.72 feet he considered the basic unit used by neolithic
surveyors. Cup-and-ring marks have also been interpreted as star-maps, solar
symbols connected with a sky cult, and so on.

Might they have served the same function as *in memoriam* messages today carved on gravestones? What are gravestones but megaliths erected above the dead? Maybe they say: 'Here lies so-and-so, son of so-and-so and so-and-so. R.I.P.'

9.   Clava to Beinn Bhuidhe Mhór *(Walk)*

This great walk nearly got away. The OS map shows a track running three miles from a minor road a half-mile southeast of Clava up Beinn Bhuidhe Mhór (548m); and also, less reliably, a second track paralleling it most of the way, a few hundred yards to the west across a ravine. At first sight, from below, this bare brown slope looks unexciting. But appearances can be deceptive. All the way up it offers views that amaze. A clear sharp day shows not only every detail of Inverness, the Black Isle, and the ridge of Ben Wyvis beyond, but carries the eye southwest from the Cairngorms to Knoydart's Rough Bounds. To the west, Strathnairn and the Great Glen presage countless remote sharp ridges along the empty 100-mile horizon. Suilven is clear in the northwest, An Teallach south of it, and further east the Fannich peaks. From a slope east of Ben Wyvis silver windmills cast the eye far up the northeast coast to Caithness. Closer, the Moray Firth and its southern shore stretch east like a giant relief map. Fort George, the Culbin Forest, Burghead and Covesea Lighthouse by Lossiemouth all show themselves while, far east over intervening moors, the Knock south of Portsoy also displays its old bald thumb.

From Suilven to the Knock? Even as the crow flies, it's a long flight. The rub is that this walk is worthwhile only on a fine, far-sighted day. The view is everything.

You can walk it from Clava but, to avoid two long road-miles at start and finish, park higher up the brae. From Clava car-park, return towards the viaduct. Turn south (right) at the T-junction. The road doglegs left under the viaduct's vast piers, then climbs a steep brae to a wooded T-junction. Turn right past a cottage and the Finglack track on the left, over a bridge, and park in the layby on the right, up from the bridge.

Start south up the Finglack track (768445). Silver birch and whin give way to open heather heath and the first fine views. At a fork, with Finglack steading 200 yards left, break right on the obvious grassy track. This curves west then south uphill through a gate into a brief stretch of forestry. With pylons overhead and the burn's deep linn or ravine to the west, the good track continues up open heathery hillside, the view north demanding frequent backward looks. With the ravine deepening, the track winds past bleached pine stumps between heather-topped peat banks. A bankside layer of peat, then sandy gravel, then peat again demands interpretation by a geologist - not me! Occasional erratics - huge boulders dumped atop the heather - suggest the ancient noisy slow grind of retreating glaciers.

With the ravine shallowing to the west, a left fork leads east up Saddle Hill (376m: 787435). Keep right, curving west past a wooden hut near the head of the ravine, then south again, crossing the ravine as it diminishes. With the track steepening, at two rough little marker-cairns leave it for a path through short heather 200 yards to the summit trig point. Enjoy vast views from a nearby wind-sheltered hollow. On the A9 below to the west, down there in the other world, cars like tiny fast little metal beetles reflect the sun.

Fooled by short summit heather and by the map showing a track parallel to and west of the upward route, rather than descend the same way, and using the Black Isle's Munlochy Bay as a direction-marker, we aimed over rough ground for the top of the parallel track, shown on the OS map as starting at 773421 by a burn west of the ravine. Bad idea.

Floundering down over deep heather-hidden ditches then through boggy sinks, we found this track - sort of. Abandoned and overgrown with ankle-breaking hidden holes, it descends under pylons through forestry to a main forestry track. A right turn here past huge old dry-stane dykes past Drummore of Clava leads to the road, then right again back to the car. Not recommended. I prefer circular walks, but here suggest you return as you came. On this walk the view is everything; so why choose a return route so rough you see only your feet? - though the ravine is worth a side-trip. Less awesome than the Ailnack Gorge above Tomintoul, it matches that cut by the Riereach above Cawdor (**80**), or those of the Leonach and Rhilean Burns above the Findhorn at Dulsie (**96**).

On a clear day, this walk is a continuous visual feast. But be sure it's a clear day. On a dreich day, you'll end up wet, disgruntled and viewless. So check the forecast first.

10.   The Curse of Moy *(Route, History)*

Now to Moy, ancestral home of the Mackintoshes of Clan Chattan. From where you parked under Beinn Bhuidhe Mhor continue southwest beside the railway along Strathnairn's wooded south slope four miles to the Moy B9154 (junction: 730391), and turn left. This is a pretty back road.

Or, from below the Culloden battlefield, take the westbound B851 to Daviot via Strathnairn's broad wooded, farmed north slopes. At the A9 (723401) six miles southeast of Inverness, turn left. In scant yards the main road sweeps past elegant Daviot Church (1826) with its golden weathercock, and over the Nairn to the Moy B9154. Turn sharp left (719385).

The Moy road meanders pleasantly east then south past new bungalows and old cairns, hut circles and woods. Past Meallmore Lodge nursing home (748379: this 1861 ex-shooting-lodge once hosted Edward VII), and a pretty lochan to the left, the road joins the railway by a broad flat heath - thus 'Moy' (*magh*, plain). Here, north of Loch Moy nine miles from Inverness and east of the road, Moy Hall (1957: not open) is the chief residence of the Mackintoshes of Clan Chattan (Clan of the Wildcat, an old Highland confederation).

Moy's colourful history includes a family curse, a cursed bed, and feuds galore. One of the latter begun in 1424 when Comyns hanged Mackintoshes. The Mackintosh chief, Malcolm, raided Nairn Castle to kill Comyns. In reprisal the Comyns drove the Mackintoshes onto one of Loch Moy's two isles, then dammed the loch to raise the water-level and drown them. But by night a Mackintosh swam to the plank-dam, bored holes in it, plugged them, then with ropes pulled out all the plugs at once. Camped under the dam, the Comyns were swept away by the resulting flood.

A feud with the Grants led to the curse. With peace guaranteed by solemn oaths, the Mackintoshes broke their word by abducting Grant of Urquhart and a lesser Grant chief, Alva, betrothed to Grant's daughter. Forced to choose the death either of father or lover, the agonised young woman chose to save her lover. With both men hanged before her eyes she cursed Moy, predicting that never again would there be a direct heir. Scott's ballad has it that, when at last a male heir is born to Moy, an old hag reminds all present of the curse, then leaves before at dawn next day the infant dies. Yet the Curse seemingly lacked the power of the notorious Seaforth Doom (**57**). Brothers or nephews often inherited over the years, but sons succeeded fathers several times.

As for the cursed bed, the tale is that, around 1900, in the time of the 27th chief of Clan Chattan, among the guests at Moy were three old ladies. Noting that it was 19 years since all three had last been at Moy together, when 'that dreadful thing' happened, one told how, at the earlier party, she'd come down late to breakfast one morning. She'd apologised to her host, saying she'd rung repeatedly for her maid who'd not appeared, so that - horror! - she'd had to dress herself! The maid's locked door was forced and the girl found dead in bed, the imprint of a large body in the sheets beside her. At this the old housekeeper said this was the cursed bed, and should never have been used, for there was something very wrong with it. Usually kept in a lumber-room, with so many guests in the house it had been brought out and used. After this tragedy, the bed was taken out that very day and burned. So runs the tale.

A less eldritch story involves 'Colonel Anne', alias Lady Mackintosh, a fervent Jacobite who, on Sunday 16 February 1746, greeted the arrival at Moy of Prince Charlie. Learning of the Prince's whereabouts, Lord Loudon in

Inverness sent 1500 men to seize the Pretender. The government troops got as far as where now, amid forestry, the dual carriageway ends (or begins) at 745346. Amid a thunderstorm the Moy blacksmith Donald Frazer, posted there by 'Colonel Anne' with four other men, saw the redcoats crest the skyline. From behind different peatstacks they fired their muskets, yelling as if they were not just five but 500. Convinced amid the thunder and lightning that a regiment faced them, Loudon's men fled back to Inverness. Two days later the Jacobites took Inverness and Fort George was surrendered, to be blown up by the French engineer who killed himself and blew his dog over the river (see **2**).

At Moy on the first Friday and Saturday of August the Highland Field Sports Fair is held, and occasionally, on the Saturday, a full gathering and march-past of all the clans in the Clan Chattan confederation - the Mackintoshes, Macbeans, Farquharsons, Macphersons, Macgillivrays, Macphails, Davidsons, Shaws, Macqueens, and Macleans of Dochgarroch.

11.   The Findhorn east of Moy *(Route, Walk)*

Past Moy Hall and halfway along Loch Moy with its two isles (on one a 70ft.-high granite obelisk erected in 1824 in memory of Sir Aeneas Mackintosh; the other a crannog, or artificial isle, long used as a prison by Mackintosh chiefs), a left turn leads to Moy Parish Church (772342). With an early 19th-century watch-house to deter 'Resurrection Men' (profiteering grave-robbers), this plain building on its ancient lochside site dates from 1795.

Soon, now in Strathdearn, the B9154 rejoins the A9 north of Dalmagarry farmhouse (788323), once a King's House on the old military highway. These inns were built every ten miles or so as rest houses, with refreshment and a change of horses. Some 400 yards on past Dalmagarry, a left turn (790320) descends a wooded brae to a humpbacked bridge over the Funtack Burn at Milton of Moy. The little road continues up a broad open strath to where the burn meets the Findhorn (*fionneren*, the 'white water').

To my mind the region's (if not Scotland's) most spectacular river, this is not our last encounter with the furious stream. It's fairly placid here, but not further on at Dulsie (**96**), Relugas, or Sluie (**93**)

For a longer or shorter walk, park by Ruthven steading (*ruadh bheinn*, 'red mountain': 814331). Follow the road east into a bare, heathery glen above the river and a white-harled farmhouse. Unsurfaced beyond a gate with a sign asking you to shut it, under sprouting juniper the track descends to the river in its narrowing glen then, below silver birch and huge rocks, climbs high where the river bends north. Crossing flat heath under steep crags, ahead you see a vast, forbiddingly-bare scarp of scree plunge to the river.

With a bonny burn tumbling from the left, descend to the ruined steading and 'rope-bridge' at Shenachie (827348). Posted warnings about using this scary contraption - a wooden box with trolley-wheels atop two parallel hawsers: you crank it high over the river to the east bank - are redundant: we found the box padlocked and the crank removed. Maybe just as well, but it stopped us in our tracks. The east bank track continues three miles past Ballachrochin and Quilichan to a ford, then returns to the west bank before Drynachan Lodge (864396: see **81**). At Ruthven I heard of a difficult path along the steep scarp ahead, but saw no sign of it. Incidentally, this empty area is part of the vast Cawdor Estate. The tiny county of Nairn contains 104,252 acres: of these 49,400, mostly bleak grouse moor, are Cawdor land. Also, of course, there's the Macbeth connection and Cawdor Castle itself (**79**).

From Shenachie, return as you came or, for a longer circular walk, break west up the bare heathery glen down which the burn tumbles to the Findhorn. At first we followed the burn's south side via sheep-paths up Tom na Slaite, to fine views above the burn's deep cut. With a dense belt of forestry ahead the going got messy. We crossed the burn to its heathery north bank: it may be better to follow this north bank to start with.

At the shallow head of this barren glen, keep right (north) of the burn to avoid the boggy flats ahead. Soon, with a ravine above right, on the bare slope ahead (west) you see the cut of an estate track. Where a fence crosses the burn, follow the fenceline briefly southwest (left), then northwest between two knolls over rough wet ground and up - thank God! - to the sandy, rutted track (816346). From here the left turn south leads gradually downhill a mile back to Ruthven through a glacier-gouged, bog-bottomed glen which, my notes tell me, 'is utterly without any redeeming aspect'. Maybe I was jaundiced by the freezing January gale and stinging rain. Still, this walk makes it awesomely clear just how barren these high moors are, so I include it, as the route from Ruthven to Shenachie is certainly pretty.

12. Strathdearn to Strathnairn via Glen Kyllachy *(Route)*

Next, from Tomatin Distillery two miles south of Dalmagarry on the A9 we head southwest up Streathdearn. But first I'll sketch the route on to Carrbridge (**99**), the last visit of this tour.

Past Tomatin and Murdo Paterson's railway viaduct over the Findhorn (lesser than his Culloden Viaduct, but still impressive) the A9 climbs southeast towards Aviemore over the Slochd ('Pit': 840252), a bare pass 1328ft. high and the northern boundary of Badenoch, 'the drowned place'. With the Cairngorms looming, the road descends to the edge of the vast flat Féith Mhor ('Big Moss').

To south and west bare Monadhliath ('Stony Moor') hills patrol a desolate horizon. The name of the highest, Cairn Mairg (3093ft.), means something like 'deplorable heap', which says it all. Soon (241876) the A938 turns east to Carrbridge, beyond which the Forres B9007 breaks north over moors so bleak they might as well be on the moon. Amid them, in a glacial trench, is Lochindorb (**97**), once lair of the Wolf of Badenoch (**98**).

Backtracking, from Dalmagarry head south and after a mile or so watch for a minor road on the right (794303) by Tomatin Distillery - Scotland's largest, with the biggest bonded warehouse, also with a visitor centre (01808-511444). Other than distillery advertising, nothing indicates where the road goes. Part of the old A9, it soon curls west under the Paterson viaduct through Tomatin ('hill of the juniper bushes') to the ugly 1926 concrete Bridge of Corrybrough (810292) over the Findhorn. The road beyond the bridge (near it the stumps of the 1833 span built after the original military bridge was washed away by the 1829 Muckle Spate: **94**) returns to the A9 near the Slochd summit.

By the bridge, turn right at the sign: 'Garbole 4 Coignafearn 10'.

Up a wooded brae southwest past Kyllachy House above the Findhorn's flat alluvial pastures, in three miles the single-track road passes Dalarossie Church (1790: 767243). Dedicated to St Fergus, Wick's 8th century patron, from its haugh by an open riverbend it is overlooked from the far bank by a ditched and banked earthen barrow - one of the few in North Scotland. This can be reached via a track over the bridge at Dalmigavie a mile upstream, beyond which the road ends at Coignafearn Lodge.

Past Dalarossie (photo below) and over the Kyllachy burn (756244), an even narrower road turns north up Glen Kyllachy. Signposted 'Farr 7', this old drove-trail (see **29**) soon recrosses the burn via a picturesque plank-bridge, then climbs steep through dense forestry to primeval moor high above the burn. With views west and north to Ben Wyvis, from a 1518ft. summit it descends into

Strathnairn past peaceful, rhododendron-rich Loch Farr. Beyond Farr House, it reaches the B851 at 679318 amid the scattered roadside community of Farr.

Leaving the A9 (718378) immediately south of the Nairn and the Moy turn-off, the B851 winds above the river past forested crags through Farr to more open, wilder land beyond Brin Rock (658294). Past turns to Dunlichity (**13**) and the Loch Ruthven RSPB sanctuary (**14**), it crosses the moorland watershed between Nairn and Farigaig, so leaving Strathnairn. Over the Farigaig, it sheds the Abersky road (607245), which loops north to the B862 via Ruthven Farm and Tom Buidhe (604274), a promontory mound above the crannog (see **28**) near Loch Ruthven's western shore.

A bare mile on and now in Stratherrick, the B851 is taken up by the B862 from Dores and Inverness. High above Inverfarigaig (**18**) and Foyers (**19**) beside Loch Ness, this route south continues through Errogie past Loch Mhor (**17**) and through Whitebridge to Fort Augustus (**28**).

To reach this junction the B851 has passed a hidden upland region of lochs, forests and crags high above Loch Ness. Many little roads crisscross this fascinating upland which, easily missed, is among the region's secret treasures. Sometimes called the 'Inverness Lake District', it demands more than a passing wave...

13.   Round Dunlichity & Loch Duntelchaig *(Routes, Walk)*

Ten miles south of Inverness, this six-mile circular walk starts from the old kirk at Dunlichity (660329). It follows quiet lochside lanes and an open forest track that climbs to wide views, west to the Affric hills, north to Ben Wyvis.

Between the A9 and Loch Ness three roads from Inverness enter this area. The B862 via Dores is explored soon (**16**). The other two, the B861 and the unnumbered Essich route, both approach Dunlichity (660329) from the north. A minor road leaving the B851 at Farr approaches from the east:

1) From Culduthel Road in Inverness the B861 climbs Drumossie Muir past Tomfad Cairn (678374: Orkney-Cromarty). Just before meeting the back road from Daviot (**6**) at Balnafoich, it passes Gask Cairn (679358). Dominated by a tall monolith and with an outer ring 126ft. wide (the largest area of any Clava-type cairns: **8**), it is clearly visible in a field east of the road, which south of Balnafoich crosses the river to join the B851 (690348). A right turn at Balnafoich leads past Tordarroch two miles to Dunlichity.

2) For the pretty Essich road, take the Dores B862 to the town limit. Turn left along Holm Road (650422) to a roundabout. Turn right, south. This (Wade's first, 1726 route: **15**) passes a right turn to Torbreck, also a plaque in the dyke to the left (657414) explaining why the Knocknagael Boar Stone (a Pictish symbol stone: **66**) now graces the Highland Council building in Inverness, where you can see it - the carving was fading. Up the brae at Essich (647396), at a fork turn left, southeast off the Wade road, up rough pasture to the 600ft. level. West of the road Carn Glas (Grey Cairn: 649381), the region's biggest neolithic burial mound, is not one cairn, but three, its tumbled stone above a bleak tarn serenaded by a lone juniper bush (see below) midway along its near-1000ft.-length. The views are fine, too. From here, Dunlichity is three miles south via forest and moor. Past Mains of Bunachton (656352) and south of Loch Bunachton, descend a steep wooded brae to a junction. Turn right. Park by the kirk.

3) From the B851 at Farr, the Dunlichity turn (684332) is between two houses, one blue-roofed, the other white-harled; the sign hidden when I was last there. Over a rocky heath past Tordarroch Cairn the road curls down past Tordarroch, the restored white-harled towerhouse home of the Shaws since the 15th century. Beyond the hump-backed bridge over the Nairn turn left (southwest) a mile, and park by the kirk.

The first church in this hidden vale was dedicated to St Finan, or Finian, alias 'Bald-Pate', a 6th-century Irishman possibly in Scotland before Columba. The present white-harled building (1569, rebuilt 1784) occupies a mossy-bouldered graveyard with walled enclosures containing Shaw, MacGillivray and other Clan Chattan headstones. With the remains of Drumbuie Mill over the tumbling Allt a'Chlachain nearby, this is an older, slower world. Yet the kirk watchhouse reminds how, 200 years ago, there was real risk of grave-robbery.

Start southwest on the dipping, winding road up a wooded valley to Loch a'Chlachain, with fine views over Strathnairn to the Monadhliaths. Crags tower over heather, bracken and wild rose. Beyond this lovely loch, the road climbs a saddle to Loch Duntelchaig, along with Loch Ashie source of the Inverness water supply. Passing a dead-end track (walkers welcome) over a bridge southwest to Letterchulin, the road follows the broad, placid loch's northeast bank through pleasant woodland. Soon, amid open pasture (and two 'clearance cairns'; piles of stone gathered prior to cultivation), the road climbs from the lochside to the Easterton track entry (633239: room to park nearby).

Turn right, up to the steading, then left through a wooden gate between steading and ruined buildings. At first faint, the mossy, maybe boggy path climbing the treeline with views over the loch is one of two shown on the map as leaving the steading: be sure to take the more easterly, with clear slopes on the right. The plantation is young (1998), not oppressive and, near the crest, the view back over Loch Duntelchaig and past the hidden Great Glen to the Glen Affric hills is superb. Over the crest, before meeting the northerly track with the bare slopes of Creig a'Chlachain (365m) above right, views open up north over pasture and moor to Ben Wyvis. Descending past Clachindrum (left), the track meets the Bunachton road, Loch Bunachton ahead. Turn right (south) and follow this road a wooded mile downhill past the brows of Creig a'Chlachain, and at the junction turn right a hundred yards to Dunlichity.

This is ideal cycling territory, and many other walks can be invented amid these quiet back roads.

14.   Loch Ashie & Loch Ruthven *(Routes)*

From Dunlichity the road just walked continues northwest past the Easterton track to Loch Ashie and the 1726 Wade road back to Essich. Beyond the Easterton turn-off, at a shallow moorland crest above Loch Ashie's southern verge, to the left of the road is Midtown. Here the farm-track south leads to West Town Cairn (621325), maybe once an Iron Age smelting-hearth. Just beyond, in forestry south of the road, is Buaile Chomhnard ('Fold of the Battle': 621332). Huge boulders surround a circular enclosure, perhaps used by drovers (see **29**) to pen cattle. A half-mile north, over the forestry fence left of the road where it swings by Loch Ashie, is Clach-na-Brataich (Banner Stone: 621343), connected with a phantom battle said to be visible after dawn on a May morning. Any connection with the phantom car said to haunt the moorland road to Essich from the crossroads just above?

At the crossroads (the lane opposite soon degenerates) this short loop connects with another, longer circuit via the Loch Ruthven RSPB sanctuary

(637281). For this, at the T-junction opposite Dunlichity Church turn southeast (Brin 2¼). The road crosses a boulder-studded moor west of the Nairn to the B851 under the fine crag of Brin Rock (658294). Turn right (southwest) over the river past the Grouse and Trout Hotel to a junction (651278) by East Croachy. Turn right a mile to the (signposted) Loch Ruthven RSPB sanctuary. In the lochside car-park an information board describes how, between April and August, you can meet the beautiful Slavonian grebe. First nesting in the UK in 1908, a quarter of Britain's 60 known pairs nest here. Red-throated diver, coot, tufted duck, goldeneye, mallard and teal are also resident. Buzzards and hen harriers often visit, and ospreys enjoy the fishing. There is a short trail, but you are discouraged from further exploration, as the grebes are touchy.

The lonely road continues west up a steep brae above the loch then descends to Loch Duntelchaig's southern shore. Here it joins the B862 under the sheer eastern crag of Tom Báilgearin. You may see crazed paragliders swooping free and high on thermals above the awful plunge. A right turn north leads in a mile to Ashie Moor and the Essich road (597315). Amid rough ground between road and loch is Lag na Cailliche (Witch's Hollow), with a haunted spring, Fuaran na Fuathasaich (Spectre Well). Who or what haunts it I know not, but the many hut-circles and cairns hereabouts can surely spare a spectre or two. By the road-junction is Dun Riabhachaidh (601316), a prominent, multi-walled hill-fort dated c.700BC, a grim-looking place that doesn't encourage any day-trips to 700BC.

Turning right (north) over Ashie Moor above Loch Ness (just a mile away but invisible in the Great Glen below), the straight road reaches the crossroads above Loch Ashie. Continuing over the allegedly-haunted moor to a fine view of Inverness below, it descends past Essich back to the modern world via the route Wade laid out nearly three centuries ago...

15. Wade's Military Roads *(History)*

It's hard to avoid the military roads built by General George Wade (1673-1748) and his successors, notably Major William Caulfeild - yes, Caulfeild is how it's spelt. Throughout the Central Highlands they and their bridges were built to link Hanoverian military outposts established after the first two Jacobite uprisings (1689, 1715). Made to aid the movement of troops, baggage and gun-trains through wild, formerly roadless terrain, they are named after Wade. In fact he oversaw about 250 miles of road and 40 bridges; his successor Caulfeild 1000 miles of road and 800 bridges. Yet Wade invented and masterminded the network, and created the major routes. These include the roads from Inverness to Dunkeld, Inverness to Fort Augustus, and the spectacular route over the Corrieyairick Pass, originally a drove-trail.

Descending to the south end of Loch Ness at Fort Augustus from above Loch Laggan, this 18-mile route is his masterpiece, with 13 (some say only 11) hair-raising hairpin-bends over a 2500ft. pass. Walk it (I haven't) to work out how many hairpins there are. You might also wish to invoke the phantom piper and other fearsome spectres said to haunt the route.

Planning and surveying these routes himself, Wade preferred fords to costly bridges (though not stinting when it came to the Tay Bridge at Aberfeldy) and, where possible, like the Romans, drove straight. The road-building soldiers got double-time, save on the many days when bad weather made work impossible, and they didn't get paid at all...

Grandson of a man whose Irish lands had in Cromwell's time been granted in lieu of pay, Wade had risen steadily through the ranks of the British Army. A proven soldier in the field, later an MP and intelligence agent, his time came when in 1724 the wily Simon 11th Lord Lovat (**36**) self-seekingly sought to raise Highland Companies to control Jacobitism. But nobody trusted the 'Old Fox', he'd already switched sides too often. Warned against him, King George I sent Wade north to: 'conduce to the quiet of his Majesty's faithful subjects'. Later stripping Lovat of his company for pocketing pay due to his men, Wade, now Commander-in-Chief North Britain, developed the strategy that made his name.

Arriving in Inverness in 1725, first he tried to drive a road south via Essich, but found it too circuitous. This route runs out just north of Errogie. In 1732, he tried again, getting as far as Foyers (**19**) along the lochside before the geography defeated him. At one section by Inverfarigaig - the Black Rock - over 2000 yards of conglomerate precipice dropping sheer into the loch had to be blasted. The miners dangled by ropes from the top while drilling charge-holes. Yet at Foyers he had to abandon the lochside and pursue the high road south through Stratherrick, now the B862.

Leaving Scotland in 1740 he became a privy councillor in 1742 and a year later was promoted to field-marshal. Dying in London with a fortune of £100,000 (he held shares in the lead and strontium mines at Strontian), he was buried in Westminster Abbey. Yet he lived long enough to see his work aid the final crushing of Highland society after the 1745 revolt.

In the 'British' National Anthem (in a verse now diplomatically ignored), the hope is expressed that Wade will: 'like a torrent rush, rebellious Scots to crush', and: 'confound their politics, frustrate their knavish tricks'. Though he seems to have been an easygoing man, some Scots may still feel ambivalent about him, his roads, and their purpose. Still, there they are, some reduced to overgrown tracks, others surfaced for modern traffic. So let's take one of the latter, to Torness and Errogie.

16.   Towards Torness *(Route, Walk)*

Following river and canal, from Inverness the B862 follows Wade's 1732 route southwest past several interesting sites. Holm Motte (653421), a 12th-century timber earthwork crowned by Scots Pine, its east ditch unusually deep, is east of the road above Holm Burn and just west of the start of the Essich road at the edge of the burgh. A little further on and also east of the road, Torbreck stone circle (645404) is the area's only free-standing megalithic circle.

A mile on between road and river is Borlum (623400), a private house on land once owned by the notorious Mackenzies of Borlum. One, 'who surpassed them all for fiendish ferocity', was the husband of Bessy Innes, alias 'The Witch of Borlum' - not a woman to cross. In 1618 Provost Junor of Inverness did just that, so she sent her two sons to kill him, which they did. The last laird, Edward, fled to France before the 1789 Revolution, leaving his illegitimate brother Alistair to hang for Edward's many crimes. This spectacularly nasty family was redeemed only by 'Old Borlum', Brigadier William Mackenzie (1662-1743), a staunch Jacobite whose life and adventures included an escape from Newgate to France.

Another mile on, east of the road amid rough ground, Kinchyle Cairn (621389) is a passage-grave visited by Boswell, though Johnson disdained it. Aldourie Castle (603376: not open), a Victorian pile built round an older tower, overlooks the north end of Loch Ness near Bona (**23**), where drovers from the

Aird forded the Ness before the canal raised the water-level. South of the castle, where the loch expands to its full width, the road reaches Dores, a village built about the inn, originally a King's House. Here the route forks.

Wade's lochside road (B852) continues south to Inverfarigaig. With deep black water one side and steep forested slope above all the way, this road for Nessie-spotters lacks variation or opportunity to escape it. Its virtues are twofold: scarce traffic and, after some miles, good views over the loch to Urquhart Castle (**26**).

More interestingly, from Dores the B862 climbs to Ashie Moor, taking up the 1726 Essich road by Dun Riabhachaidh and the Spectre Well (**14**). Rounding Loch Duntelchaig's southern end near the turn-off to Loch Ruthven, it continues under Tom Báilgearin (crazed paragliders, remember?) past narrow Loch Ceo-glas (*Keglish*) to a broad moor. With impressive conglomerate cliffs above, it crosses the bridge over the Farigaig at Torness.

The prominent knoll on the heathery slope rising left above the south end of Loch Ceo-glas is Tom na Croich (587281), a hanging hill used by the Lovat Frasers to ensure respect in Stratherrick. On the bank above the road under the pylons, a stone outcrop jutting from the heather is said to be two old women who watched so many hangings they turned to stone, leaving them as you see them now. A few yards on, north of Torness, a track (577279) breaks west and down to Inverfarigaig by Loch Ness. We'll return soon to this hair-raising route.

17.   Above Loch Mhor & the Farigaig *(Route or Cycle/Walk)*

Between Torness (580270) and Errogie there is a fine six-mile back-road circuit, easily missed. Full of charm, its only drawback for the walker (it's fine for cyclists or as a detour in the car) is that the stretch south of Torness follows the B862 for a mile before meeting a remnant of the 1726 military road.

You can start from Torness (two crofts), but for the walker a better start is from near Errogie, with finer views and greater choice. So from Torness drive southeast. Past the Abersky turn-off (**12**) the two-lane road narrows to single track where it enters forestry and turns south. After half-a-mile, a forestry track breaks right to rough open rising ground. This is not the Wade road, which is met a bit further on where, with the road swinging left, a gated, boggy track continues over the bare moor (582253). Taking up the Strathnairn B851 (580243), keep south a mile on the B862 past the driveway left to Farraline. Soon after, above Loch Mhor's northern lip, a minor road to Newlands, Carnoch and Croftdhu (567228), climbs right through birchwood, then breaks sharp left at the junction with a birch-fringed track continuing straight on - the other end of the 1726 Wade road.

The back road climbs on up a stone-dyked, beech-avenued brae to Carnoch (views back over Loch Mhor), then levels along a high open slope past Croftdhu (562240), fine views over Loch an Ordain in its woods below. Descending to a track down to unseen Loch a'Bhodaich and here turning north sharply, the road again climbs, now to a broad slope above the Farigaig, paralleling the minor Inverfarigaig road (**17**) on its high bank across the river. With crags ahead and about, both river and road meet at Torness, completing the circuit.

As for the B862, it continues south to Fort Augustus. Beyond the scattered hamlet (houses old and new) of Errogie and a road down to Inverfarigaig, it follows the reedy low west bank of Loch Mhor, a crannog drowned offshore. Plain Loch Mhor is really two lochs, Farraline and Garth, their level raised by the hydro board to guarantee water for the power station at Foyers (**19**). On the east bank Farraline's brief greenery soon gives way to the wilderness. Below the war memorial a mile southwest of Errogie, a road crosses the loch's reedy narrow central channel to a few lonely crofts on poor ground. It must be hard in winter here, but at least there's the diversion of the River E. Flowing into the loch's south end, its single-vowel name beats Galloway's double-vowel Ae, and so is Scotland's thriftiest name.

Above the memorial is Old Gorthleck House (548214), where the 'Old Fox' *(36)*, met Prince Charlie after Culloden. Charlie escaped, the Fox didn't. Yet as already he'd been getting away with it for 80 years, maybe few tears should be shed.

Past Lyne of Gorthleck and Lochgarthside, the B862 reclaims the B852 from Dores, Foyers and the lochside after the latter's steep, scenic climb alongside the tumbling River Foyers. Soon, amid bare rocky land the road crosses the Fechlin, an energetic tributary of the Foyers, close by the impressive 1732 military span (489153: photo on previous page) that gives Whitebridge its name. Here too, below Whitebridge Hotel (once a King's House: in winter you may find it open when all else is shut), emerges the public footpath from Foyers. After the left turn southeast (485148) that follows the Fechlin four miles to Loch Killin's rich pastures in the hills, the next right turn off the B862 leads to Knockie Lodge by Loch Knockie. Home first of Frasers and then of Grants, this old lodge is now a hotel.

For the last few miles to Fort Augustus the B862 enjoys broad high moor before starting down past lovely little Loch Tarff. Steepening, it plunges down a final brae to the south end of Loch Ness and Fort Augustus (**28**), where it meets the A82.

18.   Inverfarigaig & the Legend of Deirdre *(Route, Walks)*

Halfway down the east side of Loch Ness, the villages of Inverfarigaig and Foyers hide under steep wooded slopes. Foyers, really two villages, Upper and Lower, was once famed for its Falls, while Inverfarigaig is dominated by the awesome crag of Dun Dearduil.

Now for that road, or track, to Inverfarigaig from the B862 north of Torness. Signposted to Bochruben and Ballaggan, at the junction (577279) there is warning of steep gradients and sharp bends 4 miles ahead. Believe it!

The narrow road runs south under wooded crags above the Farigaig. Pylons march, potholes get worse. Beyond Balchuirn, gated farm-track takes over near the old burial ground of Cill mo Luaig, Moluag's Chapel (539251) and, above it, Caisteal Cruinn (Castle Kitchie: 538253), a circular stone dun. Neither are obvious as a breathtaking view opens up. Outlined ahead against the sudden flash of Loch Ness below and the ridge of Meallfuarvonie beyond is a huge crag. Crowned by the Iron Age hill-fort of Dun Dearduil (see opposite), it looms closer as the wooded river-gorge below to the left deepens. Amid screening silver birch opposite the crag's sheer face the grass-ridged road now drops via heart-stoppingly steep hairpins to Inverfarigaig. The surface is okay, but don't try it if unsure of your brakes.

This is the definitive approach to Loch Ness.

At the lochside (giving thanks for safe delivery and scenic revelation) turn left on the B852 through the hamlet to a bridge over the river where it meets the Allt Mor (Big Burn). Turn left up the Pass of Inverfarigaig (the Errogie road), then right into the car-park of the Faragaig Forest Exhibition Centre at Fasnagruig (522238). From here, with Dun Dearduil brooding above, forest trails depart east to Stratherrick, south to Boleskine and Foyers.

Waymarked forest walks can be dull but these, with huge specimen conifers introduced from North America a century ago, are wilder than most. Leaving the Exhibition Centre, a short climb leads, via a stepped path through silver birch and pine, to a Loch Ness viewpoint. This panorama, from Meallfuarvonie (2284ft.) to Urquhart Castle further north on the far shore, is exquisite. Other walks are described in the FC pamphlet, 'The Great Glen'.

As for Dun Dearduil, a path is said to start opposite the car-park over the Allt Mor, climbing steeply through twisted birch scrub to the fort. If so, it's not obvious, and the crag looks forbidding from almost any angle. Inaccessible from east and west, remains of its stone walls (in part vitrified) are scattered down the north and south faces. I'm told that slick and exposed grass slopes near the top may be treacherous.

Legend and its name link the fort with the tragic old tale of Deirdre and the Sons of Uisnech. It's said that during their Scottish exile they lived not only in Glen Etive but here too. The tale is that long ago, when King Conchobar (born the same day as Christ) ruled Ulster, the druid Cathbad foretold that the unborn daughter of Fedlimid, the royal harper, would wed a king but cause ruin and sorrow. Refusing demands for her death, meaning in time to marry her, the king had Deirdre (for it was she) secretly fostered. She grew in beauty, but to Conchobar's

fury eloped with raven-haired Naoise, son of the champion Uisnech. With Naoise's brothers Ainnlé and Ardan the lovers fled over the sea to Glen Etive in Alba (Scotland). Luring them back with false promises which Deirdre alone doubted, Conchobar had the brothers murdered and married her. For a year she never smiled, then cruelly he gave her to Eoghan, the killer of Naoise. 'Glen Etive,' she lamented before leaping from Eoghan's chariot and dashing out her brains on a rock, 'there I raised my first house; lovely is its wood.'

Continue east up the Pass under the crag's shattered slopes. At a junction by a bridge over the burn the road ahead climbs two miles to Errogie. Turn right (south) up the pleasant Grey Glen, Gleann Liath, gently uphill through forestry, past mossy boulders and a burn by the verge of this quiet, walkable back-road to Foyers. After a half-mile, at a bridge over the burn, a marked footpath departs east to Ault-na-goire and Stratherrick. Further on, where the glen widens, the forestry trail from Inverfarigaig joins the road; a second track takes off to Foyers, and from here you can also return to Inverfarigaig via Boleskine (**20**).

With the valley still widening, a huge green pipe erupts from the hillside. This carries water from Loch Mhor to and fro the hydro-electric power station at Foyers. By day the power station's turbines are fed by water falling from Loch Mhor; by night water is pumped back up the hill to the loch to maintain the water-supply.

Impressive, but less so than the once-famed Falls of Foyers were before, in 1896, heavy industry first reached this remote site.

19. The Falls of Foyers *(Visit, History, Walk)*

Where this road meets the riverside B852 climbing from the loch to the B862, turn right into Foyers, under crags past neat white cottages, then descend through dense forest. Soon a road turns sharp left down through the forestry to Lower Foyers.

Hidden on its lochside flat, white-harled council houses fronting the now-placid river's final run into the loch, here in 1896 the first hydro-electrically-powered electric reduction plant was built to produce aluminium. The original turbine and water-wheel remained in use until British Aluminium closed the plant in 1967. Now the hydro-electric power-station dominates Lower Foyers, abstracting water not only from Loch Mhor but also the River Foyers which, snaking down from the Fechlin and other streams high up in the Monadhliaths to the southeast, in its final mile or so plunges some 430 feet.

Visit casually today and you might not even know that the Falls exist, though once *Eas na Smuid*, the 'waterfall of the smoke', was Scotland's premier waterfall. If not, as claimed in 1832 by the *Scottish Tourist*, 'one of the highest cataracts in the world', it was awesome enough. 'The most magnificent cataract...in Britain', said one critic, adding: 'it is worth walking a thousand miles to behold for one hour the Falls of Foyers.' The poet Southey compared them to Switzerland's Reichenbach Falls, and even Dr Johnson was impressed: 'We came at last to a place where we could overlook the river,' he writes, 'and saw a channel torn, as it seems, through black piles of stones, by which the stream is obstructed and broken till it comes to a very deep descent, of such dreadful depth, that we were naturally inclined to turn aside our eyes.' And in his *Reminiscences* (1883), Telford's pupil Joseph Mitchell comments that: 'The scene is peculiarly wild and grand. You stand in an amphitheatre of rugged and perpendicular rocks fringed at the horizon with waving birch and all is still except the incessant roar of the descending water.'

There are (were) not one but two falls. The Upper Fall consists of three cataracts or leaps; the Lower Fall, the renowned one, occupies a natural amphitheatre, and is best seen from Green Point, or from the west bank immediately opposite it. Of the Upper Fall, it's said that, before Telford's Caledonian Canal made Foyers more accessible, the only bridge crossing the ravine facing the Upper Fall was a tree trunk over which, once, a drunk man scrambled. Revisiting the scene, he was so appalled by his drink-taken temerity that he had a heart attack and promptly dropped dead. This tale is also told of other waterfalls than Foyers, and was probably designed to impress tourists.

The proposal to set up an aluminium works, using the Hérault process to extract aluminium from alumina, though supported by powerful men like Lord Kelvin, caused strong opposition. 'Their scheme is the greatest outrage on Nature perpetrated this century', ran one furious letter in *The Times*, while a spokesman for the company insisted that the Falls would not be injured by the scheme, only there would be no water in them.

From Lower Foyers the footpath to Upper Foyers via the Falls starts up the hotel drive from the brae up to the B852. A second footpath leads three miles east to Whitebridge (**17**).

With Loch Ness at its deepest offshore, Foyers is one centre for investigation of the Loch Ness enigma (**27**). This is a wild place, the lochside between Foyers and Fort Augustus being the only stretch without a road along it. This lonely pebbled 10-mile shore under steep wooded slopes and scree-spills is for the adventurous. Burns spout steep from cliffs above amid contorted broken strata. The only landward access is from either end, or via a path down the gorge of the River Knockie.

From Foyers the B852 north to Inverfarigaig and Inverness passes Foyers Hotel and the site of the General's Hut (507220), used by Wade when building this road. Not far on, by the road above the loch, is Boleskine Burial Ground

(508223), site of the old parish church and said to be haunted by witches. Nearby Boleskine House (not open) is also haunted, by the memory of a notorious tenant - Aleister Crowley, the 'Great Beast 666'.

20.   Boleskine House & 'The Great Beast' *(History, Hearsay)*

In 1899, with spiritualism all the rage, discarnate Scots were (along with likewise-disembodied Red Indian chiefs and Tibetan lamas) popular with society mediums as 'spirit guides'. Attend a *séance*, and you'd hear from Red Cloud, Koot Hoomi, or Jock from Balnacraggan. This was partly due to the post-Clearances Highland romance first encouraged by worthies like King George IV, Sir Walter Scott, and Alasdair Ranaldson Macdonnell of Glengarry (**43**).

Not only mediums adopted tartan fakery. Two odd English occultists, affected by yet another 'Celtic Revival', got in on the act.

One was a scholarly eccentric, Samuel Liddell Mathers (1854-1918). Founding the influential Society of the Golden Dawn, he invented a fake Scots ancestry, styled himself 'Macgregor' Mathers, and wore the kilt. Did this aid his contacts with the invisible, immortal 'Secret Chiefs'? Nobody knows. Either way, he did no real harm.

Aleister Crowley (1875-1947), the 'Great Beast' aka the 'Wickedest Man in the World', was a different can of worms. Denounced as 'an unspeakable mad person' by Irish poet W B Yeats, expelled from Sicily by Mussolini due to his practice in 'sex-magick', he died a heroin addict after a life spent shocking (or trying to shock) folk. Born to strict Plymouth Brethren, perhaps his real aim was to shock his mother. She had early drummed it into him that he was as bad as the Great Beast of St John's Revelation. All his life he tried to prove Mama right. That in many ways he possessed genius, albeit wayward, only sharpens the irony. Skilled mountaineer, dubious poet, genuinely original in much of his thought, today he is remembered mostly for his hedonism and destruction of others.

Donning the kilt in 1899 a year after joining the Golden Dawn, young Crowley rented Boleskine House, styling himself 'Laird of Boleskine' - less ambitious than his later claim to be 'Messenger of the Lord of the Universe'. He was not merely imitating other southran *glitterati* who annually holidayed at fashionable Ness-side sites like Dhivach Lodge and Temple House at Drumnadrochit (**24**). Whatever Edward VII, Lily Langtry, Ellen Terry, J M Barrie and others got up to pales by comparison with the Beast's activities at Boleskine.

Claiming to be the reincarnation of Edward Kelley, scryer to the Elizabethan alchemist Dr John Dee (1527-1608), Crowley had obtained Dee's copy of a magical rite by a 15th-century magician, Abramelin the Mage. While performing this rite at Boleskine, it's said he conjured up 'shadowy shapes' that haunted the area for decades. It's said the lodgekeeper went mad and tried to kill his children, the coachman became a drunk, and a visiting clairvoyant took up prostitution. Meanwhile, the Society of Vigilance responded to his outraged letter complaining of conspicuous prostitution around Foyers. When their observer found no evidence, he told them it was conspicuous by its absence. So much for a Cambridge education. Soon bored with such minor mayhem, he abandoned both kilt and Abramelin, and decamped from Scotland to Mexico, to annoy folk there. Yet, charlatan or not, it seems he did leave a malign atmosphere at Boleskine. One respected later owner shot himself for no obvious reason, another got involved in a national scandal, and when the lead guitarist of a famous 1970s rock group bought Boleskine, he suffered a family tragedy.

In June 1969 two American students exploring Boleskine cemetery (haunted by witches, remember?) found a tapestry under a grave-slab. Embroidered with humped, worm-like creatures, it was wrapped round a conch shell. When blown, the conch produced a harsh braying note. Had some occultist, egged on by Crowley's ghost, tried to summon Nessie?

The Beast's well-documented life fits the loch's popular aura of dreich mystery. Given Crowley, Nessie, the local presence of mysterious big black cats (**41**), plus the curses of Moy, Brahan and other sites associated with the Brahan Seer (**57**), the area's many cloutie wells (**70**) and tales of kelpies, fairies, urisks, banshees, Green Ladies and so on, it really is odd that nobody yet has set up *Weird Tours*, its itinerary devoted to all of the above.

Now *there's* an idea...

21. The Great Glen & Loch Ness *(Description, Legend)*

Sinister to some, fascinating to others, Loch Ness occupies the northern end of the Great Glen. At least 700 million years old, this massive fracture of the Earth's surface - the most prominent in Britain - divides northwest Scotland from the rest of the land and is never really at rest. Hidden forces continually groan below ground, with 56 earthquakes locally recorded between 1768 and 1906. Still occurring, these are minor compared with the quakes that shake the 'Ring of Fire' (from Chile north through San Francisco to Alaska, then south via Japan to New Zealand), or lately in China, Turkey, Armenia and Afghanistan - but that they occur at all in the geologically-stable zone of North Europe surprises many folk.

Arguments as to the extent of the fault persist. Obvious between Loch Linnhe and the shore of Easter Ross, some geologists project it northeast as far as Spitzbergen and west towards Newfoundland. As to the rock strata shattered and displaced by the fault movement, or movements, about Loch Ness these consist principally of Lower and Middle old red sandstone, Moine schist, Mica schist, and granite. Like the fault itself, argument grinds on as to how the fault really formed or behaves, but, either way, the very names of the Great Glen and of Loch Ness create an expectancy, the hope of seeing something weird just by visiting and keeping your eyes open. How many other places carry such a charge?

As to Loch Ness itself, with an estimated 263,000 million cubic feet of water it is Britain's largest volume of fresh water (Loch Lomond, with more surface area, is shallower). 22 miles long, up to a mile and a half wide, in places it is 820 feet deep - a reading of 975 feet was recorded at one spot in 1969. Its peaty waters reject the strongest light. This darkness and the steepness of its banks restrict the growth of rooted plants. 52 feet above sea-level, its temperature remains so constant (42°F) that its surface never freezes. Dreich, it is fit for dreich beasts yet, *pace* Nessie (**27**), surely pure white eels six feet long are dreich enough?

As befits such a strange place, one legend as to how Loch Ness was formed is equally strange. Once, somewhere high above the village of Milton below which the River Enrick flows past Drumnadrochit (**24**) into Urquhart Bay and Loch Ness, there lived a holy man, Daly the Druid. Down on the floor of the valley was a well, blessed by Daly so that its waters would heal virtually every illness. Capping this well with a stone he cut so that no water should be wasted, he issued a command: 'Be sure to replace the stone upon my well after drawing water from it, or great destruction and misery will befall you all'.

Inevitably came the day a woman took her pitcher to the well. Uncapping it, she heard her neighbour's warning shout. She'd left her troublesome boy-child unwatched in her house; he was playing too close to the embers of her cooking-fire. Forgetting everything else she ran to snatch him away from harm. She returned too late. Water was gushing so strongly from the well that nobody could get near it. So, with everyone desperately scrambling up the slopes, that lovely valley was drowned forever, Loch Ness being formed out of a moment's distraction. *'Tha 'nis ann'*, folk cried out, 'There's a loch there now'.

So, with similar tales also found at Strathpeffer (**58**) and Knockfarrel (**59**), Loch Ness got its name.

Next, we explore the loch's west bank, and the land beyond.

The Aird, South & Southwest

Loch Ness, Glen Urquhart, Strathglass & Beauly

22.   Introduction: The Aird & Beyond *(Description)*

The Aird ('high ground', 'promontory') is a roughly triangular region immediately west and southwest of Inverness. Hemmed to the north by the Beauly Firth, to the southwest by the Great Glen and Loch Ness as far as Urquhart Bay and Drumnadrochit, its western boundary may be defined as the A833. This runs south (528440) from the A862 near Beauly, past Beaufort Castle and Kiltarlity and over the Glen Convinth-Glen Urquhart watershed to meet the A831 Cannich road (488304) a mile west of Drumnadrochit.

Much of it forested high ground or moor crisscrossed by minor roads linking hill-farms and secluded hamlets, to the north by the Beauly Firth the Aird's slopes are gentler and there is low, fertile ground.

Rich in old field-systems and settlements (Glen Convinth), cairns (round Kiltarlity), stone duns and hill-forts (Craig Phadrig, Cnoc a'Chinn, Castle Spynie, Dun Mor Cabrich), the Aird is less spectacular than the Highlands to west and northwest, but contains plenty of interest. Moniack Castle, Reelig Glen, the moorland road south from Blackfold (shown above) to Abriachan and Loch Laide with its crannog make exploration of its easily-missed byways a pleasure. Yet good off-road walks (let alone circular ones) are sadly hard to find. Many signposts demand privacy, and with Inverness so close some parts suffer from CBD (Creeping Bungaloid Development). That said, many of the high back-roads with their wide views can be walked or cycled with pleasure.

The A833 also forms the eastern side of a wider, wilder area to the west, explored third and last in this section. In shape a distorted parallelogram and fringed about by extensive forestry plantations, the geographical centre of this largely trackless region of crag and bog and lochan amid bare moor is remote Loch Bruicheach (**34**). To the west Eskdale Moor overlooks the steep forested slopes of Strathglass; to the south Glen Urquhart and Loch Meiklie share the Enrick with Corrimony's pastures; and to the north, with the Glass now the Beauly, the river runs through a great wooded gorge past hydro-electric dams (the river diminished by them) to the town of Beauly and the final shallows of the Beauly Firth.

Absorbing in themselves, these glens and their byways lead to other delights not to be missed, like the spectacular Plodda Falls above Tomich, the wild beauty of Glen Affric and Glen Strathfarrar, and the *dun*-studded moor high above the Beauly gorge.

First, to complete the Loch Ness circuit, from Inverness we take the A82 southeast to Drumnadrochit, Urquhart Bay and Fort Augustus.

23. Inverness to Urquhart Bay *(Tour, History)*

Does someone want to hide the A82? West of Ness Bridge in Inverness it begins as Young Street, promptly becomes Tomnahurich Street then, to bypass Tomnahurich (**4**), turns into Glenurquhart Road. Crossing the canal, it becomes Glenalbyn Road. Only on leaving the burgh past Torvean Golf Course is it revealed as the A82 (Drumnadrochit 14).

To reach it from the roundabout west of the more northerly, newer Friars Bridge, turn south along Kenneth Street (Fort William 66) and right onto Tomnahurich Street.

Past the Craig Phadrig and Craig Dunain hospitals above Kimmylies to the right and with the wooded crags of Dunain Hill ahead, the A82 soon passes the ruin of Torvean mote-hill (644432). Hidden in forestry near Torvean Quarry left of the road, this old fort guarded a ford over the Ness before the canal was built. At nearby Kilvean, now-vanished St Bean's Church may be where Macbeth's wife Gruoch was buried. It's said her sleepless ghost, still trying to get rid of that damned spot, can be seen washing its hands in the river. Said to have an evil interest in the royal family, she was seen the day before King George VI died in 1952. To me she sounds not like the maligned Gruoch at all, but the *bean-nighe*, the supernatural hag whose washing of bloody clothes by a ford was a presage of death (see **56**, **86**).

Beyond Dunain Park Hotel and after two miles the A82 bears left. Here (624417) a minor road (Abriachan 7¼, Blackfold 2¼) turns right up the densely-forested slope of Craig Leach to the Aird's hidden moortop. We'll return here when done with Loch Ness.

A mile on down the A82, the wood above Dochgarroch House hides Battlefield (608405). Here in 1297 the Scots under Andrew de Moray and Alexander Pilche of Inverness defeated the English led by Sir William Fitzwarine, proud Edward's constable at Urquhart Castle (**26**). Now, with pleasure craft at anchor in the canal by the caravan site to the left, the scene is more peaceful. Past weirs where river and canal meet and over the embankment bisecting Loch Dochfour is Dochfour House, beyond it Kirkton of Bona (603385). Once a free church, the present 19th-century building occupies the ancient site of Clach Uradain, dedicated to the Pictish St Curadan, also known as Boniface. In 710, at the request of King Nechtan mac Derile, the well-loved 'Curdy' led a mission among the Picts. He built a church at Invergowrie and Restenneth Priory by Forfar before finally settling on the Black Isle at Rosemarkie, there reorganising St Moluag's earlier settlement (**65**).

So to Lochend's white-harled council houses, framed against Loch Ness with Aldourie Castle (**16**) over the water. A left turn to Bona Ferry (*Ban Ath*, the White Ford) leads to the old ford used by drovers from Muir of Ord (**29**) until the canal raised the water-level. Guarding it was Bona Castle (603380; demolished by Telford), alias Lochaleg Castle or Caisteal Spioradan, 'Castle of the Ghosts'. The latter refers to a grisly episode *c*.1450, when Macleans returned from a raid on Lochaber with Cameron captives. Who did what first is unclear, but Camerons were hanged from the battlements and their chief, Cameron of Glen Nevis, killed two of Maclean's sons before their father's eyes. Thereafter, it's said, the dead men haunted the place.

The tale makes an appropriate introduction to the great but dreich loch ahead, stretching broad and straight to the southwest.

A mile from Lochend in December 1939 a Wellington bomber on a training flight ditched in the loch when its starboard engine failed amid a snowstorm. Six trainees bailed out, one dying when his paracute failed to open. Ditching in near-darkness, by the time the pilot and co-pilot reached the shore in their dingby, R for Robert had sunk. Years later in 1976, a Nessie-hunting team using sonar recorded the outline of an aircraft, also piles of stone which some enthusiasts at first thought neolithic. In fact they'd been dumped by one of Telford's dredgers, the *Prince Regent*. With the Loch Ness Wellington Association formed in 1984, in September 1985 the Wellington was lifted from its watery grave before a huge audience.

It ended up down south, in the RAF Museum at Weybridge.

With the loch now broadening to its full width under the steep, craggily-wooded bank above, the A82 starts weaving along the narrow lochside shelf blasted out in 1933. The soft rock is prone to landslide, thus the steel protective nets from time to time. Not an easy road, this major trunk route is heavily used by commercial traffic. For first-time visitors the scenery is best enjoyed from the many parking places. This is no road for 30mph rubbernecking.

Two miles down the loch a minor road (573349) climbs steeply up to Abriachan (**30**). Here by the loch Abriachan Gardens (01463-861232: open all year) offer two hillside acres of plants from many lands. With benches and viewpoints, you can picnic here, then visit Killianan churchyard nearby (571347). Site of an early church dedicated to St Adamnan (**27,78**), it contains an elaborate medieval graveslab. Nearby is a stone once used to confirm a form of trial marriage. Joining hands in its hollow, the couple would agree to a one-year union. If after that time they remained childless or had fallen out of love they were free to part.

Passing the Clansman Hotel (01456-450326) at Brackla, in under three miles Urquhart Castle (**26**) presents itself on Strone Point the far side of Urquhart Bay. Here the road curls west, away from the bay above the confluence of Enrick and Coiltie, and into Drumnadrochit.

24.   Drumnadrochit to the Divach Falls *(History, Walks)*

By the River Enrick west of Urquhart Bay on flats under steep slopes at the head of Glen Urquhart, Drumnadrochit (*Druim na dhrochaidh*, the ridge of the bridge) both gains and loses by Urquhart Castle's proximity. A prime visitor attraction and site for Nessie-spotting, Castle and Monster together tend to over-shadow the village's own attractions.

After all, on reaching the village first you meet Drumnadrochit Hotel, prominently hosting the *Official* Loch Ness Centre (01456-450218/573/202). A few yards on, above the junction with the A831, the Loch Ness Lodge Hotel hosts, just as prominently, the *Original* Loch Ness Centre (01456-450342). That Nessie stars at both goes without saying.

Yet Drumnadrochit is more than a model monster one end and a castle ruin the other. The hub of communities north of Loch Ness, it has Temple House, Dhivach (pronounced *Jeevach*) Lodge and Falls, a unique triangular village green where sheep and cattle from the west were rested *en route* to market, a haunted hotel and, above the village, the fort-topped crag of Craig Mony. There's the old churchyard at Kilmore, the conservation village of Lewiston, and, the last Saturday every August, the Glenurquhart Highland Games.

First, east of the village, above the loch-end pier at Temple (529300) is Temple House (1851), among its guests a century ago J M Barrie, author of *Peter Pan*. Near it a stone marks the site of the Teampull, a vanished chapel once dedicated to St Ninian, a pre-Columban evangelist to the Picts. From here a small cross-slab, St Ninian's Cross, was removed to the Episcopal Church by Loch Meiklie in Glen Urquhart (**39**). By the road nearby is St Ninian's Well, a 'Cloutie' or rag well (**70**) rebuilt after the road was widened.

A mile further west under steep crofting slopes are the hotel visitor centres. Between them, at the A831 junction, the A82 turns south over the Enrick via a Telford Bridge to the green. Past post office, restaurants, and Drum Farm Centre (01456-450788) is a car-park, opposite the Art Gallery. Of various expeditions from this point, here I describe three: a walk up Craig Mony; a circular road-walk via Kilmore and Lewiston; and a short drive above Drumnadrochit to the fine Divach Falls.

(**1**) For Craig Mony (499294), from the car-park walk on to a sharp bend on the A82. Turn right, west, up Pitkerrald Road towards the prominent wooded crag. A waymarked track on the left leads through fields to two huge Douglas Firs - like Laurel and Hardy, one fat and one thin. From the fat one a path uphill into the forestry soon forks. The waymarking arrow suggests the easier righthand path, which curves up round the side of the hill. The lefthand path climbs straight up the very steep slope, thick forestry to the right, spindly silver birch to the left. Near the top this path veers left to the summit outcrop (450ft.). Along its west side is the ruin of a defensive wall - all that's left of the fort. Though tree-obscured, the view over Drumnadrochit and part of Loch Ness makes the climb worthwhile.

It's said Mony was a Viking prince who, defeated in battle here, escaped up Glen Urquhart to be slain at Corrimony (**40**). Locally the hill is called Mary's Hill. The tale is that St Columba's nephew St Drostan, when meditating up here, dedicated his prayers to St Mary. She also gave her name to Kilmore (*Cill Mhoire*), St Mary's church, which stood between the confluence of Enrick and Coiltie by Urquhart Bay. Urquhart Parish kirk since the 12th century (it's said an earlier dedication was to Drostan), it was replaced in 1838.

(**2**) For Kilmore churchyard, take the lane opposite Pitkerrald Road. Past Glenurquhart High School the Benleva Hotel (01456-450288) is reputedly haunted by a former minister from the time when this 400-year-old building was a manse. Outside it is Scotland's second largest sweet chestnut, locally said to have been the hanging tree. Further on, the large square churchyard (515295) contains a remnant of the 1630 church, now a burial vault. From here the road loops west past dense scrub concealing the confluence of Enrick and Coiltie by the bay. Via Lewiston and the north bank of the busy little Coiltie, it returns in leisurely fashion to the A82 by Borlum Bridge. A conservation area bisected by the A82, Lewiston was removed from its original site near Balmacaan House because Lady Grant, wife of its founder Sir James Grant ('The Good Sir James'), felt that the 'temporary-type thatched dwellings' were too close for aristocratic comfort. So, anxious to stop his folk emigrating, in 1808 Sir James founded Lewiston. Also founding Milton west of Drumnadrochit, and his home village of Grantown-on-Spey, maybe he felt he had to make up for his father, the not-so-good Sir Ludovic, who in 1746 had betrayed 84 men of Glenurquhart and Glenmoriston to the authorities (**39**).

In 1900 American millionaire Bradley Martin rented Balmacaan from the great-grandson of Good Sir James. Cited in the *Guinness Book of Records* for spending $369,200 on a party in New York's Waldorf-Astoria Hotel in 1897, Martin assumed all estate expenses and provided local employment, paying end-of-season wages in gold sovereigns. There is a memorial to him. As for Balmacaan, its rotted shell was demolished in 1972.

At Borlum Bridge, return to the car-park via the A82 or continue through Lewiston past the Lewiston Arms pub, once the local brewery. After a short half-mile past houses old and new, by the village's western edge the road swings right to a junction. The right turn passes new bungalows then older white-harled council housing back onto the A82, while the left turn leads in a steep mile or so to Divach Falls - a must.

(**3**) By car (preferable) or on foot, follow the Coiltie's wooded north bank. Crossing the river by an old stone bridge, the road climbs a steep brae to an open junction. A sign to Dhivach (why different spellings for lodge and waterfall?) points right. From here the view over Urquhart Bay and Loch Ness can be sublime. Soon, from a tiny car-park, a good path angles down a steep grass slope under mature wood. Levelling above the ravine cut by Divach Burn, it reaches the guardrailed viewpoint. With the rambling lodge perched dizzily on a crag above, the burn cascades down a 100-foot drop, trees clinging tenaciously to the all-but-sheer rock walls. Plunging into the ravine below, the burn hurries on to join the Coiltie.

The lodge (494273: not open) dates from 1864. John Philip RA was an early visitor, setting a fashion. Later artistic, literary and theatrical guests included John Millais, actress Kate Terry and her grandson John (later Sir John) Gielgud; Lily Langtry and (whisper it!) her royal lover Edward VII; theatrical impresario Henry Irving (the saturnine model for Bram Stoker's *Dracula*), J M Barrie (again) and Anthony Trollope, who wrote *Ayala's Angel* here. Robert Falcon Scott, alias Scott of the Antarctic, was another visitor. Like Balmacaan, Dhivach later fell into decay, but has since been restored.

Next, a circular three-mile moorland walk with fine views over Drumnadrochit and Loch Ness.

25.   Above Drumnadrochit & Loch Ness *(Walk)*

From the Falls, return through Lewiston to the A82, cross Borlum Bridge, and immediately turn right (west) up the minor road signposted Bunloit 4. This, the old road south to Invermoriston before Telford's lochside route, zigzags steeply uphill a mile through rough pasture to dense forestry. A few yards above a house

on the right advertising 'kennels and cattery' (511282), to the left is a muddy track, loosely gated, with the sign 'no fires'. This is the start. Park on the right a few more yards uphill by the broad, open, obvious entry to a main forestry road, then return to the gated track.

Past the gate the track northeast quickly reaches a high open pasture with fine views north over Drumnadrochit up Glen Urquhart, and east over Urquhart Bay and Loch Ness. Muddy and cattle-churned, dense forestry to the right, this track and its panorama continue for most of a mile. You may find the top of the sloping pasture easier than the track itself. Eventually, the forestry falling away southeast, a gate asking you to please shut it leads up to heather heath, silver birch and Scots Pine cloaking the slope ahead and below.

Ignoring confusing faint paths ahead towards a broad descending forestry track (access this way dubious), beyond the gate bear right (south) along the edge of the plantation followed so far. Soon, by scattered pine above a reedy lochan to the left, the wood again falls away, now southwest, open moor climbing left of its new line. Here, between lochan and wood, is a third gate, beyond it two tracks. The left turn (southeast) bypasses the lochan under a bank of pine to emerge above Loch Ness. The right turn follows the wood southwest for near a mile before joining the Upper Lenie farmtrack, which leads right, back to the Bunloit road.

Select neither. More spectacular is the moortop path, due south. This breaks left from the woodside track (right turn) about 40 yards west of the gate. Obvious enough, it climbs the heathery moortop to views even finer than those enjoyed already - east over Loch Ness and Stratherrick to the Monadhliaths, south to Inverfarigaig and Dun Dearduil (**18**), and southwest to the distinctive dome of Meallfuarvonie (2284ft., 696m). Scotland's second-highest peak in Old Red Sandstone (Morven in Caithness beats it, just, but lacks its bulk), Meallfuarvonie is used by Moray Firth sailors as a landmark. Why, is clear only from this angle. The broad long ridge as seen from Foyers or Inverfarigaig is, from here, more like the cone of Suilven in Sutherland.

This is a fine stretch.. But all good things come to an end. Suddenly a deer-fence blocks you. Rather than clamber south and have to pass through Upper Lenie to return to the road, turn right over broken ground northwest towards the woodside track. The deer-fence soon ends, but keeping straight is simplest. I say this because I learned the hard way, via some bog-floundering - not dangerous, but dull.

Rejoining the track, turn left (southwest) along it. Soon it leaves the forestry, curling through scattered woodland to the Upper Lenie track. Turn right to the Bunloit road, not far, then right again, down past a white cottage to where you parked.

From Upper Lenie this dead-end road continues three miles past Bunloit to Grotaig (491236). Here, east of and above the burn, the ruined walls of Dun Scriben (491235) offer wide views over Loch Ness to Dun Dearduil. Here too starts a route up Meallfuorvonie, though with no easy place to park. The Glenmoriston approach may be preferable.

26.   Urquhart Castle *(Visit, History)*

Annually visited by up to 200,000 people and in care of Historic Scotland (Castle Urquhart Centre: 01456-450551), this scenic ruin on Strone Point by the A82 a mile east of Borlum Bridge juts into Loch Ness, commanding wide views. Destroyed in 1691 to prevent the Jacobites using it, only its 17th century tower remains partly intact. Within an enclosing wall rising sheer from the loch, this broken tower (as with Eilean Donan and Castle Stalker) potently evokes the *Rob Roy* image of Highland Scotland. And if its popularity is partly due to the many sightings of Nessie nearby, the monstrosity of its history is purely human.

Vitrified remains indicate an Iron Age fort, overbuilt *c*.1200 by a Norman motte and double bailey constructed by the Durwards. Later the Comyns of Badenoch added the main courtyard. Strategically vital and often changing hands, those occupying it had a hard time, especially during the Wars of Independence.

Seized and enlarged in 1296 by Edward I, when Wallace rose in the south Andrew Moray retook it. Back came Edward's army, demanding surrender. Amid the ensuing siege Urquhart Castle's constable, Sir Alexander Forbes, smuggled his pregnant wife out of the castle disguised as a peasant. Before fleeing to Ireland she watched from a nearby hill as her husband and his men were cut to pieces. Robert the Bruce became king and the English were again ejected. They were back 30 years later in support of Edward Balliol's royal claims, but Urquhart remained secure - at least until local squabbles got out of hand again.

In *c*.1380 the castle and lands about were acquired by Alexander Stewart, the Wolf of Badenoch (**98**). This royal psychopath did as he pleased before, by torching Elgin Cathedral, he went too far. He was reined in, but others as violent coveted Urquhart. Cattle-raids, hangings, betrayals, feuds and so on were the norm, the Lords of the Isles mostly retaining possession until 1474 when Gordon Earl of Huntly was installed by the Crown as constable.

Granted the lordship in 1509 by James IV as reward for his skill in dealing even-handedly with competing robber bands, John (the 'Red Bard') Grant of Freuchie built the towerhouse, gatehouse and present courtyard walls. After the king died at Flodden in 1513. Donald Macdonald of Lochalsh, Lord of the Isles, sacked Urquhart and ravaged the glen: it was three years before the Grants got them out. So in 1520 the Red Bard sought a treaty of mutual aid with the Camerons. The bond was cemented by union between children, Donald Cameron and Agnes Grant. Their handshake led to bedding: the wedding could wait.

After the Bard died anarchy returned. His sly son Seumas's plots misfired. The terrible 1544 raid on Glen Urquhart (**39**), with Ewen Cameron, oldest son of Donald and Agnes, joining the Clanranald invaders, left the glen ransacked and the castle stripped bare. So the violence went on.

Thus in 1603 on Meallfuarvonie vengeful Mackenzies caught up with Glengarry Macdonalds who'd raided them. At slaughter's end only the Macdonald chief, Allan Dubh, was fit to flee. At the edge of the Lon na Fola (Field of Blood) he leapt a gorge. The nearest Mackenzie also leapt, but fell short, clutching at a sapling. 'I have left much with your race today,' Allan remarked as he cut through the branch, 'let me leave them that also.' The Mackenzie plunged to his death. Allan lay low in the high hills above Glengarry and, to ensure secrecy, beheaded the stonemason he'd hired to improve his hidey-hole.

Not the kind of folk you'd invite to cocktails and cheese snaps.

As for Urquhart, in 1644 it was sacked again, by the Covenanters. It must have been a relief for the suffering old stones when, having rebuffed Jacobites in 1689, on leaving in 1691 the Government garrison blew most of them up, leaving the rest to decay. With the rafters and any other useful items quickly pillaged, in February 1715 a violent gale blew down the southwest wall, which collapsed into the loch. Tales persist of hidden treasure and, weirdly, of the plague miraculously buried in one vault. And also, of course...

27.   'The monster of Loch Ness, lately seen...' *(Folklore, History)*

Nessie a tourist trade hoax? If so, it's an old one. In his *Life of St Columba*, St Adamnan tells how in AD565 Columba dismissed a monster that rose from the water with 'a great roar and open mouth'. Later, *c*.1520, a chronicler telling of the death of Scotland's last dragon after 'a sair tussle' (maybe referring to Hugh Fraser of Glenconvinth: see **36**), adds: 'No one has yet managed to slay the monster of Loch Ness, lately seen'. Further sightings in 1771 (the 'water-kelpie': **56**), 1889 and so on, were not publicised. Only after 1933, when the furore began, did local folk openly admit: 'There's many a queer thing in that loch'.

Sceptics love to point out that the first modern sighting in April 1933 was by Mr and Mrs Mackay, owners of Drumnadrochit Hotel. Their report of: 'an enormous animal plunging and rolling' in the loch below Abriachan appeared in the *Inverness Courier* on 2 May. By October, with over 20 further sightings, Nessie was world news. 'Exposed' by the Austrian government as a British plot to steal tourists, tales of this unknown beast with its tiny head, long neck and huge black body were largely dismissed until, in 1934, the 'Surgeon's Photograph' by respected London surgeon R K Wilson seemed to clinch it, though the oddly-reticent Wilson claimed only to have photographed an object 'moving in the water'. Now, with monster-hunters converging, baffled zoologists began a debate still in progress. Assuming more than one beast, what might they be? Prehistoric plesiosaurs? Giant slugs or eels? And what would they feed on? Trout and salmon maybe, but Loch Ness is sparse in aquatic vegetation or plankton. And why has no body, floating or beached, ever been found?

Believers point out reports of similar beasts in over 300 lakes worldwide, some almost as famous as Nessie, like Canada's Champ or Australia's Bunyip. Irish loughs, especially in Connemara and Galway, seem to swarm with them; and over 20 Scottish lochs other than Loch Ness are said to host them. In August 1969, two men fishing the 1000-foot deep Loch Morar were attacked by 'Morag', sighted over 30 times in the last century. One man shot at the ugly humped creature, the other broke an oar fending it off. Nor do all naturalists deny Nessie's existence. Gerald Durrell, David Attenborough and Sir Peter Scott are or were all believers, especially after 8 August 1972, when Robert H Rines of Boston's Academy of Applied Science took underwater colour photos apparently showing a diamond-shaped paddle or flipper, four to six feet long. Its rhomboid shape led Scott to suggest the name *Nessiteras rhombopteryx* - oddly enough, an anagram of 'monster hoax by Sir Peter S'.

Even so, despite admitted hoaxes and continued talk of floating logs, dead stags, ripples, and 'small gas bubbles' produced by 'the larvae of phantom midges'; few believers have recanted, even when in 1994 it emerged that the 1934 'Surgeon's Photograph' was a fake. The perpetrator wasn't Wilson, but the flamboyant Marmaduke Arundel Wetherell, alias 'Duke' Wetherell, a self-styled big-game hunter. Hired in 1933 by the *Daily Mail* to find evidence of Nessie, he'd soon found giant footprints in soft lochside mud near Fort Augustus. Proclaimed as Nessie-prints, they turned out to those of a young hippo, maybe part of an umbrella-stand. Hoaxed (or maybe hoaxer), Wetherell decided to play (or continue) the same game. 'All right,' he told his son Ian, 'We'll give them their monster.'

So they did. Its head, neck and body consisted of plastic wood moulded over the conning-tower of a toy submarine. Floated in Loch Ness shallows, they photographed it. Acting as front man, Wilson had the plates developed, not realising what might result. With his professional reputation now threatened, he refused all enquiries. The Wetherells, who'd already sunk the 'monster', were never even approached.

None of which proves that Nessie doesn't exist. But in what form? Some claim that she's not physical at all, but the projection into the present of a beast prowling the loch millions of years ago - i.e., a time-travelling evil spirit. This is not a bizarre theory for a land haunted by many old supernatural beliefs, and *X-Files* fans may find it mundane. Indeed, some say Loch Ness is cursed, and in 1973 the Rev. Donald Omand performed an exorcism. A Highland Scot, this Anglican minister's research into Nessie and other lake-monsters led him, on 2 June that year, to enact a ritual at several points round the loch. At each point he asked that: '...this highland loch and the land adjoining it may be delivered from all evil spirits; all vain imaginations; projections and fantasms, and all deceits of the evil one'.

Strange stuff. Like Ripley, believe it or not. Oh, and a final piece of absurdity. As of early 1998, a US company, RLP Entertainment of Las Vegas, claims copyright ownership both of the Loch Ness Monster and the name 'Nessie', and has warned all Scots that we may be sued if we misuse the name. Words don't often fail me, but...*this is MONSTROUS!*

28.   Urquhart Castle to Fort Augustus *(Route)*

Continuing southwest from Urquhart Castle, and if not first accosted by Nessie or a lawyer waving a writ, after two miles left of the road you see a beehive-shaped cairn. This, erected by Glen Urquhart folk, contains a brass plaque explaining that: 'This memorial is erected as a tribute to the memory of a gallant gentleman'.

The reference is to John Cobb, the cairn marking the point offshore where, on 29 September 1952, his speedboat *Crusader* disintegrated.

A London fur broker who already held the land speed record at over 390mph, Cobb had decided to take go for the water speed record too. Choosing Loch Ness for its unusual length and straightness, he reckoned the best time to be just before the autumn equinox. But, the *Crusader* being jet-powered, conditions would have to be flat calm. Unloaded at Temple Pier on 29 August, the shattering roar of her engines became a well-known sound over the following month - yet conditions were poor. After torrential rain on the 23rd, the loch's feeder rivers poured debris, including tree trunks, into the dark peat waters.

On the 29th, just before noon Cobb started the measured mile. Witnesses say *Crusader* hardly touched the water. At the end of the mile she was going faster than any boat had ever gone. Decelerating, the powerboat bounced twice then disintegrated. Had it hit a floating log? Others blamed a sudden hard ripple, or too-rapid deceleration. Cobb died instantly, though some have it that, still alive, he was carried to Achnahannet where he died near where the Memorial still stands. His tale is already part of the legend of Loch Ness.

Past the Loch Ness Youth Hostel at Alltsigh (01320-351274), the road descends to loop briefly west past the A887 junction at Invermoriston. This least-spoiled village of any along the lochside lies under the Glenmoriston Arms Hotel (01320-351206); a natural midway watering-hole for all returning from the West Coast via the A887/A87 up Glen Shiel past Loch Cluanie. Of the glen, in 1933 H V Morton wrote; 'Fifteen miles of beauty lie between hills. They are called Glenmoriston'. It is also memorable for the Seven Men of Glenmoriston (**7**); and Ludovick Grant's betrayal of its men in 1746 (**39**).

From Invermoriston's tumbling riverside nook the A82 returns to the lochside, yet from here to Fort Augustus the dense thicket between road and water leaves little to see. Passing Invermoriston Camping and Caravan Site (01320-351207), after six miles, now almost at Fort Augustus, the Abbey Clock tower visible ahead, to the left near the loch's now-shallow southern shore is 'Cherry Island'. Named by Cromwellian soldiers billeted nearby, this tree-topped mound is really Eilean Mhuireach (Murdoch's Island) - a crannog. In 1908 Dom Odo Blundell of the Abbey dived to learn that it consists of a raft of oak logs on the soft clay loch-bed; then a layer of stone held in position by heavy piles driven into the deeper gravel.

Once called Kilchuimen (St Cumein's kirk), maybe Fort Augustus should readopt this less martial name. After all, this largest of the lochside villages was long dominated by the 19th-century Benedictine abbey and school built over Wade's four-bastioned fortress (**15**), constructed in 1730 and named after the nine-year-old William Augustus, Duke of Cumberland. The walls of an earlier barracks lie higher up, in the gardens of the Lovat Arms Hotel. Buying Wade's fort for £5000 in 1867, Lord Lovat (**36**) gave it to the monks. In 1878 the monastery became a school, and in 1882 an abbey, recently closed. South of the Oich, the canal and the village-intersecting A82, its buildings stand between the loch and the B862 to Stratherrick.

In May 1746 Cumberland occupied Wade's 1730 fort, organising horse-races as his troops committed atrocities, and punishing anyone offering so much as a crust to a wretched child (see **7**). Even so, what the redcoats did to the clans was no worse than what the clans had long been doing to each other. Those now hunted down knew all about body-cleaving mayhem. The real change lay in the fact that a foreign system and technology was forced on a doomed older culture. With clan conflict ended by outsiders many joined Highland regiments fighting for a colonial policy which, begun in Ireland and Scotland, now went global.

It's a terrible irony. The fate visited upon Highlanders after 1746 next fell upon the folk of India, North America, and South Africa, with Highland regiments to the fore.

When in 1822 the Caledonian Canal was opened (from Loch Ness five locks climb through the village) the fort was still garrisoned. In 1867, with much of the region cleared of people to make way for sheep (**43**), the spoliation was so complete that the fort was redundant. It was sold for £5000 to Lord Lovat (**36**), who gave it to the monks in the early 1870s.

Wade's masterpiece, the Corrieyourick road, zigzags steeply up to the east of Kilchuimen/Fort Augustus. The onward road continues past Loch Lochy to the southern end of the Caledonian Canal under Ben Nevis. But now, back to the Aird...and the drove roads.

29.   The Drove Roads *(History, Tour)*

'The wealth of the mountains is cattle', declared Dr Johnson in 1773. Before Wade and Caulfeild (**15**) began building military roads, the only way to get about the Highlands was via footpaths or the rough trails created by cattle annually driven south to the trysts of Crieff and later Falkirk, which was more accessible to the growing numbers of English dealers.

A venturesome trade existing since the Middle Ages, made easier by the Union of Crowns in 1603 and positively encouraged after the Restoration, by

1777, 30,000 head were sold in three Falkirk sales between August and October. By *c.*1800 one Inverness-shire man, John Cameron of Corriechoille, annually sent 2,000 cattle and 20,000 sheep south; and in 1850 up to 150,000 cattle were traded at Falkirk.

The droving of cattle to these trysts, then often on via the Great North Road to East Anglia, where 30,000 'Scotch runts' were fattened annually, brought status, wealth and land to those shrewd and bold enough to succeed at it. Small traders would lay out all they had, or more, to buy herds of up to one hundred head and travel from one small tryst or fair to another. Living on oatmeal and bannocks, for weeks they'd sleep rough in all weathers, moving ten or twelve miles a day. Bigger herds bought on loaned capital earned the real rewards, but naturally the money-men sought specific qualities in the drover - known honesty, intimate knowledge of cattle and the land, toughness, initiative, force of character, knowledge of men and a strong sense of responsibility. Such men (inheriting earlier cattle-reiving traditions) aided remote communities by operating as a means for the exchange of cash, credit, and market information. Touring the margins of the land, their arrival announced through notices given out in church, they enabled the poorest clansmen to sell their beasts locally.

The term 'drove road' is misleading. Both drovers and cattle preferred the free grazing of open hillsides. The arrival of true roads (both Wade and Telford hoped their military roads would make droving easier) led landowners to charge for overnight grazing, while paved or gritted roads harmed the cloven hoof. The beasts had to be shod, with two iron crescents per hoof. Blacksmiths catered to this task at Muir of Ord, Invergarry, Trinafour and Tyndrum: at Kennethmont in Aberdeenshire the famed smith Robert Gall boasted of having shod 70 cattle in a day. However their trade and that of the drovers died out with the opening of the Highland railway lines after 1860, the last Falkirk Tryst being held in 1901.

West of Inverness, from Muir of Ord and Beauly the main drove route led over the Aird from Reelig (**31**) up to Blackfold then down to the river-crossing at Bona. At such crossings cattle were usually swum over: if boats were used, they were lined with birch-brush, or the beasts would panic at the sound of their hooves clattering on the wood.

Past Loch Ashie (**14**), the route continued south via Farr and Glen Kyllachy (**12**) to the Findhorn. Typically broad, between dry stone or turf dykes, in parts it can be followed. However the Aird section from An Leacainn (577411) past Easter Altourie is, though marked as a path on the OS map, no longer obvious on the ground - as we're about to see.

30.   The Aird: Blackfold to Moniack *(Route, Walks)*

Two miles south of Inverness the little Blackfold road (624417: **23**) leaves the A82 to climb thickly-forested Craig Leach over a cattlegrid to open moor and wide views. Barely four miles from Inverness? It's hard to believe. By a house (Blackfold: 589407) a track starts north into the forestry atop the Aird. Here too the old Inverness-Glen Urquhart high road emerges (**5**), to continue southwest to Drumnadrochit via Ladycairn and Achpopuli.

West past Blackfold the road continues over the heather moor, broad views opening up past Meall na Caiplich Bige. Just past Easter Altourie, where the drove trail shown on the map isn't and before the road crosses a burn (569399), in a field to the right are springs known collectively as the Red Spring, *An Fuaran Dearg,* their waters bright orange. The moor here is attractively open and, track or no track, invites a wander, but walkers here are not encouraged.

With views widening the road passes Ladycairn then descends a wooded slope above Loch Laide to a junction above Abriachan. Once a crofting community, now a sought-after Inverness dormitory, Abriachan occupies a high (750ft.) valley under forested hills. Here was the Croft Museum, its many relics of the old Highland way of life collected by author Katharine Stewart (*A Croft in the Hills*). With a Bronze Age cairn at the top of the brae (567347) above Loch Ness, and 18th-century crofts along the walkable way past Balmore to Achculin (568353), Abriachan repays a visit, even if you fail to stumble across one of the illicit stills for which the area was once renowned.

Back at the junction, turn left (Foxhole 3, Beauly 9) and west round pretty little Loch Laide, near its reedy northwest fringe a crannog (545345). Black-headed gulls nest on it; the Slavonian Grebes (**14**) which once visited moved to Loch Dochfour when forestry ploughings disturbed the water-table. All seems peaceful here, yet this is a stretch of water that folk once feared to pass by night, for reasons or beliefs unrecorded.

Above the loch a left turn along what looks like a forestry track leads to Achpopuli, once site of a fair. With the remains of hut circles and field systems *en route*, after Achpopuli this part of the old high road continues as a path over high bare ground past Loch Glanaidh before sloping steeply down past Wester Achtuie to Drumnadrochit four miles to the south. It was hoped this route might become part of the proposed Great Glen Way; but access problems arose, in part because of gates left open by careless walkers. Currently (1998) a new route further east via forestry tracks above Loch Ness is being negotiated.

Breaking away from one forestry belt the road climbs north over the Aird's broad central ridge to another. At a Y-junction (529379) by the second belt (the right fork leads past South Clunes), stay left, north and downhill to the staggered crossroads at Foxhole (523387). In one mile the left turn joins the B833 at Convinth (see **38**) on the Drumnadrochit road.

This pleasant high back-route via Blackfold, Abrichan and Foxhole is an ideal winding alternative to the lochside A82 route to Drumnadrochit, and offers the walker or cyclist plenty of opportunity to invent routes. The road ahead also shortly joins the A833, north to Beauly.

For Moniack and Reelig Glen (see below), at Foxhole turn right at the red phone box by the old Glenconvinth school building. Past Torranhirick, its cairns hid in thick forest, this pretty road runs northeast over level high ground with open views between the plantations. After a couple of miles, where forestry on the left falls back, the wooded slopes higher up conceal Castle Spynie (541420). Finely set on a north-facing rock with outer defences below, this hard-to-reach, near circular stone dun is best approached from Cnocanord (544415) a little way on and north of the road. This is one of several fine old forts in the area.

With the Beauly Firth below the road descends a steepening slope into a broad, shallow, wooded glen. Taking up the South Clunes lane it descends to a T-junction under the turreted towerhouse of Moniack Castle (552436: tel. 01463-831283).

With visitor centre and shop open all year (not Sundays), this Fraser seat now hosts an enterprise producing wines, liqueurs and preserves from natural local ingredients. Nine miles west of Inverness and under a mile south of the Inverness-Beauly A862 (well-signposted from it), the original L-plan towerhouse dates from 1580, later additions being made in 1830. Among several interesting stones in its gardens, one has cup-marks and an inscribed human fig-ure. Apparently Pictish, it was removed here from Kilmorack *c*.1830.

From the T-junction, the left turn leads a mile west to Dun Mor Cabrich (**33**), a fine Iron Age hill-fort; the right turn to nearby Reelig Glen and its forest walks.

31.   Reelig Glen *(Forest Walks)*

From Moniack turn right (east) a few hundred yards to a T-junction. Here, at the sign 'Rebeg 1¹/₂', again turn right, south, by the Moniack Burn. East of the burn is Reelig House, home of the Frasers of Reelig for over 500 years, fine cedars behind its classical front. 'Reelig' may mean 'burial ground', referring to a pos-sibly neolithic site in the grounds.

Where the road turns sharp left over the burn to climb through beechwood to Rebeg, turn right into the car-park for Reelig Glen Forestry Park. A Forestry Commission pamphlet, 'The Tall Trees Walks', describes the walks and the many species growing here.

Sold to the FC in 1949 by Major Fraser of Reelig, this narrow, exotically-forested glen was planted mostly by his ancestor, James Bailie Fraser (1783-1856), an author and Asiatic traveller. He also built bridges over the burn and the Grotto - a ruined folly at the furthest point of the walk, or walks; these con-sisting of several interconnecting routes. None are long or hard. The maximum height climbed is 200ft., the greatest distance 1.5 miles.

With waterfalls on a tributary of the main burn, the main attraction here lies in the impressive maturity (meaning height!) of the Douglas fir, western red hemlock, and other imported species planted over 150 years ago. As with California's redwood groves, but rarely met in Britain, these giants create the sense of a natural cathedral. Moreover, at their feet proliferate a multitude of exotic plants - ferns, mosses, rhododendrons.

With the remains of two burial cairns above the car-park (558431/2), the first part of the Low Glen burnside walk from the car-park is broad and flat, easy for all. Cross the bridge to start up the burn's east side. A footbridge half-a-mile south up the glen allows access from one side to the other, creating a circular route and making Reelig Glen an excellent place to relax.

So, with the A862 and Beauly Firth so close, to the Aird's northern shore.

32.   Inverness to Beauly *(Route)*

Before the Kessock Bridge opened in 1982, what is now the A862 was the A9 trunk route north via Beauly. Today this road along the firth's southern shore is quieter, if not much, with commuter traffic so busy.

Leaving Inverness via Telford Street (**3**), it crosses the Caledonian Canal by the Muirtown swing-bridge then, now Clachnaharry Road, bypasses Muirtown Basin where the canal begins and ends. Under Craig Phadrig it winds through Clachnaharry, a 19th-century fisher village. Bending sharp right then left to cross the railway, it starts west along the shore of the firth under a steep wooded slope. *En route* it passes some interesting sites.

Halfway along Muirtown Basin and opposite the old toll-house, left of the road up a wooded den is Muirtown Well (650461). Also called Fuaran Allt an Ionlaid ('Well of the Washing Burn'), from it the doomed Montrose drank on his way to execution in Edinburgh on 21 May 1650. A little further north and again above the road, the Clach na h-Aire ('Watchstone': 647464) offers broad views up the firth. West of it, above the bridge over the railway is the Battle Monument (645465), the base of an obelisk erected in 1821 to commemorate a 1454 battle between Clan Chattan and the Munros. Above it along the hillside the old Beauly road runs to Bruchnain a mile west, *en route* a forest track (642462) breaking south up Craig Phadrig (**5**). Finally, beyond the railway bridge on the south side of the road is Fuaran Priseag ('Precious Spring': 645465), said to have been blessed by St Cessog as a site for sore eyes.

A mile or so on, in woodland between road and firth where the landward slope begins to fall back a bit, is Bunchrew House (621459). Originally built 1619-21 by Simon Fraser, 8th Lord Lovat, later Lord President Duncan Forbes of Culloden (**73**) was born here. Also owner of Culloden House, he preferred Bunchrew. Failing to avert the 1745 rebellion, when the cause was lost he had no better luck trying to prevent 'the fiendish thirst for blood evinced by the Duke of Cumberland' and his men. Not surprisingly, he died of exhaustion in 1747. As for Bunchrew House, rebuilt in baronial style in the 19th century, it is now a hotel. Beyond it, in the firth halfway over to the Black Isle, a black pile of stones visible at low tide is Carn Dubh (618473), the remains of one of the firth's five ruined crannogs, with another at Phopachy further along.

From Bunchrew village a lane (618455) climbs south to Englishton Muir then west along Kirkton Muir, with views of Ben Wyvis. At Altnacardich (remains of burial cairns hereabouts) this route branches north down through forestry to a minor crossroads at Newtonhill (578436). A left turn here leads in a mile down past Rebeg to Reelig Glen.

Beyond Bunchrew on the A862 another left turn (608557) cuts under the railway to Kirkton, site of the old parish church of Fernua, its walled burial ground in the steading. Nearby is Tom a'Chaistel (Castle Hillock: 604449): scant stone foundations atop a rocky mound, maybe built by a 12th-century knight from the south, thus 'Englishton'. Much older, west of and above Kirkton, Cnoc a'Chinn (Hill of the Head: 597451) is a ruined oval stone dun. Before exploring any of these, it may be best to ask at the farm.

Onward under Cnoc a'Chinn at Phopachy, with a crannog offshore visible at low tide, the road hugs the shore then turns under the railway over level land to Inchmore. Here, a right turn on the B9164 by Bogroy Inn (567449: once a whisky-smuggling haunt) leads to Kirkhill, an airy Inverness dormitory, the old Wardlaw churchyard above it. West of Kirkhill, branch right on a lane past Wester Lovat steading (539461), site of Lovat Castle. Originally (c.1220) a Bisset timbered earthwork, by c.1500 it was the fortified house of the Frasers of Lovat, who later moved to Dounie/Beaufort (36). Turning west the lane follows the railway above the Beauly's final flow to the firth, a track descending to the old crossing-point at Ferrybrae. The lane rejoins the B9164, which breaks south back to the A862, so ending this interesting two-mile detour.

From Bogroy the A862 cuts inland past the first of two turn-offs to Moniack Castle. Signs make it clear that the first road leads only to Easter Moniack and Glen Reelig houses: the approved route to the Winery and the Forest Walks is via the second turn.

Following a broad slope southwest (Dun Mor Cabrich visible to the south), at a sharp bend north the A862 takes up the minor Cabrich road then, successively, the A833 from Drumnadrochit and Glen Convinth (24, 38) and the Kirkhill B9164. Swinging west, it crosses the Beauly at Lovat Bridge (1813), built near the variable site of the old Stock Ford. Hereabouts c.1110 King Alexander I defeated Heth, Earl of Moray, who claimed the throne by descent from Macbeth. Later, the west bank of this crossing was protected by a motehill of timber and earth (513448: just east of the scenic gravel pit).

Over the river the A862 meets the A831 from Cannich and Strathglass (46), then turns north through Beauly (49) to Muir of Ord, Strathconon and beyond (Section 3).

And now for the walk up Dun Mor Cabrich.

33.   Dun Mor Cabrich *(Walk)*

The region's many Iron Age forts and *duns* (the latter generally smaller: the qualification of 'fort' requires an internal area over 1300 m^2) speak of insecure times long ago. Such sites usually command wide views from remote, exposed ridges or narrow hilltops. Refuges in time of danger, their builders probably lived mostly in hut circles on lower ground, with lookouts on duty at the fort. A site like Dun Mor Cabrich, overlooking the fertile lands about the Beauly's final bends, helps one imagine how fierce the struggle to survive may have been in Iron Age times.

Cabrich, a mile west of Moniack Castle, and half-a-mile south of the A862 (turn south at 529439), is a scattered community on an open, rolling, north-facing hillside of craggily-forested heights. As for the fort (534429), enclosed by a partly-vitrified stone wall and with splendid views, on the northernmost crag at the 500ft level it is easily reached by a steepish climb from Balchraggan Quarry, which is at the west end of the hamlet.

Park off the road just west of the quarry entrance where two tracks break southeast. Take the muddy lower track (signposted 'Dunbeag 3 Cabrich'), and follow it past three houses (the last flying a saltire when I went by). After this last house - set back amid pasture to the right - the now-gravelled track passes a red tin-roofed byre. Where the field ends and the track dips left, turn right (southwest) over a low stone dyke. Climb a faint path rising parallel to the field through bracken and scrubby birch. Meeting deer-fenced forestry to the right, keep straight up through the birchwood. Where the fence ends, the path joins a deep-rutted old forestry track where the latter right-angles. Keep straight, up the track's left fork. Try to avoid breaking your ankle in the ruts made, at a guess, by Tractosaurus Rex.

With a steep open bracken slope to the right and the dun on the ridge above, the track contours left. Here, leave it. Cut diagonally right up a faint path over a downed fence and climb to the dun's rocky birch and fir-crowned height. Crushed bracken-tracks suggest previous visitors. Enter from the northeast and climb through a hollow centre past tumbled rocks to the summit knoll. With steep slopes on three sides, this commands a vast panorama west from Strathglass east over the Beauly Firth to the Black Isle and past Ord Hill (**51**) to the Moray Firth..

Beyond Phoineas House (the white house below) the Beauly winds under rugged bare hills past Beaufort Castle, hidden in its woods. This is an ideal spot to imagine the land as it was 2500 years ago - forest from sea to mountain horizon, down below a thin curl of smoke above the trees, a brief clearing with a ploughed strip, by it wooden huts so much part of the forest it's hard to see them at all. Or maybe you want something more dramatic. How about a battle? But don't get too involved, or you may fall through time for real...

Either way, on opening your eyes return as you came.

34.   Kiltarlity to Eilean Aigas *(Route, Walk)*

From Cabrich join or rejoin the A862, turning left onto it where it bends north. 200 yards further the A833 (Kiltarlity 2, Drumnadrochit 11) breaks left, south. With mature woods to the right and high stone dykes both sides, this road sweeps south past opposite entries to Dounie and Beaufort Castle (west) and Phoineas House (east). Beyond Belladrum North chambered cairn (514421: ruinous), the road forks at Brochie's Lodge, a well-known local watering-hole. The A833 continues south via Glen Convinth to Glen Urquhart (**38, 39**).

Turn right (west) to Kiltarlity, a sprawl of new housing and open pasture with its own Tom na Croiche, Gallows Hill (**16**). Shown below, this earthwork dominates the graveyard of Kiltarlity Parish Church graveyard (513413), reached via the first road south from the village. Once a motehill, it became a gallows-hill after the Frasers took possession of Dounie in 1511.

At a T-junction (505417: to Culburnie, Eskadale and Struy) west of Kiltarlity turn left up a brae past Culburnie's scattered houses. On the right the Lonbuie lane leads to Culburnie Ring Cairn (491418), its eight outer monoliths road-bisected. At the crest of the brae the left fork at a Y-junction (484414) runs west above Eskadale Wood two miles to Cruive. From there a mile-plus hike south up a bare glen leads to lonely Loch Bruicheach, by its northern inlet Eilean Bhruaich, a large wooded crannog (454369: 190x110ft). With ancient oak beam construction and vitrified masonry this was a refuge for Elizabeth, Lady Lovat, in 1589. The Culburnie road descends northwest to Hughton cross-roads (476415). A few yards left (west) on the Eskadale road a private drive descends right to Eilean Aigas House. Built in 1839 by Thomas Lord Lovat as a shooting lodge, it occupies a craggy, wooded isle in the Beauly at the mouth of the Beauly Gorge, upriver from the dams at Cluanie and Kilmorack. On it in 1697 the 'Old Fox' (then a young fox) lay low after one of the heartless escapades that 50 years later finally led him to the block (**36**).

Here too the Sobieski brothers occupied the lodge in lordly style. These clever frauds persuaded many post-Culloden romantics that their father, Lieutenant Thomas Allen RN, was the legitimate son of Bonnie Prince Charlie, courtesy of Louise of Stolberg. The elder, 'John Sobieski Stolberg Stuart', (c.1795-1872) styled himself 'Count of Albany'; his brother, 'Charles Edward Stuart' (c.1799-1880), supported him. They also said they'd fought for Napoleon at Waterloo. Did Lovat believe them, or merely indulge their posturing? Either way, their conceit got them a living. While in the lap of Lovat luxury they wrote *Vestiarum Scoticum*, an 'ancient' work on clan tartans as reliable as their claim to royal Stuart ancestry.

Just above the bridge to Eilean Aigas a forestry track forks north through Ruttle Wood to Dun Fionn (472429), a spectacular site above the gorge. Excavated c.1830 by Lord Lovat, who uncovered vitrified stonework, it is now little more than a grassy knoll. The only possible confusion comes when, curling east through the wood above a deep linn, the track abruptly enters a messy clearing with no obvious continuation. In fact it turns hard back on itself, left and west, downhill the other side of the linn a few hundred yards to the site of Dun Fionn high above the gorge. The track thereafter, though shown on the OS map as continuing two miles round the riverbend to Kilmorack power station, is not easily passable. In addition, there is now (1998) a locked gate barring the start of it. The gate is easily bypassed, but access may be debatable: best ask first.

35.   The Fanellan-Culburnie Circuit *(Route/Walk)*

A pleasant 5-mile road-circuit by foot or bike starts at Hughton, or at any other convenient point. From Hughton's red telephone box the little road climbs to Fanellan then descends, not steeply, two miles to Kiltarlity Cottages. With Ruttle Forest above pasture to the north, the road follows a broad open slope with wide views east to the Beauly Firth and southeast over the Aird to the hills beyond Loch Ness. After a mile, a big sign above a bottling plant advertises 'Lovat Mineral Water - Fanellan Visitor Centre'. Opened in 1992 but now abandoned, it was among the ventures leading to the recent collapse of the once-vast Lovat Fraser estate until lately run from nearby Beaufort Castle, hidden amid its policies by the river a mile west of Fanellan. Built in 1880, it replaced the previous building destroyed by Cumberland after Culloden.

Down the brae the road reaches a junction (496437) at Kiltarlity Cottages. The left turn north crosses the river via Black Bridge below the Kilmorack dam and power station to join the A831 from Strathglass (**46**). A mile further east the A831 meets the A862 by Lovat Bridge south of Beauly. East of the road on the south bank (497440) are the ruins of Kiltarlity's old church (1626) and graveyard. An earlier church was dedicated to an 8th-century Pictish missionary, St Talorgan.

The right turn south at this junction curls southwest between fertile flat fields past Beaufort Castle's grounds to Culburnie Bridge and a junction with the road recently taken from Kiltarlity. Continue through Culburnie and back to Hughton as already described.

36.   The Lovat Frasers *(History)*

Locally prominent for 500 years, lately visited by catastrophe, the Lovat Frasers were originally Normans from Anjou. By 1030 *seigneurs* of La Frezelière (where strawberries grew, hence the name), with Simon Frisel or Frazer owning land in Scotland by 1160, the family tradition developed that the first-born male of each new generation should be named Simon. So most Lovat lords came to be called 'Mac Shimidh', Gaelic for 'son of Simon'.

William Fraser, brother of the founder of the Lovat line, was Regent of all Scotland north of the Forth in 1288. Simon Fraser of Oliver Castle defeated the English at Rosslyn a few years later, but was captured and hideously executed in London. By 1367 Hugh Fraser, Lord of Lovat, held land near Beauly, while in 1500 Hugh Fraser of Glenconvinth famously slew a nine-foot dragon in the heather. Setbacks included a disastrous 1544 battle against Clanranald, but a later Mac Shimidh could hang a golden chain at the 'Stock Ford of Ross' (Beauly River: see **32**) and leave it there, and nobody dared steal it.

So to the notorious 11th Lord, also Simon (*c*.1667-1747). Lacking 'the kind of nature that is attracted by honest labour', the 'Old Fox' first persuaded his cousin Hugh, the 9th Lord, to nominate as heir his own father, Thomas. When Hugh died in 1696 Simon promptly tried to marry his nine-year-old daughter, Amelia, then in 1697 abducted his widow. By force he wed then bedded her, a piper drowning her screams while a kinsman cut off her buckram stays with his dirk. Even by 1697 standards this, like the then-recent Massacre of Glencoe, was too much. Outlawed, Simon fled to Eilean Aigas with his bride, unconvincingly denying charges of rape. Forced to release the lady, he fled to Skye, to become 11th Lord when his father died in 1699. Still outlawed, estates forfeit, he visited the Old Pretender in France and swore loyalty. Back in Scotland in 1703 as a Jacobite spy, he turned his coat, got involved in a plot that collapsed, and fled back to France. Jailed for almost a decade, he escaped, and in 1715 led his clan against the Jacobites.

Pardoned and regaining Lovat lands, he began 'brooding over how to make the Highlands a more profitable place for Simon Fraser of Lovat'. Advocating the formation of Highland Independent Companies to subdue Jacobitism, his command of one such company ended when General Wade (**15**) removed him for stealing his clansmen's pay.

When the '45 broke out and the Jacobites won at Prestonpans, this slippery rogue, now 78 and thrice-married (his second wife had died, the third abandoned him), sent his son to fight for Prince Charlie. This was a bad move. On the run after Culloden (**7**), he was caught near Loch Morar. In London, his eloquent self-defence was useless. As he was helped up to the block a woman howled: 'You'll get that nasty head of yours chopped off, you ugly old Scotch dog'. Calmly he replied: 'I believe I shall, you ugly old English bitch'. The last British aristocrat to be beheaded, he died with dignity, but was unusual in that most Lovats protected their folk, as during the Clearances (**43**), and in return received loyalty. Several raised special military forces. The Old Fox's eldest son led his Fraser Highlanders against the Heights of Abraham at Quebec in 1759. Over a century later the 16th Mac Shimidh (d. 1933) led locally-raised Lovat Scouts in the Boer War. Later his cousin David Stirling, the 'Phantom Major', created and led the SAS in the Sahara during World War II.

In a 1944 letter to Stalin, Winston Churchill described the 17th Lovat, also Simon, as 'the mildest-mannered man that ever scuttled ships or cut a throat'. A natural leader and showman, when World War II broke out he led Lovat Scouts. After Dunkirk he argued the need for a fiercer type of war and formed the Special Service Brigade, the commandos. At dawn of 6 June 1944, on D-Day he landed his brigade on Sword Beach, beside him his piper, Bill Millen. To the skirl of 'Highland Laddie', carrying a rolled brolly and an old Winchester rifle with the name Lovat printed on his rollneck sweater, he led his men through fierce fire to relieve surrounded airborne troops. In the 1960s epic movie, *The Longest Day*, Peter Lawford played Lovat. Surly critics said Lawford wasn't as handsome.

Recovering from his wounds, Lovat was sent by Churchill to discuss tactics with Stalin. After the war, married with six children, he rebuilt the Lovat estates. Reclaiming uplands for shorthorn cattle and reseeding low estates, by the 1960s he had over 35,000 acres of productive land, reinvesting the profits to employ local people. Historian and agriculturalist, an expert on Scottish affairs, all seemed well. Then a heart attack persuaded him to pass the estate to his first son, Simon. The rest is history. After years of financial collapse, in March 1994 his youngest and oldest sons died within ten days of each other, the first gored to death by a buffalo in Tanzania, the second of a heart attack while leading out the Dounie hunt. The 17th Lord survived them by almost exactly a year.

Beaufort Castle's new laird is, as it happens, by birth a Fraser. Creator of one of Scotland's biggest bus companies, on buying the castle she made clear her determination that 'such a great house should remain in Scottish hands' - not always the case these days.

As for the new Mac Shimidh, the 19th Lord Lovat, he remains clan chief of Lovat Frasers all round the globe. The long tale may yet have a twist in it.

37.   To Eskadale & Struy *(Route)*

West of Hughton a fine road runs above the south bank of the Beauly past Eskadale House (*c*.1830). Near this Georgian mansion a wooded oval earthwork is the site of an early motehill castle, built to defend the Aigas Ford (455505: **46**). A long mile on this road reaches the white-harled Catholic church of St Mary's, Eskadale. With east-facing rose window and unusual style it was built in 1826 by Thomas Fraser of Strichen, the Lovat who built Eilean Aigas Lodge and indulged the Sobieski Stuarts. Burial-site of Lovats and the Sobieski Stuarts, this is an eldritch place. Trees glower thick about. At twilight maybe you'd not be surprised if the headstones start seeming to *move*. For here we verge on old lands where standing stones erected long ago were once called *fir chreig*, 'false men'.

I was sorry to find the church door locked. But that's how it is now.

With river to right and crag-climbing forest to left, this lovely little road continues west another three miles above the Beauly, a broad marshy flood-plain opening out as the crags above get more rugged and the big bare hills above Glen Strathfarrar loom closer. Where the river bends southwest down Strathglass to Cannich, the road follows it to Kerrow Brae and the A831 (**41**). This was once part of St Duthac's road, a pilgrim-trail from the west coast north to his birthplace and shrine at Tain. Giving his name to Loch Duich (and maybe to the Black Isle: see **50**) Duthac died in Armagh in 1065, his remains being borne back to Tain in 1253. His preserved shirt, said to protect its wearer from injury or death, did the Earl of Ross little good at the Battle of Halidon Hill near Berwick in 1333, though the English at least returned it.

Here, where road and river bend south, a right fork (397403) descends over the river via Drochaidh Dubh (Black Bridge) to the A831 at Struy, just south of the road west up Glen Strathfarrar. Taking up Farrar's waters by Erchless Castle, the river changes both direction and name - northeast to east, and Glass to Beauly.

We return here (**45**, **46**) late on the circuit next begun: south via Glen Convinth to Milton, west up Glen Urquhart to Corrimony and Cannich (via Tomich and Glen Affric), northeast up Strathglass, then via the Beauly's north bank to the town of Beauly itself.

38.   Glen Convinth to Milton *(Route)*

From the Kiltarlity-Eskadale-Cannich road rejoin the A833 at Brochie's Lodge (**34**) or a half-mile further south (via Kiltarlity Parish Church) at Tomnacross. Opposite the second junction, where the Belladrum estate road branches east, Meg's Stone may be a removed remnant of the ruined chambered cairn at Belladrum South (516415).

By Belladrum Burn the brae climbs steadily to the broad mouth of Glen Convinth. Crossing the burn (now the Allt Dearg) at White Bridge the A833 takes up the minor Foxhole road (513376: **30**) near ruined Convinth Church. Traditionally founded by one of Erchard's bell-carrying companions (**46**), parts of the thick walls of this large (75x25ft) building still stand. The pre-Gaelic name 'Convinth' (from 'Coinmed') implies hospitality or waiting-upon; the local 17th-century Coan's Fair suggests that the dedication was to St Comgan, an 8th-century Leinsterman traditionally associated with Turriff in Buchan.

With old hut-circles and field-systems high above the brae where the glen narrows, the road climbs to a dark moorland watershed between Glen Convinth and Glen Urquhart, a wilderness of crags and lochans to the west. More hut circles lie east of the road near Garbeg, where in 1974 an unusual cairn (511319) was excavated. Roughly square, it was surrounded by straight ditches not meeting at the corners, at each corner was a single stone. Up here, it may be, lived Daly the Druid (21)

From open moor the A833 descends steeply to the A831 on the north bank of the River Enrick in Glen Urquhart. With Drumnadrochit (24) a mile east, to the left above the A831 is the pretty, white-harled village of Milton, once Milntown. Developed c.1811 by 'The Good Sir James' who also founded Lewiston as a centre of weaving, Milton was not completed until after 1820: the last mill closed in the 1930s.

39.   Glen Urquhart to Corrimony *(Route, Walks)*

From here the A831 runs west through Glen Urquhart, first past the beech-hedged drive to Polmaily House Hotel. Here, it's said, c.1540 a local armourer, the Big Smith of Polmaily, was given a filly by his friends - the fairies of Tor-na-Sithe, a hill-fort two miles further on. The agreement was that this fey beast would plough tirelessly, if yoked only to a plough. Inevitably, one day she was given a cart to pull, and her powers vanished.

More brutally real, in 1544 the Smith's sons and many others died during the Great Raid, when Macdonald of Clanranald fell on the glen. He seized Urquhart Castle (26) and stole huge numbers of livestock - 3000 sheep and lambs, 1500 cattle, nearly the same number of goats, and 300 horses. There is no such animal wealth here now.

With forestry cloaking both sides of the narrowing glen, south of the road where it bends north under the steep wooded slope of Tor-na-Sithe (452297), is an old meal mill, the Mill of Tore, restored in 1976. As for Tor-na-Sithe (Fairy Crag), little is left of this large rectangular fort. The *Daoine Sidhe* (Men of Peace), also called *Sleagh Maith* (Good Folk) - terms used by the wise Gael to placate these mischievous otherworld entities - seem to have moved on from this densely scrub-wooded conical hill.

Round this bend on the left is a Forest Enterprise parking space by a track over the Enrick. Beyond it forestry trails climb south above Lochletter or west past Loch Meiklie to Shewglie and Shenval. Shewglie (418297: mostly 1762) recalls a major betrayal. In 1746, Grant of Shewglie and his son were among the 16 Glen Urquhart men and 68 from Glen Moriston abandoned to Cumberland by their chief, Ludovick Grant. Of these 84, by 1749 only 18 remained alive, as prisoners in Barbados, Shewglie and his son not among them.

Back on the A831, on the left where the river leaves Loch Meiklie a narrow road over a three-arched humpbacked bridge leads to Lochletter House.

Further on, Affric hills visible ahead, the road passes St Ninian's Episcopal Chapel (432304). Stop. Don't be put off by the plain whitewashed exterior. Originally thatched, this 1853 building was designed by Alexander Ross, architect of St Andrew's in Inverness, also of so many other churches it is said in jest that the Diocese of Moray and Ross was named after him. Within the peaceful interior, set in the altar-front is St Ninian's Stone from Temple by Drumnadrochit (**24**). The stone panel about it is inscribed 'From the Knight's Templar's Chapel, Temple House'. But the donor, confusing the Gaelic *teampull* with 'Templar', got it wrong. The Templars, associated with Kilmartin by Loch Awe, Kilmory in Ardnamurchan, and most famously with Rosslyn (home of Dolly the cloned sheep) south of Edinburgh, were never here.

An informative leaflet here is well worth the few pennies asked.

West of the loch, the large white house over a bridge left of the road is Shewglie. A few yards on the narrow Buntait road breaks right (north) up to high ground and Char's Stone (398311). With three round cairns to the east, this fallen monolith commands fine views west to Glen Affric.

40.   Corrimony *(Route, History, Waterfall Walk)*

Back on the A831, a mile past a left turn (south) to Shenval, the Corrimony road (394302) breaks left over a new girder bridge replacing the humpbacked old White Bridge of Aultmulloch. After half a mile through pleasant pastures past Corrimony Church, a white-harled building with black tin roof, the lane reaches Corrimony Cairn (383303).

Advertised from the A831 and obvious by the roadside, this scheduled Ancient Monument is a Clava-type passage grave, but better-preserved than any at Clava (**8**). With a near-complete outer circle of monoliths about the 50ft.-wide cairn, a low, partly-lintelled passageway through corbelled walls enters an inner chamber 13ft. across, open to the sky. The large slab atop the mound is probably the original capstone. Excavated in 1952, on the ground was found the faint image of a crouched burial, but no more.

Continuing, the road reaches a fine old humpbacked bridge over the Enrick. On the north bank (376303) the Old Grange of Corrimony dates from 1740. After the '45 it was one of many houses the redcoats were sent to destroy, its owner Alexander Grant having raised troops for the Jacobites. He was out when the troops arrived. His wife, Jane Ogilvy, faced them. The officer in charge also being an Ogilvy, the house was spared.

In the steading is the Cruck Barn, a listed Ancient Monument, its cruck-framed structure consisting of five bays. The timber crucks, not the later stone walls, support the roof. Late 17th-century, it has been called 'the finest cruck building in Scotland.'

Continuing past the Old Grange and the humpbacked bridge, the now-pot-holed riverside road swings left past a second, flat bridge over the river. Soon, walking to Corrimony Falls, we cross this bridge, start of the drive to Corrimony House, a Victorian manse demolished after a 1951 fire.

First, though, at the end of the road is Clach Churadain (377300), a walled burial-ground dedicated to St Curadan (St Curdy: **23, 65**). On the east wall (built in 1890) of this peaceful Highland cemetery a Gaelic inscription refers to its building. The hollow stone below is Clach-an-Tullan, the font of an earlier, now-vanished church. The ruined building beyond was a bobbin-mill, active in the 19th and early 20th centuries.

Park here for the waterfall walk. Cross the concrete bridge over the Enrick. Past a metal gate, on the left by the start of the old driveway, avenued by tall Wellingtonias, is Mony's Stone (374300). Here the Viking prince defeated at Craig Mony (**24**) was slain. Almost at the top of this fine avenue, a track cuts left - the start of a track to Tomich. Follow it up through sheep-pasture above the Enrick. Where it swings hard right above the river at the start of a gorge, on the left a path, not too obvious, breaks away up the east side of the steep-wooded gorge. This is an interesting walk. Paralleled on the far side by another path, soon its fence falls away. Step carefully above the ravine for what seems a mile but isn't, steep falls and cataracts below. At length the path descends to a ruined power-house under Corrimony Falls. Plunging almost 100 feet past rusting pipes, its remoteness is oddly emphasised by the abandoned effort to harness the torrent. In the bank above is Mony's Cave, a Jacobite hideout after the '45.

The return (or an easier way to it) is simple. From the highest point of the path before the falls, a foot-beaten path climbs the wood to a forestry track. Turn right past a mossy concrete water-tank to the Corrimony-Tomich forestry track, earlier-abandoned, by an old wooden double gate. Return east as you came down through the sheep pasture.

To find the falls while avoiding all but the last bit of the path along the gorge, follow the Tomich track up to the double gate, turn left immediately, then, just beyond the tank, with the roar of water in your ears, take the path on the left, down through the trees.

Yet these fine falls bow to those at Plodda, south of Cannich and Tomich nearby. Truly breathtaking, they're the next stop - at least, after a word or two about another local mystery.

41.   Big Black Cats *(Route, Wildlife Mystery)*

From Corrimony the A831 sweeps up Kerrow Brae through broad open land, Affric and Glencannich hills ahead impressive. Entering Kerrow Wood after two miles, the road descends steep to Strathglass and Cannich. Below a forested right turn north up Strathglass to Struy and Eskadale (**37**, **45**), with Cannich visible ahead, by a bridge (345314) over the Affric/Deabhag is a road on the left: Tomich 3^1/$_2$ - the way to Plodda.

Take it. A mile southwest down the broad flat strath is Clachan Comar (Kirktown of Comar: 335306), a ruined 16th-century church and walled grave-yard, scrub-trees sprouting from it, this on a site dedicated to the 6th-century St Bean or Beathan. Here too are the sites of crofting townships deserted after the Strathglass Clearances. Their own chiefs evicted the folk of Clan Chisholm to Canada (**43**), but the sheep are still here.

So, more oddly, are big black cats not known as native to Scotland.

In 1980 a puma, 'Felicity', was caught nearby, to end her days in the Highland Wild Life Park near Kingussie. Maybe she'd been freed in secret from a private zoo. Yet other large felines of no known species have lately been seen in Glen Urquhart and throughout the Highlands from Argyll to Sutherland, especially on Speyside and in Moray.

In 1983 at Kellas near Elgin (by the Hill of the Wangie, meaning 'wildcat') a big cat was shot as it stalked pheasants. Jet-black, spaniel-sized, it stumped the experts. Several such 'Kellas cats' were later shot, one in 1984 at Revack by Grantown, another in 1985 at Advie by the Spey, one labrador-sized. With biologists and zoologists silent, the sightings and sheep-maulings continue. The obvious answer is that imported big cats later released have, over generations, mated with local wild felines to create mutations surviving in the deep cover of forestry plantations. Yet such reports are not new. Back in January 1927 a wave of mystery predation in the Inverness area was attributed locally to large black cats of unknown origin, while the 16th-century chronicler Ralph Holinshed, source of Shakespeare's *Macbeth* (**86**), remarks oddly that: 'Lions we have had very many in the north part of Scotland'. The possibility that beasties unknown to science have for centuries lurked not only in Loch Ness but in Highland forests may be reinforced (I like to believe it, anyway) by the folk-tale of Ailean nan Creach ('Alan of the Forays') and the cats.

Associated with the River Lochy at the south end of the Great Glen, the tale is that in old age this violent Cameron chief, a killer of many men, so feared for his soul that he asked a local witch to help him. She, for whatever reason, advised him to spit and roast his housecat live. He did so, but its screams attracted a horde of other cats to the open slope where he'd lit the fire. They did not attack, but waited about the now-terrified old man. Soon arrived a gigantic black cat with fierce yellow eyes. Scattering the fire, it glowered over the cowed Ailean, then told him: 'We will not kill you because you are a stupid and credulous man. But we will spare you on one condition only.'

This was that he should build seven churches, one for each of his murderous forays, where no church had been built before. And this, it is said, he did. As for Felicity, nobody has ever suggested that she was other than natural.

42. Tomich & Plodda Falls *(Route, Waterfall/Forest Walks)*

Soon after Clachan Comar a road breaks right over the Deabhag a few yards to Fasnakyle power station, there joining the Cannich-Glen Affric route. We go that way soon, but first there is Plodda. Continue by the river's south bank through a brief gorge and over a cattle-grid into Tomich, with its small hotel, post office, few houses, and wrought-iron black lamp-posts along the single street. An estate village laid out in the 19th century by Sir Dudley Marjoribanks, first Lord Tweedmouth, this was the junction of medieval pilgrim-trails, specifically that from the west coast to the shrine of St Duthac at Tain (**37, 50**). Over the pass from Loch Duich (Duthac's Loch) and along the south side of Loch Affric, this trail descended past Knockfin to cross the Deabhag by a bridge just south of Tomich.

On a steep wooded slope north of the bridge (302268) is Laragh Tigh Fionn, the Ruined White House (306279), an old stone fort. Also near Knockfin is or was the 'wishing tree' - an elder tree with a round hole through its trunk. Once local children were, as infants, passed through this hole to bring them good luck for life.

Where the road forks south of Tomich, the route three miles further to Plodda Falls is clearly signposted, here and at forks higher up. Climbing steadily, the road degenerates into a potholed track that tests your enthusiasm for waterfalls. Amid pasture high above the strath the track passes Hilton, a neat white lodge over a wide pond (284245). Soon, with footpaths on to Cougie and Glenmoriston, is the car-park by the Eas Socach burn.

(Note: this new car-park replaces its predecessor below the falls, reached from Tomich via ruined Guisachan House. Older guide-books mislead through no fault of their own, but no confusion need result: simply follow the clear signs from Tomich.)

About Guisachan (Gaelic for 'pine') hangs an odd tale. A Fraser stronghold bought in 1854 by Lord Tweedmouth, in the 1930s the then-Lady Tweedmouth tried to convert it into a 'Centre of Excellence', inspired by 'New Age' ideas and her association with Kurt Hahn, founder of Gordonstoun School. Horrified at such goings-on, her neighbour at Hilton bought the house and let it fall into ruin. Now the roofless ruin is unsafe.

From Plodda car-park interweaving waymarked trails wind through fine woodland, including European larch and Douglas fir (planted 1895-1900), the latter among the best quality in Britain - the masts for Scott's restored 'Discovery' at Dundee came from here.

The shortest way to the falls is via the path downhill, following the burn. An initial 25ft. cascade leads to an ornamental iron bridge. Built by Lord Tweedmouth in 1880 and restored in 1984, this spans the lip of the falls. There is no sign of them before you reach it. But look over the guard-rail and you'll gasp. The Socach plunges 90 feet sheer to the gorge below where the Deabhag boils round a horseshoe bend. Immediately after the Socach strikes it, there is a further 30ft. fall on the Deabhag itself.

From the bridge a steep-stepped, guard-railed path twists down almost to the foot of the falls. This awesome scene, amid exotic woods and lush spray-enriched vegetation, roots you to the spot. Plodda is majestic.

Less majestic were the people responsible for the Clearances.

43.   The Highland Clearances *(History)*

The Clearances all but depopulated the Highlands. From Strathnaver to Ardnamurchan tens of thousands of folk made way for *na caoraich mhor*, the Great Sheep - the Cheviot. Cross-bred in the Borders, this beast yielded a third more wool and meat than known breeds. Crucially, it could endure harsh upland winters. By 1790 the first Cheviot and Blackface sheep reached the Northwest, and the evictions began. Many were enforced by the clan chiefs of those they ejected. Men like The Chisholm, or Alasdair Ranaldson Macdonnel of Glengarry, full of southern disdain and diction, no longer saw themselves as protectors of their folk, but as the owners of empty lands demanding 'Improvement'. Fixated on increasing their personal wealth, they treated their tenants as vermin.

Between 1785 and 1850 Clearance involved two types of removal. Told to fish or kelp, tenants might be driven from old communal rigs and grazings to marginal coastal land. Or, due to destitution, starvation, rent arrears, or failure in fishing and kelping, they emigated 'voluntarily', often in plague-ships: a process the Kirk approved. Ministers reliant on lay patronage exhorted their two-legged flocks to give way to the four-legged variety. The disgust felt by others at this kowtowing to landlords helped lead to the 1843 Disruption and creation of the breakaway 'Wee Free' (**64**).

Worse were men like Patrick Sellar. Factor of the Duke of Sutherland, human life meant little to him. Clearing Strathnaver in December 1813, he came to the house of William Chisholm, whose mother lay bed-ridden. 'Damn her, the old witch, she has lived too long,' he declared. 'Let her burn.' The house was fired. Carried out in flaming blankets, she died five days later. Tried for murder in Inverness in 1816, Sellar, aided by the landlords, got off 'scot-free'. Later granted an estate in Ardnamurchan, he expelled another 20,000 people, and died a happy man.

The Strathglass evictions began in 1801. William, 24th Chisholm, was ruled by his wife Elizabeth, whose mother had already evicted 500 folk from Glenquoich. She made a deal with Thomas Gillespie, a Lowland grazier renting most of nearby Corrimony. That year, almost half the clan was evicted. By 1803, of 5000 emigrants leaving Fort William for Canada, up to 1000 came from Strathglass. In 1809 another great Strathglass clearance further swelled the Canadian population. In 1817, William died. Coming of age in 1831, his son Alexander proved as merciless. Summoned to meet him at the Inn of Cannich with their rents due to expire, the remaining men of Strathglass waited, and waited, but The Chisholm failed to appear. He had already secretly let the best farms and grazing lands. Half the remaining population was turfed out. Some found refuge on Lovat estates, but most left for Canada.

In 1832 the Canadian exiles sent The Chisholm an address of loyalty. If hoping to shame him, they failed. Alexander and his brother Duncan cleared Strathglass from Glen Affric to the Beauly. The 1858 death in London of Duncan, 26th and last Chief of the direct male line, at least answered the curse of an old Glen Affric bard, delivered on boarding the emigrant ship: 'May a shroud be spun for the chief who runs after money!'

Among the worst of the evictions were conducted between 1782 and 1830 by Marjorie Macdonnell of Glengarry (*Marsailidh Bhinneach*, 'Light-headed Marjorie') and her son Alastair Ranaldson. From the Great Glen to Knoydart mother and son threw out 20,000 of their kin. From the profits Alastair, always in full Highland dress with piper, bard, ghillies and henchmen at hand, promoted the romantic Highland myth. Forming the Society of True Highlanders, he invented the Glengarry bonnet, held barbaric Highland Games, then (deep in debt) died leaping from the wreck of one of the new-fangled Caledonian Canal steamers he hated. Amid thunderstorm his coffin was carried to the grave by four men with flaming torches as his blind bard sang: 'Blessed the corpse that the rain falls upon!' Those with other opinions were by then over the seas and faraway.

The climax of this deeply nasty episode came with the potato famine of 1846. With the Northwest all but emptied of folk save those clinging to the shore, the crofters' plight and the famine relief measures at last brought the issues before a wider public. It was another 30 years until the Napier Commission and the Crofters' Holding Act ended Clearance, but after 1855 it was rare.

44.   Glen Affric: Dog Falls & Beyond *(Route, Walks)*

Glen Affric is said to be 'the second most beautiful glen in Scotland'. The most beautiful? Your own, naturally. Meaning, don't miss Glen Affric!

From Plodda return through Tomich. Cross the Deabhag to the road junction by Fasnakyle power station (318296). Open to visitors, its bulk is redeemed by the Pictish-style carvings of animals high on its front facade. Turn left (south) past an old church and the drive to Fasnakyle House, on the north bank of the Affric where it joins the Deabhag. Below the road nearby is Eas nam Broc, Badger Falls (308285), named after the many badgers once resident hereabouts. A delicate 30-foot spill, some prefer it to Dog Falls.

The single-track road climbs steeply through Chisholm's Pass. Once Chisholm land, by 1858 the last six tenants shared it with 30,000 sheep. Now, with a wooded ravine below, spectacular views open up over native pinewood to high hills ahead. With the Affric tumbling over huge rocks below, Dog Falls car-park is soon reached. Here a plaque describes how Glen Affric contains one of the largest surviving remnants of the Caledonian Forest, dating back almost to the last Ice Age. In 1994 designated a Caledonian Forest Reserve of over 9000 hectares, this is a wildlife haven, with roe, sika and red deer, pine marten and red squirrel, adders, and many bird species including capercaillie and golden eagle. The plaque (its information in an FC pamphlet), also describes local history, conservation projects, and walks from this car-park.

These, graphically depicted *in situ*, may be combined into a four-mile circuit.

Over a bridge by the car-park, the main track climbs a half-mile west to where, with the hill escaping its tree cover, there are wide views west over Loch Beinn a'Mheadain (hydro-electrically dammed) and up the glen to the high peaks west and north. Turning east, the track continues a forest mile to a fork. The left turn descends towards Dog Falls: stay right for the longer route. This curls south then northeast round Coire Loch. Under a rocky outcrop, this pine-fringed lochan nurtures crested tits and many species of dragonfly, including the rare Northern Emerald, with only one other known habitat in Scotland.

The track returns downhill (west) to a stile and footbridge over the river below Dog Falls. Its final section crosses the road to loop up through commercial woodland before descending back to the car-park. Total height climbed about 350ft. - nothing strenuous. A direct, shorter route from car-park to falls follows the riverbank before looping above the road then down to the viewpoint. As for Dog Falls (288283), the power of this cascade lies less in its height (30 feet) than in its mystery and setting. Nowhere fully visible due to intervening rock and the narrowness of the gorge, it is as much imagined as seen. If not 'the finest set fall in all Scotland', as has been claimed (to my mind it's not a patch on Plodda), this has to be taken in context: the river and its surroundings are magnificent.

The road runs on seven miles past Loch Beinn a'Mheadain and the Clan Chisholm monument near Chisholm Bridge. Beyond, now unmetalled, it continues to a car-park and picnic place (200233) at the start of the private drive to

Affric Lodge. Here a short circular waymarked walk climbs to views of the peaks north of Loch Affric - Sgurr na Lapaich, Tom a'Chòinich, and other giants with names to confuse all but Gaelic speakers and serious Munro-baggers. You can drive no further, but the way west is open to walkers. So why not do the 10-mile walk round Loch Affric? The route is simple, but this is wild land where bad weather can quickly swoop, so be prepared.

Follow the drive through a gate to the right of the lodge (184230), where during a wet holiday Sir Edwin Landseer painted sporting scenes on the dining-room walls. Trek west over open moor north of the loch, past lone pines under the heights of Sgurr na Lapaich ('Peak of the miry moss'). The rough path may be boggy in parts, but offers no other problems. At the west end of the loch the path forks.

Leading to Loch Duich on the west coast, the right-hand track runs past the youth hostel at Alltbeithe (079203) over an 1800ft. pass behind the Five Sisters of Kintail, long ago frozen by a wizard into mountain-form to await their promised Irish lovers. They still wait.

If less ambitious, keep left over a suspension bridge past red-roofed Athnamulloch Bothy (133206), once a droving stage-post, later part of a sheep farm, now accomodation for conservation workers. Pine stumps in the peaty open slopes indicate the scale of the old forest. Cross the bottom of the glen to the forestry track running east above the loch's southern shore, and return to the car-park via the bridge over Allt Garbh.

Return past Fasnakyle power station to Cannich (337318) for the next stage of this journey, northeast up Strathglass then east to Beauly, with side-visits to Glen Cannich and Glen Strathfarrar.

45.   Strathglass: Cannich to Struy *(Route)*

Sited by a bridge over the river that pours from Glen Cannich's narrow, wooded defile, the functional little village of Cannich (hotel, shop and youth hostel) owes its development to Comar (334312). Probably 17th-century, this plain house south of the village was home to Chisholm chiefs, known as the Chisholms of Comar, but never of Erchless (below). As to their appellation, The Chisholm, it used to be said the world knew but three with 'The' before their name: The Chisholm, the Pope and the Devil.

South of the bridge (337318), a road climbs eight miles west up Glen Cannich past Mullardoch House and the shooting lodge at Cozac, now a hotel (231317). Soon after it ends at the dam containing Loch Mullardoch (221316). Scenically, this glen suffers by comparison with Glen Affric four miles south, being bleaker and more bare-ribbed.

Back in Cannich, cross the bridge to follow the A831 northwest up the the west bank of Strathglass, steep slopes both sides densely forested. Combining Deabhag, Affric and Cannich, the river is now the Glass (but which *glas* - Gaelic *grey-green*, or Brittonic *water*, or both?)

Soon, at Glassburn, near a big stone house with triple-pitched roof set back of the road, is the roadside cairn and well of St Ignatius (370346). Less ancient than St Ignatius, the well (restored in 1955) dates from 1880. Drinking from it is not a good idea. Another three miles on, high up the steep forested slope (the east slope now bare, full of scree-shoots) west of the road and before Struy, there are two duns - Dun Coille Struy (Fort of the Wood and Stream: 396397, designated on the map as a broch), and Dun Struy Beg (397392). Both can be reached by starting along the track opposite the hotel: the more northerly is strikingly sited on a crag above the valley.

Past the junction with the Eskadale-Kiltarlity (**37**) road by Struy Inn, Struy Bridge (a Telford design: 1809-17), spans the Farrar. Immediately over it a narrow private road to the left heads 17 miles west up Glen Strathfarrar to Loch Monar Dam, where you can park. Stop at the gatehouse of this National Nature Reserve for permission to drive in (not Tuesdays or Sunday mornings), and arrive early: there's a daily limit on the number of cars. There's no limit on walkers and cyclists, though during the stalking (August-October) season you are asked to keep to the road. This is wild, beautiful country with many fine hill-walks described in numerous mountaineering guides.

On a flat between the confluences of the Farrar then Erchless Burn with the Beauly, all-but-hidden amid its policies from the A831 (now running east through the woods above) is Erchless Castle (410408: not open). Dating from *c.*1610, its towerhouse was probably built by John Chisholm of Comar, a descendent of Sir Robert de Chisholm, Constable of Urquhart Castle (**26**) in 1359. Nine years later in 1368 Sir Robert married Margaret del Ard (of the Aird); a family recorded in 1296. Their home was probably the old motehill castle atop Cnoc an Tighe Mhoir or Hall-hill (411411) north of the road, later the burial-place of Chisholm chiefs. The timber castle was defended to the east by a ditch, and to north and west by the Erchless Burn. West of this site up the steep wooded slope is the ruin of Dun Coille Mhor (404411), but prominent Private No Entry signs discourage exploration.

46.   Erchless Castle to Lovat Bridge *(Route)*

The road continues east above the river under wooded crags past Craobhnaclag ('Tree of the Bell': 431405). The tale is that the saintly Erchard, a disciple of St Ternan who himself had followed St Ninian (see **24**), noted that a white cow in the herd he tended did not graze with the others but instead gazed at a particular tree. Yet, oddly, she seemed as well-fed as the others. Digging at the foot of the tree Erchard found three bells, 'new and burnished'. Taking one himself, he gave the others to his two companions, telling each to go off alone and build a church wherever his bell should ring of its own accord for the third time. One went east to found his church in Glen Convinth (**38**); the second got as far as Broadford in Skye, and Erchard settled in Glenmoriston at Clachan Mhercheid. Later, returning from Rome a bishop, he died at Kincardine O'Neil, the church being built over his grave. It's said that after the church was moved his bell, said to possess healing powers, was kept on an old tombstone at Dalcreichart, until in 1873 it was stolen.

The road widens past Aigas Quarry, Craig Dhu Dun (449408) on a knoll above, Eskadale House (another Sobieski Stuart haunt) visible over the river. Hereabouts Aigas Ferry (455405) was used by Catholics from north of the river to reach Eskadale Church. To the left, well-advertised, the Victorian Aigas House (458414) hosts Aigas Field Centre, where folk study the countryside, and maybe practice their swing on Aigas Golf Course. With wooded Eilean Aigas below at the lip of the Beauly Gorge (a shadow of its former self since the dams were built downstream), the road winds past Crask of Aigas by the gorge, a spacious parking place just north of Crask of Aigas opposite Dun Fionn (**34**).

A half-mile on, just past the first dam and power-station, on the left is Cluanie Park (475439: tel 01463-782415/782534), a visitor centre for lovers of birds of prey. Between April and October there are daily demonstrations starring *Haliaeetus albicilla*, the White Tailed Sea Eagle. Ring to find out opening and demonstration times.

Still above the gorge, at 477442 a minor dead-end lane starts steeply north up the west bank of Breakachy Burn past little Teanassie School to Tighnaleac Farm. Beyond the farm is a spectacularly-sited stone fort, Dun Mor Tighnaleac (**47**). After the Breakachy turn-off, the A831 continues three miles to join the A862 south of Beauly by Lovat Bridge (**32**). *En route*, lanes break left up steep slopes to broad-viewed crofts and bungalows. Higher up, hill-farms fringe the bare moors of Farley Forest. The first such lane (487445), under a mile east of the Breakachy road, climbs past Torgormack to the start of the Loch nam Bonnach walk (**48**). Another (493444) breaks uphill beside the old parish graveyard at Kilmorack, a hamlet above the dam and the road over the Beauly to Culburnie and Kiltarlity (**34**). This graveyard is the site of the ancient church of obscure St Moroc, thus Kilmorack.

East of Kilmorack the Beauly loops south of Balblair Wood then north under Lovat Bridge. This loop contains a complex little area. A minor road by Lovat Bridge enters it past a camping/caravan park *en route* to Groam of Annat. The name 'Annat' may refer to the church of a forgotten saint, or (with no sign of any church ever there) may be older. *Annwn* was the Welsh/Brittonic underworld; *Anu* was the mother of the old gods of Ireland, and the hag-goddess *Annis* is uneasily remembered in the English Midlands. As for Croiche (Gallows) Wood nearby...

Yes. Definitely time for a walk.

47.   Dun Mor Tighnaleac *(Walk)*

If intending to visit this dramatic old fort, first ring Breakachy Farm (01463-782116: ask for Robbie Short) to find out if it's okay. This is not only because you'll have to park in or pass through his steading (there are other, more difficult approaches); it's for your own good. Red deer are bred on the moor about the fort, and at certain times of the year stags do not behave like Bambi. That said, there is no other objection.

So, from the A831 at 477442, just east of the Cluanie Bird of Prey centre, drive north up the west bank of Breakachy Burn past Teanassie School. In under a mile the road climbs west from woodland over rough pasture to a T-junction between two houses. Turn right (north), down over a burn, then up west past a deer-paddock to Tighnaleac Farm. The fort (at 457451) lies half-a-mile due north, over the brow of a low intervening hill. You'll need good walking-boots or wellies: the deer-and-cattle-churned ground is also naturally boggy. The route north from the steading is straightforward, save for the beasts and deer-fences. Get on-the-spot advice on how to negotiate both.

Crossing the first rise north, you see the dun ahead. On a knoll above intervening heather moor, from afar its tumbled stone ramparts resemble Noah's Ark stranded on Ararat. North of it, defining it, though not obvious until you get there, there is a plunge down to the Breakachy Burn, far below. Whoever chose this site was no fool. At the 600ft. level, the ruinous oval fort has extensive, tumbled walls. Measuring 80x50ft. (24x16m.), it was entered from the southeast. Below and about it are the remains of encircling defensive walls, the outermost enclosing the entire rocky knoll. The view west towards the wilderness of Erchless Forest and beyond is lonely and spectacular.

Over the gorge to the bare north and northeast are old cairns and field systems, also the forts of Farley Forest - hard to reach from here, but not so hard from Drumindorsair.

48.   Drumindorsair to Loch nam Bonnach *(Walk)*

This five-mile circular trek up an old drove-road to an empty heather-and-forestry fringed sink of glacial water with views beyond of mountain and moor may sound dull, but isn't. Its western section is a bare mile from Dun Mor Tighnaleac; but the gorge and rough intervening ground separate the two walks. There are two stone forts close by this track up to 'Farley Forest', now mostly bleached tree-stumps amid the heather. Forestry as such (a third fort amid it) occupies only the final part of the circuit.

To start: from the A831 take any of the three lanes north mentioned above (**46**). The most direct (487445), to Drumindorsair via Torgormack, leaves the A831 a half-mile west of Kilmorack. Ignoring all turns, follow this steep, twisting lane to its highest dead-end (482458). At the wide parking-space a high stile sends you over a wooden gate onto a rough track. This climbs a bare heather slope with wide views opening up from the Beauly Firth to the river below and bare empty land beyond to the west.

Keep left at the first fork, then up left (northwest) through a sheep-pen past Dun a'Chliabhain (477460) on its isolated rock just south of the westbound track. Measuring 77x36ft., it lies within a wall about 12ft. thick and still three courses high.

The track swings north round the unnamed hill-flank, the wild brows of Sgurr á Phollain and Beinn á Bha'ach Ard five miles away to the west, the land between turbulently broken, empty but for heathery knolls, little stands of fir in dark hollows, gleaming serrated outcrops of ancient rock shining in the watery cloud-thinned sun. When I was last up here the wind blasted so hard from the west the heather rippled like a stormy sea. Almost blown off my feet, I wondered at the the old cattle-drovers, out for weeks at a time on tracks and in weather like this. Past white wind-dried tree-stumps as surreal as a Salvador Dali landscape the track twists and climbs; now along a deer-fence; now by an old dry-stane dyke of rose-marbled stone. Nearby, behind crags on an outcrop to the west, reached by a steepish climb up an old 'peat' road, is another old fort, Dun Garbhlaich (466466), with a fine view south over the Beauly valley.

Soon the track crests the empty rise. Bare Loch nam Bonnach lies below, wind-swept blue in its lonely moorland trench, two miles beyond it the transmitter mast on Cnóc Udais (**52**).

The boggy track curls east above the loch's tussocky southern verge into the forestry fringing it, then swings south, passing the largest fort in this area, Dun Fhamhair, the Giant's Fort (484471). On a height amid the forestry, with a ruinous outer wall, it's said to command a fine view over the Beauly Firth. I say 'said', because I haven't sought it out. The track twists in and out of the forestry, a dull stretch but at least out of the wind, until a sudden right bend leads out of dense forestry over a high stile back on the top road by Drumindorsair House.

Turn right on this road for half a mile, then right again at the T-junction, the Beauly winding below, and another quarter-mile sees you back to your car.

And so to Beauly.

49.   Beauly *(Visit, History)*

On rich land at the head of the firth bearing its name, this attractive old stone-built town occupies a brief flat between the river's final westward bend and bungalow-crowded slopes above. With the old main road relegated in status from A9

87

to A862, Beauly does not seem to have suffered. Headquarters of the trade organisation Made in Scotland, also of a renowned tweed shop, the town is almost as close to Inverness as to the high wild land immediately west of it.

Laid out in 1840 by Thomas Fraser of Strichen, Lord Lovat (architect of Eilean Aigas Lodge and Eskadale Church (**34**, **37**), it embraces a widening of the main road to form a spacious market-place, mostly now given to car-parking, the ruin of Beauly Priory at its north end.

Like Pluscarden near Elgin, this priory was established in 1230 by Valliscaulian monks from the Val des Choux ('Cabbage Valley') in Burgundy. Unlike Pluscarden (but like Fortrose Cathedral: see **67**), it is now a roofless shell due to a familiar tale of neglect and vandalism. With lead removed from the roof in 1582, by 1633 the structure was 'badly decayed'. In the 1650s Cromwellian troops removed stone from it to build the new fort in Inverness which, as soon as it went up, came down (**2**). The Priory is open daily (no charge), and near it, in the square, the inn named after it will look after you.

The name 'Beauly' is from the French *beau lieu* ('beautiful place'). The romantic tale has it that Mary Queen of Scots, back from France, came, saw and exclaimed: *'Ah! Quelle beau lieu!'* In fact the name was given by the Lovat Frasers, long the area's chief family (**36**). Their influence here remains visible, as in the 1905 monument in the Square commemorating the raising of the Lovat Scouts for service in South Africa by Simon Joseph, 16th Lord Lovat.

Next? North and northeast lie Muir of Ord, Strathconon, Strathpeffer and Dingwall, not forgetting the mysterious Black Isle which, as folk never tire of remarking, is neither black nor an isle...

North of Inverness

Strathconon, Strathpeffer & the Black Isle

50.   Introduction: Land of Enigma *(Description)*

From Inverness and the Kessock Bridge the A9 sweeps northwest past Ord Hill and over the fertile whaleback of the Black Isle towards the Cromarty Firth and the far north.

The enigma of the Black Isle begins with its name. It is not an isle, but a peninsula boundaried by a neck of land running from the Beauly Firth's north-west verge through Muir of Ord to Conon Bridge, where the River Conon meets the Cromarty Firth. As the crow flies, from Muir of Ord to the tip of the penin-sula is about 13 miles - not far, but somehow the Black Isle can make it seem so, in time as well as in space. Even though now bisected by the A9, this easily-bypassed region remains oddly remote, hidden and secretive.

Boundaried to the north by the Cromarty Firth and the Easter Ross hills beyond; and to east and south by the Moray, Inverness and Beauly Firths, the peninsula is ridged by the Millbuie - a high moor, now largely forested, that runs its length. Its northern slope down to the Cromarty Firth is mostly gentle, but the southeastern shore - a continuation of the Great Glen faultline - is craggy, especially between Cromarty and Rosemarkie. In between, fertile farmlands and extensive woods also beg the oddity of the name - the not-quite-an-isle is not exactly 'black' either. So why the name?

The usual explanation is that, being low-lying and largely sea-girt, its mild climate denies winter frost and snow, so that its fields stay 'black' while sur-rounding mainland hills are white. Or, it may be, the Gaelic 'Eilean Dubh' is a corruption of 'Eilean Duthac' - 'Duthac's Isle': St Duthac of Tain (see **37**) being linked to many local sites. Or again, the name may derive from the dismal look of the vast Millbuie Ridge before it was ploughed and planted. Hugh Miller (**64**) of Cromarty often referred to this dominating moor as dark or black, this when farming was mostly coastal, and Millbuie's high peat-digs were still common ground.

Yet the name fits. The Black Isle *is* 'black' in that it remains mysterious, dark and hidden; and an 'isle' because, before the arrival of rail, road and bridge, it was as insular and cut-off as any isle. Now, with easy road access, it is easily explored - or is it? Maybe there's more hereabouts than meets the casual eye.

After a walk up Ord Hill, this clockwise circuit starts not with the Black Isle as such, but with the area immediately west and northwest, with particular attention paid to Strathconon and Strathpeffer - land on the edge of wilderness, land of the kelpie, land of the Brahan Seer and the Seaforth Doom. Thereafter, via Dingwall, the route enters the Black Isle from the north, swings east to Cromarty, then explores the southeast coast via Rosemarkie, Fortrose, Avoch and Kilmuir.

51. Ord Hill *(Route, Walk)*

A forested crag dominating the north side of the Kessock Bridge as if guarding the land beyond, Ord Hill (633ft., 190m) is crowned by a ruined Iron Age fort, twin of the one atop Craig Phadrig (**5**). The fort is one reason to climb it. Another is the enchantment of the many crisscrossing paths and trails under a cool tall canopy of mature woodland. This enchantment is heightened by the contrast of ancient and modern; of Inverness and the busy A9 so close to the peaceful, high-ridged fort. Sunlight slanting through the trees above the mossy tumble of stone, as pictured below, offers dazzling half-glimpses of firth and bridge. Equally striking is the contrast between bird-song on the ridgetop and the roar of traffic so close below. It's like being in two realms at once but, atop Ord Hill, it's the modern world that seems unreal.

Trails are explained on the 'Ord Hill Wayfaring Course Master Map' at the car-parks, or in the Forest Enterprise pamphlet, 'The Forests of Inverness'. There are two car-parks from which these trails depart. One (655482) is by the A9's fast final southbound swoop down to the Kessock Bridge. With dual car-riageway traffic here invariably intense, entry from the northbound lanes from Inverness demands care. The car-park on Ord Hill's north flank may be prefer-able. This is reached by taking - with care - the first right turn (646487) a mile northwest of the bridge. Signposted Drumsmittal/Kilmuir, it is easy to miss. Keep an eye out after passing North Kessock tourist information centre on the

91

left. When over the southbound lanes and safely up the wooded brae, turn right on the Kilmuir road towards Ord Hill. A sharp left turn at the edge of the wood (ignore the track straight ahead) leads, via a signposted right turn, to the car-park in the wood (653488). Phew!

The following route is a variation on the waymarked trails:

Head uphill, due south, over one junction to a second. Ignore tracks to left and right: take the central path straight uphill. Next, at a diagonal crossing, a left turn up the curving track leads faster to fort and summit - but keep straight on up to a slightly sunken path running southwest-northeast just under the ridgetop. Again, you can turn left here, but it's worth continuing up to the wooded crest for tree-obscured views over the Kessock Bridge, a trig-point on the rocky out-crop nearby. Half-buried under lichen and heather, this outcrop looks vitrified - an outpost of the main fort?

Now follow the ridgetop track northeast. At a blue marker-post, bear right a few yards downhill for a brief open view over the firth, then return to and con-tinue along the cool, pleasant ridgetop. Soon, through well-spaced pines, views west demand another sidetrip, to enjoy views over the treetops to the Beauly Firth and peaks beyond. Back on the main track, a path to the right climbs to the fort's tumbled remains. Once this was a structure about 830ft. long by 390ft. wide (265x115m), but now little is left. With road-noise now muted under the pines, the track reaches one forested summit knoll, descends, then climbs to a second.

From this point glorious views stretch west then north to Ben Wyvis and points east. Sunlight reflects from windmills on a bare slope far to the north. Eyesores? Personally, I find them (shades of *Don Quixote?*) oddly enchanting, their silvery whirling blades hypnotic. Enjoying the good feel of this place on a bright October day, I was about to continue down the steeply wooded northeast slope towards Kilmuir, meaning to return by one of the various routes about the flank of the hill, when I felt my pocket, and - *Where's my wallet?*

Despite police warnings posted at the car-park, DO NOT LEAVE VALU-ABLES IN YOUR CAR, and so on, I had done just that. With pleasure in the walk instantly destroyed, I fled back to the car-park...to find that, in changing from jacket to anorak, I'd left my wallet on the dashboard, in full view. It was still there. Nobody had smashed the windscreen. The moral? DO NOT LEAVE VALUABLES IN YOUR CAR!

52.   North Kessock to Muir of Ord *(Routes, History)*

Back at the A9, the northbound road continues in three miles to the major round-about at Tore (603525), with options southwest to Beauly/Muir of Ord; northwest past Conon Bridge to the West Coast; north via the A9; or east via Munlochy and Fortrose to Cromarty.

Alternatively, on rejoining the northbound A9, immediately turn left down into North Kessock for the minor road west along the Beauly Firth shore. This village, where the ferry once docked, was founded *c*.1828 by the laird of near-by Redcastle, Sir William Fettes, also founder of Fettes College in Edinburgh.

The road departs west past Charlestown's raised beach and old fisher cottages. Skirting pleasant farmland and the firth's bird-rich flats, in four (walkable) miles it reaches Redcastle, a hamlet by an old pier used to ship local stone over the Firth during the building of the Caledonian Canal. A crannog amid the mud-flats can be seen at low tide, while the ruined 19th-century mansion (584495) incorporates a towerhouse rebuilt *c*.1641 by Rory Mor Mackenzie. This may be the site of Eddrydour Castle, built by William the Lion in 1179 yet, if so, there is no sign of it (see below).

Dated *c*.1450 but rebuilt after 1800, nearby Killearnan Parish Church (577495) had one 18th-century minister who kept falling asleep amid his own sermons because, he claimed, two local women were sticking pins in a clay image of him. Luckily for them, belief that the best cure for such activity was at the stake was on the wane by then.

Just before Spital Shore (site of an early 'hospital' for pilgrims making the ferry crossing) this road joins the A832 from Tore to Muir of Ord.

Two miles southwest of Tore and a mile east of this junction, at Newton (584585), a minor road breaks north from the A832 up a broad slope almost a mile towards Kilcoy Castle (576513), a Z-plan 1618 towerhouse restored and reoccupied in 1968. Beyond the castle drive and a few yards east of a minor junction, a rough track leads north between fenced fields up a broad slope to Carn Glas, the Grey Cairn (578521). The remnant of an Orkney-Cromarty type high-ground cairn, entry to its double burial chamber is from the east. Nearby, among other neolithic burial monuments and circled by eight monoliths, is Carn Urnan (566523), the only example of a Clava-type cairn north of the Beauly Firth.

Continuing west on the A832 from the Spital Shore junction, soon a lane turns south to Tarradale House, near it (553487) another possible site of Eddrydour. Here where river joins firth the crossing was commanded by a mote-hill, the timber fort atop it probably destroyed by Bruce's men in 1308 to prevent the English reoccupying it.

Past the B9169 crossroads (and a short-cut south to Beauly), the A832 enters Muir of Ord. Sited on a plain of glacier-deposited gravels and pebbles under slopes to west and east, this grey village is one long main street either side

93

of the northbound A862. Due to the good drainage it was once an ideal stance for cattle-drovers (**29**), but the old Market Stance now is a golf course, and the village lacks focus. With Conon Bridge to the north and Beauly to the south, it is sandwiched between an industrial estate by the Beauly road and Glen Ord Distillery (1838) on the continuing A832 to Marybank and Strathconon.

Muir of Ord features in prophecies allegedly by the Brahan Seer (**57**), most seeming to do with the coming of the railway. *I would not like to live when a black, bridleless horse shall pass through the Muir of Ord*, runs one. A second relates how: *After four successive dry summers, a fiery chariot will pass through the Muir of Ord*. Even more apocalyptic, and referring to a time when there should be two churches at nearby Ferintosh:

> *Soldiers will come from Tarradale*
> *On a chariot without horse or bridle*
> *Which will leave the Muir of Ord a wilderness...*

In fact soldiers were stationed at Tarradale during World War I, and doubtless arrived by train. As for Ferintosh, locally it had a bad reputation. In the mid-17th century four Ferintosh women branded as witches underwent the ordeal of being 'pricked'. Their fate, as with Isobel Gowdie of Auldearn (**85**), is unrecorded. And at the Muir of Ord market in November 1877 a hare appeared, pursued by a pack of dogs. A local newspaper reported how, on seeing the hare, a local woman exclaimed in Gaelic that, as the hare must be one of the old Ferintosh witches, the market would be a bad one.

All of which leads to a subject central to old Highland lore.

53.   The Second Sight *(Folklore, History)*

'The Second Sight is a singular faculty of seeing an otherwise invisible object', wrote Martin Martin in his *A Description of the Western Isles of Scotland* (1703), 'without any previous means used by the person that sees it for that end; the vision makes such a lively impression upon the Seers, that they neither see nor think of anything else, except the vision, as long as it continues: and then they appear pensive or jovial, according to the object which was represented to them.'

Long associated with Highland culture, *an da shealladh* ('the two sights') involved unsought vision, omens of impending disaster, and physical changes affecting the seer. Well into historical times its reality was taken for granted, though seers were ambiguously regarded, especially by the Kirk. Men like Thomas the Rhymer (**4**), Coinneach Odhar (**57**), or John Morrison the Petty Seer (**74**) cannot have made comfortable neighbours. Too often the Sight involved misfortune, while typically the seer was not master but slave of the unwanted gift. As Martin, factor to the Laird of Macleod in the Outer Isles, continues (I quote selectively):

'At the sight of a vision, the eye-lids of the person are erected, and the eyes continue staring until the object vanish....There is one in Skye, [who] when he sees a vision, the inner part of his eyelids turn so far upwards, that after the object disappears, he must draw them down with his fingers....This faculty of the Second Sight does not descend lineally in a family...neither is it acquired by any previous compact. And...I could never learn...that this faculty was communicable any way whatsoever.

'The Seer knows neither the object, time, nor place of a vision; and the same object is often seen by different persons, living at a considerable distance from one another. The true way of judging as to the time and circumstance of an object is by observation...

'If an object is seen early in the morning...it will be accomplished in a few hours afterwards. If at noon, it will commonly be accomplished that very day. If in the evening, perhaps that night...

'When a shroud is perceived about one, it is a sure prognostic of death: the time is judged according to the height of it about the person; for...as it is frequently seen to ascend higher towards the head, death is concluded to be at hand within a few days, if not hours....If a woman is seen standing at a man's left hand, it is a presage that she shall be his wife....To see a spark of fire fall upon one's arm or breast, is a forerunner of a dead child to be seen in the arms of those persons....To see a seat empty at the time of one's sitting in it, is a presage of that person's death quickly after.'

Remarking that some seers who had never met him had foreseen his arrival 'at some hundred miles distance', Martin comments that: 'All those who have the Second Sight do not always see these visions at once, though they be together at the time. But if one who has this faculty, designedly touch his fellow-seer at the instant of a vision's appearing, then the second sees it as well as the first.'

This remark, that visions could be shared simply by touch, as by contagion, impresses by its matter-of-factness. Martin is reporting, not speculating; speaking of something as taken for granted as rain or birth and death. Other 18th-century texts are similarly down-to-earth. *A Treatise on the Second Sight, Dreams and Apparitions* by 'Theophilus Insulanus' (1763) catalogues hundreds of cases of prevision and their results, all laconically. The secretive author (maybe the Rev. John Macpherson of Skye) accepts that 'deists and freethinkers, who deny all revelation', will inevitably refuse to credit Second Sight, and 'raise what dust they can to cloud and discredit it'. Yet he finds it 'lamentable' that the Church, being based on 'Sacred Oracles', should also deny the truth of revelation.

So why is the Sight so rare today? There are a few known seers, but the faculty, if not quite extinct, seems to have waned in parallel with the rise of the kind of society we live in now. The subtleties of second sight have little in common with the garish materialism of supermarket and superhighway.

Soon we'll meet the Brahan Seer, and later the Petty Seer - I predict it. But now, the backlands either side and north of Muir of Ord require description.

54.   Muir of Ord to Strathconon *(Routes)*

Southwest of Muir of Ord a mazy sub-moorland network of high lanes links hill-farms, crofts and smart new houses. With fine views east over the firth, these lanes knit the slopes above Beauly (**49**) with the A831 at Balblair and Kilmorack (**46**). To the west beyond Farley Forest and Loch nam Bonnach, bleak moorland and hills contain Orrin Reservoir.

Northeast of the village, the neck of the Black Isle is high ground bisected by the Tore-Conon Bridge A835 and the B9169 to Culbokie (**61**). Farms and new bungalows overlooking Strathconon and the hills beyond share this backland with neolithic cairns, as at Carn Glas (**52**).

From the A832 east of Muir of Ord the B9169 climbs two miles to the Rootfield crossroads (551523), where a very odd monument stands. Like a two-stage stone rocket, it was erected by friends of Major-General Sir Hector Macdonald who, locally born in 1853, died by his own hand in 1903. Rising from the ranks, as 'Fighting Mac' he is also claimed by Dingwall, where another monument to his memory crests the cemetery atop Mitchell Hill (**60**).

A mile further on, the left turn north onto the A835 leads south down a broad slope past

Kinkell Castle (554543), a Z-plan towerhouse built in 1594 by John Mackenzie of Gairloch (restored 1969). With grand views of Ben Wyvis and the Cromarty Firth, the A835 sweeps on past Conon Bridge over the rivermouth to the Maryburgh roundabout. Dingwall (**60**) lies on the A862 a mile northeast; the Ullapool road past Brahan and Contin departs west.

Facing Maryburgh over the Conon's lowest crossing three miles north of Muir of Ord (A862), Conon Bridge is an attractive village with a well-known fishing hotel. South of village and river, and west of the road, elegant Conon House (534538: built 1790-99 by Sir Archibald Mackenzie to succeed Kinkell Castle) overlooks the old graveyard of Logie-Bride. By the river opposite Dunglass Island, this oval enclosure contains a mound, atop it the remains of the medieval (1256) kirk dedicated to St Bride or Bridget of Kildare.

With numerous other Scottish dedications, Bridget is enigmatic. The historical St Bride (*c*.452-524), born to the Christian slave of a pagan bard, traditionally founded a community open to both sexes. Yet her feast on 1 February falls a day before the old pagan Candlemas, and her legend - she is born at sunrise, her house blazes with light, fire shoots from her brow when she takes the veil - is that of Brigit, 'The High One'. This older figure was the fire-goddess of the mythic Tuatha de Danaan ('Children of Danu'), and daughter of their king, the Dagda, his ever-full cauldron a precursor of the Holy Grail. The Celtic equivalent of Roman Minerva or Greek Athene, she was the Muse of Irish poets. Did ancient Gaelic bards seek inspiration from her here at Logie-Bride?

Starting from Loch Achonachie in Strathconon, the next walk is easily reached from the Maryburgh roundabout. Take the A835 Ullapool road west past Brahan (**57**) four miles to the A832 junction by the 1894 Moy Bridge (482548) over the Conon. Turn south over the river to Marybank (481537), a hamlet from which the Strathconon road departs west.

From Muir of Ord there are two roads to Strathconon. The A832 northwest to Marybank is pleasant, but the minor route via Aultgowrie on the Orrin is the route of choice.

North of the railway bridge in the village turn west off the A862 onto the A832 (Marybank 8). At Glen Ord Distillery (visitor centre), again turn left (Aultgowrie $2^3/4$). The walkable wee road winds towards and past a domed hill, a transmitter atop it. This is Cnoc Udais, seen from Loch nam Bonnach (**48**). Past more new bungalows, amid forestry and rough pasture the road descends a steep brae over Allt Goibhre ('Burn of the Blacksmith'?). Here in a wooded glen the hamlet of Aultgowrie hugs the south bank of the Orrin, a busy river tumbling down from the reservoir five miles west. Upstream from the old bridge are the Falls of Orrin, long reckoned Scotland's highest salmon leap - meaning a sheer leap, in this case about 16 feet. The map suggests access via a Fairburn Estate track on the north bank, but the old wooden gates by the elaborate 1877 lodge are locked.

The road climbs from this tranquil backwater over a broad crest past Fairburn Tower (469524) a mile to the west. This 16th-century Mackenzie towerhouse was replaced in 1874-5 by Fairburn House. A baronial mansion (455530) amid wooded policies above the Orrin, it is now a nursing home. With views over Strathconon the road descends to Marybank to join the A832 from Muir of Ord and Urray.

Here, by the century-old (still open) village post office and shop, the dead-end road up Strathconon departs west upriver, 20 miles past Scatwell shooting lodge to Scardroy. Yet first, in just over two miles it reaches the Torachility hydro-electric dam and fish-ladder at the east end of Loch Achonachie - a good place to start and finish a fine circular walk.

55.   Loch Achonachie: Round Torr Achilty *(Walk)*

A walk for a windy day, low-level and hill-protected, this circular six-mile route round craggy Torr Achilty to Contin returns southwest past Loch Achilty and along Loch Achonachie's north bank (start 446545).

Park above the dam (second entry). Cross the parapet past the viewing gallery of the fish pass. There's no sign of the map-indicated path from the west along the loch's steep north bank, but don't worry: it's there but for the final section, a rocky bracken-slope, not too hard. Start east above the river along a tarmac track under Torr Achilty. Beyond a metal gate the track turns north over flat boggy pasture towards Moy Wood and Cnoc Mór. A hovering kestrel and scruffy

black cattle hock-deep in mire give you the once-over; Ben Wyvis hulks above Contin, snug under pine-dark slopes. As shown in the photo, the track curls down to Torachilty steading (453557): beyond it a tarmac road bends north into the village, its three-arched 1812 Telford bridge over the Blackwater now replaced. Nearby Coul House (1819-21: 463564), now a hotel and the third house on the site, was once the seat of the Mackenzies of Coul.

In Contin (where you can as easily start this walk), turn left 200 yards west along the A835, then left again (south) on the minor Loch Achilty road (450567). (Note: from just east of where you meet the A835 amid the village, forest trails depart north above the Blackwater to the Rogie Falls or to View Rock: see **58**).

Under forested crags, the silver birch-fringed road swings northwest a mile over flat heath past neat bungalows. At Loch Achilty's wooded northeastern verge a minor road breaks back northeast past Craigdarroch Hotel (444573) to the A835 north of Contin. The lochside road continues southwest a mile to a picnic site at the loch's lower end. It's a marvellous mile. The crags tumble down through bracken-rich scrub-oak to giant lochside trees, the water a mirror reflecting the surrounding mountains with utter clarity.

150 yards beyond the picnic site at the end of the loch a forestry gate gives access to Torrachilty Wood. Ignoring forestry tracks on the left, follow the track along the forest fringe, boggy open heath to the right. This bends southwest into Strathconon at a point where the track meets open riverside pasture, reedy in the middle (423557). Here, cut east over the pasture to a riverside stile and red fishing bothy, then follow a main forestry track east. Where this bends hard left, an old grassy trail continues east above the river then Loch Achonachie. Crossing under pylons up into denser wood, this fine trail continues through dark mossy tree-tunnels past stands of pencil-thin silver birch above the loch.

With Torachilty dam visible under a half-mile ahead, the track peters out on the steep slope between loch and forest. Step carefully through bracken and whin, then down a tumble of mossy boulders to the road over the dam. Keep higher longer for easier descent. About six miles long, on a fine day this walk is beautiful.

But a word of warning: the Conon is notorious for its *eachuisge* (kelpie; water-horse); also for other weird and hostile beings....

56. The Kelpie of the Conon *(Folklore)*

Sole outlet for the dammed waters of Lochs Achonachie, Meig and Luichart in the hills to the west, the Conon pours east from Torachilty to the Cromarty Firth. A renowned short salmon river with a broad flood-plain, the rush of its peaty waters in controlled spring-melt spate can still suggest why once it had such a fearsome reputation.

When the River Conon floods three times, goes an old prediction attributed to the Brahan Seer, *the river will go back to its old course by the church.* Another runs: *When there are three bridges over the Conon, a coachload of school children will go down when the bridge collapses.* So in recent years one careful school bus-driver made children walk over the new road-bridge while he drove over it alone, picking them up the far side.

The Conon is said to have been plagued by a fierce *kelpie.* Possibly related to the Irish *peiste* and to Nessie (**27**), this weird beast, once guardian of many a Highland river, appeared as a wild-eyed black horse browsing by a ford. Tempting a weary traveller to mount in hope of a dry crossing, it would throw him off to drown in the flood. Yet, though supernatural, it was not invincible. If caught in horse-shape, it could be harnessed to work with a bridle on which the sign of the cross had been made. This was a rare event. Usually it evaded capture, being the spirit of the raging river. In daytime it might also appear as a handsome young man, its fairy origin betrayed by the water-weed, sand or rushes caught in its hair.

A near cousin was the *bean-nighe* ('washerwoman'). With feet webbed like a duck or goose she squatted by a ford, washing the bloody clouts of those about to die in battle. To let her see you before you saw her was fatal, though in parts of the Highlands it was said that only those about to die could see her at all. Similar was the *fuath*, a water-spirit with webbed feet, yellow hair, a tail, a mane, no nose, yet wearing a green kirtle. Are the fey folk vain?

As fatal was the *bean-sidhe* (banshee, 'fairy-woman'; in places also known as *cointeach*, 'keener'), a bloodless, boneless, snow-haired hag with huge hollow eye-sockets. Tattered white rags flapped about her as she keened mournfully outside the door of the dying. All the best clans had their own private banshee. Lesser folk had to make do with the raucous doom-laden croaking of the rapacious hoodie crow.

Other weird Highland sprites included the *urisk*, a shaggy satyr haunting lonely places, especially waterfalls; the sorcerous *gruagach* (the 'long-haired one') placated until quite recent times by offerings of milk; and the *ly erg*. Haunting Glenmore in the form of a soldier with a red hand, any wayfarar meeting its challenge to fight was sure to die soon after. The *fachan* had 'one hand out of his chest, one leg out of his haunch, and one eye in the front of his face'; while the *bocan*, leaping on unwary travellers, mutilated them dreadfully.

Yet the kelpie was bad enough, and that of the Conon (also plagued by a tall, scowling woman dressed in green who, leaping from the river, urged travellers to their doom) was deadlier than most. Some 300 years ago, it is said, harvesters by the Conon heard a voice cry: 'The hour is come, but not the man'. Then they saw the kelpie, lurking in the 'false pool' under the old kirk, vanish into a lower pool even as a man rode up to the ford. They tried to warn him, but he rode on. To save his life, they locked him in the kirk until the danger-hour was past. Yet later they found him dead, face down in an old stone water-trough. Seized by a fit, he had drowned, as fated and foretold by the kelpie of the Conon.

In the foaming peaty water of a Highland river you might easily see the kelpie's black tossing mane. Likewise in riverbank willow or alder with their trailing fronds, the beckoning arms of the green-clad river-demon are easily seen. So, should you meet a handsome stranger or wild black horse by the water, take care! And, while on such weird subjects...

57.   The Brahan Seer & the Seaforth Doom *(History, Legend, Walks)*

Under the trees and above the Conon on the south side of the A835 a mile east of Moy Bridge is a stone memorial. It marks the spot where in 1823 Lady Caroline Mackenzie was killed, thrown from a runaway pony-trap driven by her sister Mary. Her death ('and she is to kill her sister') all but fulfilled an ancient curse said to have been laid on the proud and wealthy Seaforth Mackenzies, once owners of land from Easter Ross to Lewis.

Not far on, also south of the road (512552), a sign welcomes visitors to Brahan, now Matheson-owned. Below the estate office are wooded riverside walks and, under Brahan House, an empty pasture where Brahan Castle once stood. Long the Seaforth seat, its demolition in 1950 completed the terms of the curse. This, it's said, was cast by Coinneach Odhar Fiosaiche - Swarthy Kenneth the Enchanter, the Brahan Seer (see **53**).

Yet Coinneach is as shadowy as the alleged events behind the curse. The tale is that in the reign of Charles II (1660-85) he was executed at Chanonry Point (**68**) by order of Isabella, wife of Kenneth, third Seaforth Earl. A Lewisman who (unusual among Highland seers) owned a hollow white vision-stone, despite his low status as a Brahan cottar (field-worker) he openly despised his betters. Earl Kenneth (also allegedly second-sighted) protected him; but Lady Isabella hated him for his lack of respect. With Kenneth away on royal business in Paris, Isabella trapped Coinneach into insulting her publicly by second-sightedly reporting how, at that very moment, Milord was 'on his knees before a fair lady, his arm round her waist, and her hand pressed to his lips'. The infuriated Isabella had him executed horribly, in a barrel of burning tar. In revenge, before he died he uttered the Seaforth Doom. This predicted the extinction of the Seaforth line in the time of 'a chief, both deaf and dumb...the father of four fair sons, all of whom he shall follow to the tomb', the remnant of his lands to be 'inherited by a white-hooded lassie from the East, and she is to kill her sister', all this in a time of 'four great lairds', one buck-toothed, another hare-lipped, another half-witted, and the fourth a stammerer.

In 1816 Francis Humberston Mackenzie (b.1755) died, two months after the last of his sons. Two had died in infancy, a third at Brahan in 1813. Soon the fourth, William, MP for Ross, fell ill and also died. Francis, deaf since childhood, struck 'dumb' by the loss of his sons, sank rapidly. His eldest daughter Mary, widow of Admiral Hood, returned from India to inherit what remained of the Brahan estates. Seven years later the pony carriage bolted and Caroline died. Mary's second husband sold the Seaforth lands on Lewis; a later Brahan laird died without issue, and two nephews - the last of the line - died within a day of each other in World War II. A few years later, Brahan Castle was demolished.

There is some evidence of the curse being known throughout the Highlands before 1816. In *Memoirs of a Highland Lady* Elizabeth Grant of Rothiemurchus mentions in her diary for 1815 how at the Northern Meeting in Inverness the identity of the 'four great lairds' was 'the only topic spoken about'. Duncan Davidson, Lord Lieutenant of Ross, asserted in writing that during youthful visits to Brahan, long before the deaths, he had often heard the family refer to it. Sir Walter Scott and Sir Humphrey Davy were both believers.

So we have a curse, but who was Coinneach? There is no record of a 'Coinneach Odhar' being executed in the late 17th century. Isabella, an unpopular early 'Improver', tough and thrifty, seems to have been victim of an inventive calumny. The legend may date from events a century earlier, when the scheming Catherine Ross of Balnagown hired sorcerors to commit magical murder. These sorcerors included 'Keanoch Owir', in 1578 arraigned as 'principal enchanter' in a trial following Catherine's conspiracies. Two of his partners in crime died at Chanonry in November 1577, and it seems likely that he too perished - though a century earlier and for different reasons than the legendary Coinneach.

Perhaps his death earned Keanoch the name to which, over time, many anonymous prophecies became attached. In 1877 Alexander Mackenzie of Inverness wrote these down and, assuming a single source, called him 'the Brahan Seer'. Many of the 'prophecies' referred to events - the building of railways, bridges and canals - which by 1877 were already history, and so are suspect. Others unfulfilled typically warn of disaster. *When there are seven bridges over the Ness, Inverness will be consumed with fire from the black rain and tumble into the sea.* So the start of construction in 1984 of a new Inverness bridge brought many anxious letters to the *Inverness Courier*.

Of predictions attributed to Coinneach, those involving the 'Black Rain' still excite most speculation. *Sheep shall eat men, men will eat sheep, the black rain will eat all things; in the end old men shall return from new lands*, is the short version of the best-known. A longer version, date unknown, details takeover of the Highlands by sheep (**43**), desolating the country, whereupon: *the people will emigrate to Islands now unknown, but which shall yet be discovered in the boundless oceans after which the deer and other wild animals in the huge wilderness shall be exterminated and browned by horrid black rains. The people will then return and take undisturbed possession of the lands of their ancestors.*

Much has been read into this, from the Clearances to acid rain and nuclear devastation. Yet it remains as ambiguous as the Seer. With tales of the hollow vision-stone he threw when about to die into Loch Ussie (or into a cow's muddy hoofprint, from which Loch Ussie welled up), Coinneach remains as mythically vague as Merlin, Fingal or Ossian. Maybe it's best like that. After all, 'History is the lie commonly agreed upon', and who wants too much truth?

Alexander Mackenzie's *The Prophecies of the Brahan Seer* (1877), and Elizabeth Sutherland's *Ravens and Black Rain: the Story of Highland Second Sight* (1985) tell the story in much more detail than there is space for here.

58.   Strathpeffer: Round Rogie Falls & Auchterneed Glen *(Walk)*

Now for two circular walks to shake off the cobwebs of kelpie and curse. Both start and end at Strathpeffer, a pretty Victorian spa resort on the Dingwall-Contin A834. From Brahan you get there by taking the A835 west towards Contin. A mile past Moy Bridge turn north up a minor road (470552) to the A834, and turn right past Jamestown to Strathpeffer's mile-long main street, descending west to east.

Snug under Ben Wyvis to the north and Knockfarrel to the southeast, the village expanded when the railway arrived in 1885. Now fading grand hotels and villas flank lush hillside gardens with monkeypuzzle trees. The village heads a flat, fertile valley along which a mountain burn, the Peffery, flows past Castle Leod (see below) to Dingwall, seven miles to the east.

For the first, eight-mile walk, park at the square (tourist centre: 01997-421415). Start uphill on the A834 past the old pump house. Opposite a youth hostel (01997-421532: March-Sept.), on the right is a sign: 'Public Footpath to Garve 7'. Follow the lane through beechwood to Kinellan Farm, and beyond bear left through a gate to Loch Kinellan with its impressive, thickly-wooded crannog. At the loch's marshy western end the track bears right, up rough ground past a wooden gate through thick gorse to a stile. Reaching the forestry

(464576), keep it to your left. Follow the muddy track northwest through brack-en and scrub, mountain views opening up. Where the wood turns north (462577) by a gate, continue straight on into it via the forestry track to a fork (green way-marker).

The left fork leads in a half-mile up to View Rock, thence south to Contin or east back to Strathpeffer. For Rogie Falls, here turn right downhill along a broad track west then south (left at each junction), to a main forestry road (blue waymarker: 452577). Again, the left turn leads south to Contin; the right turn north to Rogie Falls. After half a mile north, the roar of the Blackwater fighting traffic noise, a blue-coded track steep on the left leads down to the Falls (444584). With a car-park by the A835 (another possible start), here, *en route* from Loch Garve to the Conon, the Blackwater tears through a wooded gorge. From a footbridge you can see wild salmon fight their way up a fishladder to reach their spawning grounds, this between July and September.

For the full circuit, from the Falls return to the main track above. Turn left, down to the river, as shown below - a lovely spot to picnic. Leaving the river for open pasture, the track passes Rogie steading (443593) to a forest-edge junction. Turn right then, after a few yards, sharp left up a lesser, grassy track. This bears north through a glade of silver birch and juniper bushes into dense forestry, then under the Inverness-Kyle of Lochalsh railway (442598). On open heath at a main track crossing above the bridge turn east, railway to your right, for a mile through shallow Glen Rogie to white-harled, derelict Glensgaich Lodge under Creag an Fhithich (Raven Rock: 874 feet).

104

By the lodge a whin-hemmed path descends to a ramshackle wooden bridge over the Rogie Burn, then diagonally right between forestry and a heathery slope to the railway under Raven Rock. After several hundred yards east the line curves over a wooded ravine, above Allt Dearg. From a gate the far side of the ravine emerges the path mentioned below. I don't recommend this as a shortcut, though both Lodge and Rock are worth a look.

Above the lodge the track loops northeast then crosses Allt Dearg (465613) to meet a track from the south. Turn right down this secondary track, which crosses then follows the burn down to the railway (469606). Cross the track and follow it east (left) a few yards to join the opposite path. This descends steeply through dense forest, then bears right through a clearing to a wooden bridge over Allt Dearg (470605). On the south side bear left (east) on a rutted track to follow the flank of deepening Auchterneed Glen. After a long mile through mixed woodland rich in mosses and lichens, you descend past a sawmill and private road to the Auchterneed road. Turn right (south) past Castle Leod (486594), seat of the Mackenzie Earl of Cromartie. Based on the original 1616 Z-plan tower by Sir Rorie Mackenzie of Coigach, this prominent pile with its corbelled bartizans and wallhead parapets occupies lush parkland.

At the A834, turn right (west) into Strathpeffer. At the start of the village on the right a hedged, signposted path climbs to the Eagle Stone (486585). On a grassy knoll facing Knockfarrel, this small Pictish symbol stone (see **66**) is dated 6th century. Legend says it has fallen twice and, if it falls again, there will be such a flood that ships will be able to sail up to Strathpeffer. Hopefully not today. On the other side of the A834, the old railway station contains the Highland Museum of Childhood (01997-421031: mid-March-31 October). After this trek, you may well find the cafe here welcome.

59.   Strathpeffer: Knockfarrel Vitrified Fort *(Folklore, Walk)*

With spectacular all-round views the vitrified fort at Knockfarrel is a must. From Maryburgh roundabout (544570), take the A835 west and turn right up either the first or the second of two minor roads to Loch Ussie/Knockfarrel. Once above the pretty loch turn first right (508578), then first left, then first right again between two cottages. Knockfarrel, unimpressive this side, is the ridge ahead, due north. Park by a farmhouse under a gate (503583). Beyond the gate follow a track, right, up the ridge.

More rewarding is to walk from Strathpeffer via Blackmuir Wood and Cnoc Mór. Again, park in Strathpeffer and walk west up the A834. At the youth hostel sign (478574), take a broad track left to Blackmuir Wood. The marshy pool on the right was once a curling pond, dating from Queen Victoria's Jubilee

Year. Beyond, at a junction on the left (the 'Touchstone Maze' advertised) begin colour-coded woodland trails. Keep straight on (right) past holiday chalets (Cnocmor Lodge) to a forestry gate. A sign welcomes walkers onto a track curling southeast up through the wood. Where this turns hard left and levels off (the direct route to Knockfarrel), take a rough path on the right (beside a sign indicating a car-park downhill) east up a fire-cut.

This path soon swings south, contouring Cnoc Mór's wooded lower slope to a fenced field. Turn uphill over a stile through brief forestry to a devastated open slope, felled but uncleared. Bear diagonally south up a rutted path to a main forestry track. Here, rounding a high bare flank with fine views back over Strathconon, suddenly you're above swan-rich Loch Ussie's wooded islets.

Winding east round Cnoc Mór's folded flanks and forestry clutter the track descends through coniferous gloom to a wooden gate, then up along a narrow heathery ridge, slopes steep down to Strathpeffer one side, to Loch Ussie and Brahan Wood the other. Bare save for a few windblown firs and silver birches, by the trig point the design of a modern symbol stone suggests some ancient goddess. In fact it replicates a stone carved in 1989 and set up in the local school to commemorate a visit by young earthquake-victims from - was it Armenia?

Straight ahead, a shallow dip between, is the narrow spine of Knockfarrel, its rocky north face almost sheer. The path joins the main track (see above), then climbs the ridge up spills of glassy, fused rock to an information plaque. Dated *c*.700-500BC, Knockfarrel (or 'Knock Farril') commands unrivalled views. Jagged Munros march the western horizon. To the north, like a stranded whale Ben Wyvis dwarfs the field-chequered slopes (see photo) above the green strath below. East beyond Dingwall and the Cromarty Firth the Black Isle stretches out; to the south Loch Ussie sparkles.

250 metres long and at most 50 metres wide, with 'pour-marks' where the fire-melted rock ran downhill, the fort is vitrified round much of the perimeter. What caused such fierce heat (**5, 51**) is here explained by folklore. One day, with Fingal and his warriors out hunting, the unpopular Conon was left in charge. Finding him asleep, the women staked his seven braids of hair to the ground, then rang the alarm bell. Leaping up, Conon left half his scalp behind. Enraged, he drove the women into the fort. Torching it and them, he left it as we find it now.

Another legend concerns Fingal's Well. Amid the topmost grassy sink within the remains of low slag walls (allegedly up to 23 feet high when first excavated in 1774) is a reedy depression. It's said (shades of the Loch Ness (**21**) and Eagle Stone (**58**) myths) that removal of a stone plugging this 'well' will cause Loch Ussie to burst up and flood the valley below. As for Fingal, this ancient Gaelic hero with seven-league boots needed only one step to stride from

Knockfarrel to Ben Wyvis. I wouldn't try it, myself.

Returning to the saddle between Knockfarrel and Cnoc Mór, take the track west down the north flank of Cnoc Mór. With Strathpeffer visible all the way you may be tempted to short-cut across the fields. Don't. Even where, under Cnoc Mór's rocky scarps, the bracken-fringed track starts uphill again, keep to it. Soon after it enters the forestry, take the path running down-hill, right. After another hundred yards, a second down-hill junction leads to the Touchstone Maze. Based on old labyrinth designs and sun/moon alignments as found in megalithic stone circles like Callanish and East Aquhorthies, this imag-inative construction is an ideal outing for geology classes. All the stones of the region, with their geological history, are set up and explained. Hidden just inside the wood, below it over a stile a path through a field leads to a steep brae facing Strathpeffer's Victorian architectural oddities. A spired Italianite church, windows outlined by soft warm stone, catches the eye as the now-metalled road takes you back down to where you started...

60. East Through Dingwall *(Route)*

Now we head east through Dingwall to the 1980 Cromarty Firth Viaduct and south onto the Black Isle. The A834 following the River Peffery along the wood-ed strath past Fodderty is pretty enough, but the higher back road via the Neil Gunn memorial up the Heights of Brae has the views. This, signposted to Achterneed (the memorial also indicated: 492590) breaks left from the A834 just east of Strathpeffer, passing Castle Leod before climbing steeply past scattered crofts opposite Knockfarrel, impressive from here. After a long three miles you reach the memorial to one of Scotland's best-loved authors, Neil Gunn (1891-1973).

The memorial is sited here because during the 1940s Gunn and his wife Daisy lived in nearby Braefarm House, just down the road towards Dingwall. His daily walk brought him to this splendid viewpoint to gaze over the hills he described so poetically in books like *Highland River*, *The Silver Darlings* - a joyous read - and *Young Art and Old Hector*. The friend of Edwin Muir, Leslie Mitchell ('Lewis Grassic Gibbon'), and especially Maurice Walsh, he moved about a lot but ended his days on the Black Isle. As so often, it took his death to restore him to fashion. Most of his books are now back in print and well worth your attention for their lyrical intensity and deep love of the Highlands.

The road now drops steeply to Dingwall, a medieval market town at the head of the Cromarty Firth and by the mouth of the Peffery. Once a thriving port before mud choked the harbour, and perhaps Macbeth's birthplace (see **86**), its name derives from the Norse *thing* (parliament) and *völlr* (place). Quiet enough today, save round the market square any Wednesday, or during July's annual highland gathering, this is the county town of Ross and Cromarty. It is a functional place, the through road dominated by a sprawling car-park. There is a fine little museum in the 1730 Tolbooth on the pedestrianised high street. A special exhibition commemorates 'Fighting Mac' - General Hector Macdonald (1853-1903), a local man who made his name at the Battle of Omdurman. Visible for miles around, the battlemented tower atop Mitchell Hill (the local cemetery) was erected in his memory, as was the lesser-known monument at his birthplace, Rootfield (**54**). The view from the monument is splendid. Also impressive is the Free Church (1867-70). As for the Old Parish Church (St Clement's), it dates from 1799-1803, its predecessor having burned down after someone took a pot-shot at a pigeon on its heather-thatched roof. In its graveyard is a cross-slab tombstone dated 1531 and, by the gate, a weathered Class 1 Pictish symbol stone (see **66**). Built back to front by Davidson of Tulloch following a dispute with the Kirk Session, it faces Tulloch Castle, a stolidly unexciting edifice overlooking the town from a rise to the north.

Continuing up the north bank of the firth, the A862 from Dingwall parallels the railway to meet the A9 and the route north past the oil fabrication yards at Invergordon to Tain, Dornoch, Brora and Caithness. But that's for another day.

On meeting the A9, turn south over the viaduct to the Black Isle.

61. The Black Isle: Culbokie to Udale Bay *(Routes, Short Walk)*

On reaching the Black Isle shore the A9 sweeps past the coastal B9163 turn-off northeast to Cromarty. Bypassing the village of Culbokie, it tears on to Kessock Bridge and Inverness, interrupted only by the Tore roundabout, where the A832 breaks east past Munlochy to Avoch, Fortrose, Rosemarkie and Cromarty.

Our route is to Cromarty. First, though, two routes not otherwise mentioned. One is the B9163 from the A9 southwest to Conon Bridge. This soon passes the ruined church at Urquhart (581585). Here St Maelrubha (the 'red priest': 642-722) may have died before being buried at the monastery he founded at Applecross. Foundations of the oval enclosure of the early Christian community survive within a walled cemetery. A mile on, above the steep den of Castle Burn, Drummondreoch Fort (583576) is a circular Iron Age ruin with a dilapidated stone wall, two outer ditches, and an earth rampart 20 feet wide.

The minor road along the Millbuie ridge is also easily missed. Leaving the A9 bare yards (602528) north of Tore, it runs east past Killen to the Balblair-Rosemarkie B9160 (710607). With several junctions amid dense forest or on broad high farmland, it offers fine views south over Munlochy Bay and the Moray Firth. There are chambered cairns at Balnaguie (628547) and Belmaduthy (644560). The road from Killen south to Fortrose (**68**) and Avoch (**69**) swoops up and down through hidden little bowl-like valleys before a Y-fork leads to impressively steep, scenic coastal descents, especially to Avoch.

As with the Nairn backlands (**81**), everything about the Millbuie feels hidden, old, remote and haunted. Something about it raises a shiver. Absorbing even bright sunlight with a sense of shadow, if the 'blackness' of the Black Isle is anywhere, it is up here.

For Cromarty, as soon as the A9 reaches the shore, turn left onto the B9163, which takes up the B9169 from Muir of Ord northeast of Culbokie. This straggling hamlet on its bare slope once had a fair, but little happens there now. In Culbokie Wood to the south, Glascairn Fort (603587) lies by a road to Fortrose via Mount Eagle, while just north of the village is Findon Dun (609603).

The B9163 follows open farm-slopes above the firth past Castle Craig (632638), a ruined 16th-century tower built by the Urquharts of Cromarty. Cullicudden burial ground (649650: nothing left of the 1609 church) has Urquhart and Gordon enclosures. Local neolithic remains include Cnoc nan Taibhsean, Ghosts' Hillock (673661). It's well-named, for this is a wind-blown landscape almost as bleak as Buchan.

At the hamlet of Balblair the road curves south then east past the mud-flats of Udale Bay, a mecca for birds and bird-watchers alike. Teal, mallard, shelduck and widgeon are present; likewise heron, winter greylag, waders and dunlin. The time to visit is August to October, when vast flocks of migrating birds pour through *en route* from far north to far south. Facing Invergordon over the firth, the mudflats here constitute half of a National Nature Reserve, the other half including the tidal flats on the opposite shore. Park by the shoreline ruin of St Michael's Chapel (706658) to walk a mile north to Newhall Point. Here the view over the firth to Ben Wyvis and beyond is especially fine. This track continues a half-mile west to a pier. A junction halfway along leads south through Balblair past the Ferry Inn (*c.*1835) to the B9163 and back to the start.

Avoid the flats - the mud is treacherous.

Past Newhall, an 1805 Georgian mansion, the B9163 crosses Newhall Bridge. Beyond the B9160 Rosemarkie (**65**) road and Jemimaville, a row of 19th-century cottages named for the wife of a local laird, it continues along the edge of Udale Bay to Cromarty, the view dominated by huge gantries towering over oil platforms in the fabrication yards at Nigg, close across the firth. They look like they've just lurched out of *War of the Worlds* or *Independence Day.*

So, with impressive headlands (the North and South Sutors) towering either side of the entry to the firth bearing its name, to one of Scotland's best-preserved old towns.

62. Cromarty & the Sutors *(History, Museum)*

Cromarty is a jewel - rich in history, folklore, striking vernacular architecture, and grand views of seven counties from the headland above it. So don't do as I did, and visit on a day of driving rain and zero visibility. Secluded as it is at the tip of the peninsula, you may not come this way too often. A tiny two-car ferry to Nigg offers an alternative route north to Tain, but lately the service has been in doubt. Withdrawn in early 1997, it has since been restored under private ownership - but, if meaning to use it, best check in advance.

Over 700 years old and mostly rebuilt in the late 18th century when hemp and flax were imported from St Petersburg; home of 17th-century eccentric Sir Thomas Urquhart (d.1660) and 19th-century geologist and author Hugh Miller (**64**), the town nestles under the South Sutor (406 feet), a craggy headland facing its neighbour (the North Sutor) over the firth's narrow deep entry. These, it's said, were two giant shoemakers who threw shared tools to each other over the channel - maybe over the dolphins (see **68**) in the area (call Dolphin Ecosse at 01381-600323 for boat-trips), or the mermaid once often seen near the stalactite-rich Dripping Cave east of the town. It's said that *c.*1710 John Reid, a local sea-skipper, caught this slippery lady, letting her go only when she promised that no man in any of his boats would ever be lost at sea. It's also said this promise was kept.

Also along the rocky shore, in a bank two miles east of Cromarty is Fiddler's Well, (808673), one of the Black Isle's healing wells (**70**). It is named after William Fiddler, whose friend died of consumption. The night after the funeral Fiddler, also consumptive, dreamed his dead friend invited him to the site, where a bee flew round his head. Its buzzing told him: 'Dig, Willie, and drink'. Awakening, he went to the place, found the spring, drank, and regained his health. This is another tale recorded by Hugh Miller.

To call Cromarty *charming* is the truth, but only part of it. The survival of its ruddy-stoned town houses and rows of terraced cottages gable-end-on to the street is due as much to poverty as policy. Two centuries ago, Cromarty was rich; a port well-placed to trade not only with other parts of Britain but Europe and the Baltic. Bought by George Ross in 1772 (the year the 15th-century Castle of Cromarty was demolished), for a time the town flourished. A harbour was built, and factories producing cloth, rope, nails and spades, and the Gaelic Chapel for the Highlanders who came seeking work. Yet by 1850 this 'jewel in the crown of Scottish vernacular architecture' was in decline, sidelined by the the railway and loss of demand for its products. For years it languished, the old buildings crumbling until lately their restoration was begun. So the old brewery is now an arts centre; part of the old ropeworks has been converted into housing and a restaurant; and the Courthouse on Church Street is an award-winning museum. Animated figures and audio-visual displays tell Cromarty's history; and personal stereos, a tape, and a map are available to help you tour the town on foot. Open all year (though for fewer hours in the close season: ring 01381-600418), the Courthouse stands near the town's other main attraction - the cottage where Hugh Miller was born, which we visit shortly. First...

63. Round the South Sutor to McFarquhar's Bed *(Walk)*

To mount the Sutor, start east from Shore Street past the old brewery/arts centre along Miller Road. Where the road swings right at Clunes House take a path left to the shoreline. Note the posted warning about difficult footing and the need for care. After half a mile, cross a stile and start up the boggy, wooded slope via wired wooden walkways and over eighty steps. Through bracken, scrubwood and past big trees the path mounts the dizzy slope past a concrete pill-box. Another fifty steps bring you - at last! - to the top of the bare headland (808670), by the end of a (drivable) track from the Mains Farm.

The concrete buildings nearby are the remains of gun-emplacements above Sutors Stacks. Dating from Churchill's 1914 visit, the fort was extended during World War II, when a metal anti-submarine net stretched underwater between the Sutors. I found them a useful shelter (807670), until realising the pouring rain wasn't going to stop.

Failing to find the track the OS map shows as leading southwest past Blue Head to Red Nose, amid dense fog I squelched over open sheep pasture southwest along a fence-line to the Gallow Hill trig-point (156m). Not pausing for one of the finest views I never saw, a mile on I hit the track south from Cromarty Mains Farm. Via an avenue of trees this descends to McFarquhar's Bed (801653), a bay with caves, a spectacular natural arch, rich plant life and (according to folklore) a thriving colony of mermaids. On the shore under the cliffs a mile southwest is another cloutie well, St Bennet's (see **70**).

From McFarquhar's Bed the track returns north through the steading of the Mains Farm, past terraced estate cottages. Turn right and immediately left down a tarmac road past Cromarty House's interesting stable block and Cromarty House *(c.*1780) itself, and so back into town via the pretty Old Manse.

Before duplicating this route best check the weather forecast and also ask locally. It probably makes sense to forget the Gallow Hill pasture and instead follow the track east from the headland, then take the signposted route to McFarquhar's Bed. As for the views, I hope you have better luck than I did. If not, you can always duck inside Hugh Miller's birthplace.

64. Hugh Miller & the Old Red Sandstone *(Biography, Geology)*

'In the course of the first day's employment,' writes Hugh Miller in *The Old Red Sandstone*, relating his early life as a stonemason in coastal quarries near Cromarty, 'I picked up a nodular mass of blue limestone, and laid it open by a stroke of the hammer. Wonderful to relate, it contained inside a beautifully finished piece of sculpture...'.

Born in 1802 amid Cromarty's prosperity, the Black Isle's famous son was more than a self-taught geologist delving into local fossil strata. A folklorist, journalist and author whose *Scenes and Legends of the North of Scotland* remains a useful source-book, he became the leading lay member of the Free Church of Scotland after the Disruption of 1843; a schism over lay patronage that led 451 of the Scottish Kirk's 1200-odd ministers to abandon their livings and establish the Free Church. Denouncing the Kirk's connivance with 'improving' landlords (see **43**), often this meant they had to worship in hiding, on bare hillsides or in coastal caves. Leaving Cromarty for Edinburgh, as editor of *The Witness*, official organ of the 'Wee Free', Miller built it up into Scotland's second biggest newspaper.

Yet he too was divided, between faith and science. The conflict was inherited. His father, much older than his mother, had passed on the canny, practical outlook of the east coast sea skipper he was. His mother Harriet, grand-daughter of a second-sighted Gael, filled him with religion and legends. These contrasting inheritances both made and unmade him. Unable to reconcile scientific insight with religious faith, on Christmas Eve 1856, three years before Darwin published *On the Origin of Species*, he shot himself dead.

Today Miller's fame as a great naturalist is as intact as his birthplace on Church Street (open May-September, not Sundays: 01381-600245). Long, low, newly-thatched with crow-stepped gables, its tiny upper windows are all but buried in the eaves, as shown on the next page. Built in 1711 by his piratical great-grandfather John Fiddes and restored by the National Trust, it contains memorabilia, collections of his writings, belongings and geological specimens.

It's worth a visit, as are his books, the two cited above being the best-known. Concise, elegant and clear, his undated prose offers vivid entry to a vanished world. Of his first job as an apprentice stonemason in a Cromarty Firth quarry, he describes how 'Ben Wyvis rose to the west, white with the yet unwasted snows of winter, and as sharply defined in the clear atmosphere as if all its sunny slopes and blue retiring hollows had been chiselled in marble'. When one of the quarry's 'inferior strata' is blown up (he finds the explosion 'highly amusing'), amid the rubble he discovers 'two dead birds, that in a recent storm had crept into one of the fissures, to die in the shelter'. One 'was a pretty cock goldfinch, with its hood of vermilion, and its wings inlaid with the gold to which it owes its name, as unsoiled and smooth as if it had been preserved for a museum'.

It was at another coastal quarry-site, between Cromarty and Eathie, that he split the nodule of blue limestone and found his first fossil. 'My curiosity, once fully awakened, remained awake.' After working for almost a decade as a mason he drew his first, self-taught conclusions about the area's geology. At the time, the existence of the Old Red Sandstone as a unique formation was disputed. Researching the local strata, Miller put it on the scientific map. Among his most intriguing finds was the fossil of a winged fish named after him by the great

Swiss geologist Louis Agassiz: *Pterichthys milleri*. 'My first-formed idea regarding it was, that I had discovered a connecting link between the tortoise and the fish.'

His earlier *Scenes and Legends of the North of Scotland* (subtitled *A Traditional History of Cromarty*) opens a window on his time. Fifty years before Mackenzie, Miller places the Brahan Seer (**57**) in an Easter Ross context. Sir Thomas Urquhart of Cromarty, John Reid and the mermaid, Thomas Fiddler and many others come to life. His words remain as vital as the shoreline between Cromarty and Rosemarkie where he made so many discoveries - the shoreline we visit next, maybe to find an ammonite or two.

Hugh Miller couldn't have found them *all*.

65. Rosemarkie: Coastal Cliffs & the Fairy Glen *(History, Walk)*

North of Chanonry Ness (**68**) with Fort George (**75**) a bare mile away over the Moray Firth narrows, Rosemarkie was long called 'Rosemarkney', perhaps from the Gaelic *ros* ('point') and *maircnidh* (possibly *marc*, 'horse') - thus 'Point of the Horse Burn', a stream tumbling down the Fairy Glen past the site of the first settlement. Later reorganised by St Boniface (**23**), this was founded by St Moluag of Lismore, who died here in 592. In 1125 David I founded the first Cathedral of Ross on its site, where the 1821 parish church now stands (737576). Nearby Fortrose later got the see, but Rosemarkie remained a local centre of trade, boat-building and linen production until the railway arrived. Later a popular seaside resort, the neat old streets, the Groam House Museum (the Rosemarkie Stone the finest of its many Pictish symbol stones), and the cliff-hemmed shoreline with its wealth of geological riches make this a place to explore.

Ten miles southwest of Cromarty on the A832, this old settlement lies snug under the Red Craig, a mass of glacial deposits. The road descends above the Fairy Glen, a wooded ravine below The Dens. Cut deep in the glacial moraine by fast-flowing water, these raw ravines are famed for their earth pillars, created when a boulder, exposed by weathering and erosion, protects the clay below. The surrounding clay erodes and a pillar is formed.

An alternative route with wide views breaks left from Newton a mile south of Cromarty. By a white house and gigantic hedge, this turn is signposted to Eathie/Navity. Climbing high along the peninsula's steep, forested southeast slope, after three miles a steep lane (769636) descends from it to the Eathie salmon station. There is little room to park or turn here but, given care, the eight-mile shore between Eathie and Rosemarkie can be walked.

The next, circular, 7-mile walk explores this shore north of Rosemarkie, either going to or returning from Hillockhead (748597), the minor Eathie road and the Fairy Glen. But two *caveats*. First, check the tide is out or on the ebb. Second, the cliffside path up to Hillockhead is steep. Fitness and good boots are needed. To exchange the climb for a descent, reverse my description and walk this route clockwise.

From Marine Terrace start northeast along the beach to steps up a wooded bank. Continue past ivy-choked trees then descend to the rocky, sandy shore. With Scart Craig's wooded cliffs rising above and Fort George and Ardersier construction yard close enough to touch over the firth, the rocks grow fantastic in colour and shape. Gulls and oystercatchers wheel; cormorants hang out their wings to dry as the going gets rougher. Past a wooded defile (745596), and by the first cave shown on the map (the second, Caird's Cave (748598) was inhabited until *c.*1900), is a point where at high tide the sea briefly meets the cliff. Here you turn back, swim, or time it right, tidewise. The stretch of shattered rock beyond is a geologist's paradise, the more so the closer you get to Eathie's fossil beds, but no joke for the unfit or poorly shod. So to Hillockhead Cliff Path (signposted: 754604). Starting amid thick bracken, if you miss it, retrace your steps on reaching old anchor placements by the burn before the off-limits track up to Learnie.

Not for vertigo-sufferers, the steep path is stepped. The first 50 steps climb scree, the last 20 approach the top amid scrub-wood. So to Hillockhead (01381-621184), an SSSI (Site of Special Scientific Interest). Open to the public, with 25,000 broadleaf trees planted in 1994 and Old Scots Pine regenerating naturally, this gorge-torn woodland high above the sea is precious. Please respect it as you walk through.

Over a clifftop stile follow blue markers 20 yards through rough pasture to a fork, Hillockhead farmhouse and holiday cottages to the left. Turn right into mixed woodland of sessil oak, rowan, birch, silver birch, hazel, ash, willow, alder and Old Scots Pine. At the first fork keep left (white marker) for the shorter route out to Hillockhead summit and the Eathie road. The right turn (also white marker) loops briefly through the wood to become the main path. Now above a ravine and bearing west, at the next fork the left turn (white) leaves the wood for a heath-top path on level ground. The right turn (red marker) zigzags down a steep bank to bridge the ravine by a waterfall spraying a dark, cressy hollow. Two steep steps up the far bank lead to a path through sweet fey woodland, boardwalks crisscrossing the burn. Rejoining the white trail by the heath, its native pine regenerating, continue over the heath towards the hillock. At the next fork, either turn up to its summit to enjoy panoramic views, or continue directly to the farm track. Here, turn right up to the Eathie road (733600).

If doing this walk clockwise, you'll know the Hillockhead entry by the carved birds of prey on the gateposts.

Descending gently west, after two miles the road curls left and down to the wooded A832. Cross to a pedestrian gate posted 'Fairy Glen Nature Reserve'. Steep steps descend to a footbridge under a fine waterfall. The path, at first rocky, descends the glen under a cool high canopy of leaves. Further down are the remains of ponds: 'the pows', where local flax was steeped before being turned into linen. With water from the mill-lade, once they also provided ice for preserving salmon.

Finally the path joins the A832 into Rosemarkie. By the old Plough Inn (1691) just before the museum, turn left down Mill Road to the seafront where you parked. Before leaving, visit Groam House Museum. Open daily May-October (01381-620961), here you can make rubbings of Pictish symbols, play

116

a Pictish harp, hear the Brahan Seer's prophecies, and admire the great Rosemarkie Stone - centrepiece of a fine collection of local symbol stones. And as you eye this intricate cross-slab, the inevitable question arises: just who *were* those 'mysterious' Picts?

66. The Picts and their Symbol Stones *(History)*

The ancient megalithic folk (**8**) built stone circles, not stone forts. There is no evidence of war before, *c.*1500BC, the climate began to fail and, with it, the old culture. For centuries Scotland may have been almost empty. Then, *c.*700BC, the first hill-forts appear, along with the initial infiltration of an aggressive, iron-working, horse-riding warrior society. Soon these continental invaders were everywhere. By 500BC stone *duns* and timber-laced stone hill-forts were also everywhere. P-Celtic speakers (Brittonic/Welsh, as opposed to Q-Celtic Gaelic), these folk came in waves, maybe via Orkney, overwhelming (and presumably mating with) the descendants of the former folk. Later Irish story cycles suggest a violent culture, flamboyant and superstitious. Head-hunters who'd fight to the death for the Champion's Cut of meat at a feast, the women as fierce as the men, their kings and champions were bound by *geasa*, contradictory magical taboos. Governed by druids preaching immortality of the soul, reckoning the spirit-world more real than the everyday, they were remote from the pragmatism of the Romans, Germans and Anglo-Saxons who successively divided then drove them back to the 'Celtic Fringe'.

The Romans subdued Celtic Britain only as far as Anglesea and Carlisle. The Irish Scotti ('pirates') and the Caledonian tribes of the north remained free. After establishing a few military camps and in *c.*AD84/5 defeating tribes led by Calgacus (a Celtic name) at Mons Graupius, maybe Bennachie in Aberdeenshire, the Romans withdrew behind the Walls of Hadrian and Antonine. The latter, between Forth and Clyde, soon fell, but the former remained provocative. The tribes responded, their warships regularly raiding the coasts south of the Wall, and in AD297 the Roman chronicler Eumenius refers to them as *Picti*, 'painted people' - the first known use of the term, and similar to the Gaelic name for them: *Cruithni*, 'people of the designs'. So the folk of the north, by now Celtic in custom and speech, became 'Picts', and by AD500, with the Romans gone, were known as such.

With Pictish territories covering north Scotland, 664 saw the birth of the Kingdom of Fortriu. Other kingdoms rose and fell as north and south Pictland competed for power. At Nechtansmere in AD685, a Pictish army defeated the Anglo-Saxons. But since *c.*450 the Scots, Ulster Gaels, had been infiltrating the land, initially via Argyll - *oirer Gaidheal*, 'coast of the Gael' - while Norse attacks began after 790. Squeezed by Scots and Norse, by the mid-9th century the Picts 'vanish', leaving no written records save late king-lists in Latin. Their legacies are place-names (*pit*, 'piece of land'), and their symbol stones.

Unique to north Scotland, their purpose and meaning unclear, many display impressive artistry. In the earliest (Class 1) abstract symbols and zoomorphs (birds, beasts, etc.) are cut into rough-hewn boulders. The 'dressed' Class 2 stones show symbols in low-relief joined by human figures, a Christian cross on the obverse. Class 3 stones (*c.*800) portray only human figures and a cross. The simple harmony of, say, the early Eagle Stone (**58**: shown here) contrasts with the complex design and elaborate knot-work of later cross-slabs like the Rosemarkie Stone. Yet, early or late, there is no sure interpretation. The antiquarian Kenneth Jackson suggests that specific symbols in varying combinations depict dynastic alliances between local Pictish kingdoms.

Or they may have been territorial notice-boards, or memorials, or statements of land-charter. Nobody knows.

The Maiden Stone under Bennachie in Aberdeenshire is among the most evocative, with its comb, mirror, and odd Nessie-like beast, while at Forres (**92**), a 23-foot-high monolith, Sueno's Stone, is the last and greatest Pictish symbol stone. Or is it? In carved bands is depicted a bloody battle, with fleeing and beheaded warriors. Long thought to celebrate a Pictish triumph over the Norse, it may instead (Jackson again) be a propaganda coup by the first Scots king Cináed (Kenneth) mac Alpin (d.858), set up to remind the beaten Picts who now ruled the roost. Yet they never 'vanished', but were dispossessed and assimilated. Today, their ancestors no longer carve symbol stones. More likely, they use Windows 95 or drive a mud-spattered Daihatsu.

118

67. Fortrose & the See of Ross *(History)*

From Rosemarkie the A832 crosses a brief plain above Chanonry Ness to Fortrose. Despite their proximity these two burghs could not be less alike. Sited on the southwest side of Chanonry Ness, above a small harbour with red sandstone quays, Fortrose projects the quietly self-satisfied air of a place with a long history and the architecture to prove it. Large Victorian villas amid sloping gardens overlook the narrow High Street and the 18th-century houses flanking the ruined cathedral and its green. A rash of new houses and bungalows shows how the Kessock Bridge has made the Black Isle more accessible to Inverness commuters. South of the old town, the golf course occupying the narrowing spit of the Ness reaches out towards the bartizans of Fort George.

The name 'Fortrose' (stress on the first syllable, not the second, though nowadays the second is usually stressed) may be among the few things the village shares with Rosemarkie; i.e., the Gaelic *ros* ('point' or 'promontory'). Once called Shendrey, it entered history when *c.*1240 the Cathedral of Ross, dedicated to St Boniface (Curadan/Curdy) and St Peter, was transferred from Rosemarkie by Bishop Robert (1214-49). The new cathedral was begun. Within half a century, chancel and chapter house were complete. The nave and south aisle followed. Yet, like Elgin Cathedral and Beauly Priory (**49**), later it fell into ruin - another case of vandals who, exalting their eyes, saw only the profit to be got from the lead of the roof. With the rest reduced to mere foundations, only the roofless, late-Gothic vaulted south aisle and the transept with its Rood Tower still stand. One of three table tombs under arched canopies in the surviving south aisle is said to be that of Euphemia, Countess of Ross (d.1395).

This unfortunate lady, Countess in her own right, was cynically married then rejected by Alexander Stewart, Earl of Buchan, alias the Wolf of Badenoch (**98**). He took up with one of her maids, Mariott Athyn, who bore his children, most of them as bad as he was. The Church took issue with him when he rejected Euphemia, but mainly because this feral son of King Robert II was seizing its property. And in 1390, even as she endowed Fortrose Cathedral, he sacked and torched Elgin Cathedral - an odd symmetry.

About the cathedral was the Chanonry of Ross, thus the name of the peninsula. Here, from large mansions, godly men governed the spiritual needs of nearby parishes. Now replaced by housing, this area conformed roughly to that enclosed by High Street, Academy Street, Rose Street and Union Street. The site of the Bishop's Palace lies within the walled enclosure at the corner of Academy and High Street. Set in the pavement close by is the Cross, an octagonal pillar almost nine feet high. Another survival from this denuded past is the arched building at Rose Court. More recent is the 19th-century Episcopalian Church of St Andrew, overlooking Fortrose Bay and the Firth. Nearby, Fortrose Academy

(1791), continues the earlier tradition of the burgh grammar school, and is now the focus for all secondary education in the area.

All summer long (especially during the St Boniface Fair in August) folk visit Fortrose to explore the cathedral grounds and village before driving (or walking) out to the tip of Chanonry Ness - which sounds like a good idea...

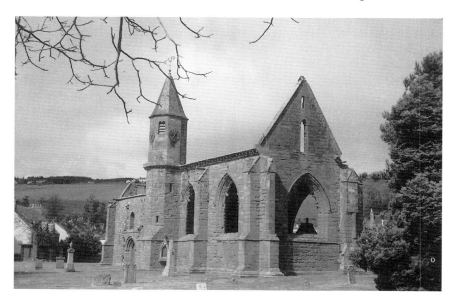

68.   Chanonry Ness: Dolphins & Dunlins *(Walk, Natural History)*

Park in the car-park up Station Road and walk the High Street to Cathedral Square, or park in Cathedral Square itself. Turn left down Academy Street then, by the church, right into St Andrew's Walk. Above the harbour turn left (east) along the shore (if the tide is in, just follow Academy Street) to a caravan site. Follow the road southeast through the site to a sharp left turn. Continue straight ahead on the grassy track signposted 'pedestrians only'.

This shoreside track leads past the golf course to the car-park, lighthouse (1846) and double-compartmented ice house at Chanonry Point, also to the jetty once serving the Chanonry Ferry from Ardersier, just over the narrow strait dividing outer from inner firths.

To explain this unusual spit of land, folklore invokes a wizard who, planning to bridge the narrows, assembled a band of fairy engineers. They did fine until a passer-by wished them 'God speed'. At this the fairies fled, leaving the work undone. More likely the Ness is what's left of a huge glacial moraine, marking the limit reached by a tongue of ice thrusting down from high ground during a return of the cold over 10,000 years ago.

But this is no place to be prosaic. Here, cast in 1969 by pupils of the Academy, a plaque set in a standing stone commemorates the Brahan Seer (**57**). It is said that here Coinneach perished in a barrel of flaming tar, whether in the reign of Charles II or in 1577. Another possible site of his incineration is by the Cross of Ness (742524), on the golf course near Point Road - a stone perhaps marking the boundary of cathedral territory.

The Point is also a place to spot Moray Firth dolphins. Several herds, maybe 130 individuals in all, of the bottlenose dolphin (*Tursiops truncatus*) range the firth from Kessock and Cromarty to the open sea off Aberdeen. Travelling fast in search of cod, herring, salmon or mackerel, up to four metres long and 350 kilos in weight, these warm-blooded and very smart mammals navigate by echo-location, can stay submerged up to 20 minutes and may live 40 years or more.

Tales of dolphins rescuing drowning mariners by guiding or towing them to land led some early folk to believe them semi-divine. In ancient Greece it was a capital offence to kill one even by accident. Called 'lowpers' or 'lowper dogs' along parts of the Banff coast, it's told how in the 1950s a herd chased a school of herring into Burghead harbour and onto the beach, providing the Brochers with a welcome free fish supper.

Often seen bow-riding pilot whales or large ships, with its short, prominent beak and sickle-shaped dorsal fin the protected bottlenose is the Moray Firth's best-loved denizen. Yet at least four other dolphin species visit the Firth; sperm whales have lately grounded by Cullen and near Nairn; a hump-back whale was seen off Lossiemouth in 1983, and an orca (killer whale) off Hopeman. The grey or common seal is often seen; also the shy harbour porpoise, bullied and even sometimes killed by our friend the bottlenose - behaviour more human than we might care to admit...

Might the old tales of mermaids hereabouts refer to sightings of *tursiops truncatus*?

Chanonry Ness is also rich in bird-life. Lapwings gather here in July, autumn brings skuas and a variety of waders, while dunlins, shearwaters, petrels and short-eared owls are among the winter visitors.

Return to Fortrose via Point Road through the golf course past the Cross of Ness or, a little way up the road, turn right (east) down a marked path to the shore. Follow the shoreline northwest towards Rosemarkie as far as the golf clubhouse, here turning left up to Point Road, and so back to where you parked.

Either that or, for a longer walk, follow the shore road into Rosemarkie. There's no lack of possibilities here.

69. Fortrose to Avoch *(Fisher History, Walk)*

Next stop down the coast is the fishing village of Avoch (*Auch*), barely two miles southwest of Fortrose along the A832 - here a tricky stretch of narrow road with a low stone dyke between it and the water, meaning you'd better steer straight. A prettier route between the two villages is via the higher Insch-Knockmuir back road. This can be driven, of course, but is also the first half of an elongated loop walk with splendid views, the return to Fortrose being via the old railway line.

From the Station Road car-park start up Church Street (from the High Street signposted: Killen 4). This road swings left, southwest, and up a high brae past the cemetery. Above the final bungalows turn left onto the back road to Insch. Between fields high above the firth, looking past Munlochy Hill and Ord Hill to the mountains beyond, in just over a mile this road curls past Knockmuir above Avoch down to the Killen-Avoch road. From here the view of and beyond Avoch is superb.

Descend the brae to the village, keeping left to Braehead and Avoch Old Church, the burial place of Sir Alexander Mackenzie (1763-1820). From Stornoway, Mackenzie was the first European to traverse the great Canadian river bearing his name. A plaque in his walled burial enclosure in the atmospheric churchyard tells how, in 1789, from a fort on Lake Athabasca, he reached the shores of the Arctic Ocean, returning safely with all his men after an epic canoe-trip of over 3,000 miles. In 1793, again with native aid, he reached the Pacific Ocean - the first European to cross the North American continent. Later he retired to Avoch House (698558: burned down in 1833) north of the village.

Also buried here are the Fletchers, rich colonial planters who succeeded to the old Mackenzie estate at nearby Rosehaugh in 1864. Now demolished, Rosehaugh House was by 1900 a palace with swimming-pools and tiled Turkish baths. The opulent rooms were heated by a steam boiler which, blowing hot air through grilles, burned a ton of coal a day. This fabulous Shangri-La, built from the wealth of rubber and tea, did not last. Over 40 folk were employed indoors and in the vast gardens, but the largesse ran out. Demolition in 1959 was preceded by dispersal of the luxurious internal fittings to other fine houses.

To return to Fortrose, continue past the church above Avoch harbour. At the end of the road turn left up a track by a house onto the bed of the old railway line. This runs straight back to Fortrose through farm and woodland. Crossing Bishop's Road via a small bridge at the edge of Fortrose, turn down steps onto the road. A left turn under the railway line leads to the High Street.

But why not first explore the 'streeties' of Avoch's sea-town?

To the casual eye Avoch (maybe *Abhach*, the 'river-place', meaning the Goose Burn) is a typical small fisher-town. Overlooked by Gallow Hill (698549), the feudal justice seat, and with a Telford harbour (1813-15), the seatown's small parallel streets with cottages gable-end to the sea resemble those of East Coast ports. Bearing the forenames of members of the Mackenzies of the big house at Rosehaugh, these should be walked, not driven. The close-knit fisher-folk, once never far from poverty, have their own dialect. Famed for their seamanship, sailing in-shore 'skufteys' or small, open, clinker-built 'scaffies' locally built of Black Isle larch, they'd venture as far as Northumberland without chart or compass. Later, needing larger vessels to pursue the deep-water herring, they adopted the 'Zulu'-type drifter, designed at Lossiemouth in Moray in 1879. These became the mainstay of the fleet. Steam drifters came into use after 1900, but sailing vessels worked out of Avoch until the late 1920s, long after other Moray Firth ports had abandoned them.

Living on fish, potatoes and oatmeal, their water came from communal pumps and their fuel (via 'burdeens' of twigs and branches) from the local woods. It was the job of the women to carry their men-folk out to the fishing boats so the men could start their voyages dry-shod. A tale is still told of Katie Gak, who rowed passengers to land from a steamer offshore, completing the last few yards by piggy-back. One day she carried an estate keeper who'd chased her out of the woods where she'd been gathering firewood. Uniquely, this time somehow she slipped. The man was drenched. The local laird had her portrait painted: it hangs in the Avoch branch of the Bank of Scotland.

70. Munlochy Bay: the Craiguck Well *(Folklore, Walk)*

Potent among old rural beliefs is the power of sweet wells to cure the sick or fertilise the barren. Long holy, such bubbling sources traditionally represent access to Mother Earth, or to wise but terrible underworld powers. Today, a casual penny may be thrown into a wishing-well, but once the sacrifice could be of life or limb. Two human bodies found buried head-down in a well at Goadby in Leicestershire emphasise Celtic legends of decapitated heads sunk in wells to placate the well-spirit or to prophesy the future.

In Scotland, the rags (clouties) hung about wells by sick folk seeking cure usually stay in place. Popular belief has it that anyone destroying or removing the clouties will assume the donor's illness.

Of several Black Isle healing wells, best-known is the Cloutie (or St Boniface's) Well (641537). It trickles from a bank by the A832 half-a-mile east of Munlochy. An estimated 50,000 clouties are tied to branches about and above it. The sight is unlovely, many of the more recent offerings being of non-biodegradable modern fabrics.

Another well, near Munlochy's Cloutie Well but more interesting in its mystery and location, is Craiguck or St Bennet's Well (681532) by the east side of Munlochy Bay - focus of a circular 5-mile walk from Avoch (or from an intermediate point for a shorter walk).

Park in Avoch. Follow the sea-front road past fisher cottages to the south-west end of the village then climb a wooded brae past farm-tracks first to the right then to the left. The beech-hedged left turn to Castleton leads, via a gate on the left just before the steading, to a prominent flag-poled mound (Lady Hill), atop it the turf-covered foundations of Ormond (or Avoch) Castle (696535), once a De Moravia (**76**, **78**) stronghold. Invited by King David I (1124-53) to settle in the Laich of Moray and building Duffus Castle there, by 1200 this family was potent in the north. Andrew de Moray, with Wallace commanding the Scots at Stirling Bridge in 1296, died there, but his son Sir Andrew Moray, regent during the on-off reign of David II (1329-71), inspired the Scots during the Second War of Independence. The castle was later owned by the Douglases, Earls of Ormond, and thereafter by the Kings of Scots.

Beyond this site a track loops west then north round Ormond Hill to join our on-going track - another route where it may be best to ask first.

Past the Castleton turn-off the road reaches a Y-fork: turn left, southwest past the junction with the Ormond Hill track. Beyond Ballone and Matheson's Stone (681533: a red sandstone pillar once known as Clach Bhenneit, Bennet's Stone) the road deteriorates. With a massive old stone dyke one side, it descends west through woodland towards Bay Farm, the tidal mud-flats of Munlochy Bay below. Where rough pasture slopes steeply down to a wooded bank above a narrow bay-inlet, look for a prominent mound by the lower fence. This, maybe the site of St Bennet's Chapel, lies above the well. Through a wooden gate (reach Bay Farm and you've gone too far) bear diagonally downhill over the pasture, left of the mound. Over the fence a faint path sinks right to a wooded flat above the bay. Turn left to a little rough causeway under a bank. Here, water trickles from a hole capped by a sloping slab. This is Tobar Chragag, Craiguck Well, the 'well of the little rock' (679539).

Said to protect against disease, witchcraft and fairies, taking the waters here (the time to visit was the first Sunday in May) involved the supplicant spilling water three times on the ground, crossing him- or herself, then tying a rag to the bush by the well before drinking. The idea was that the disease would pass to the sacred tree. Attributed to the Brahan Seer (Telford may have built everything hereabouts, but it seems Coinneach foresaw it all first), a rite to predict likelihood of cure required the supplicant to place two straws in the water.

If these whirled in opposite directions, recovery was sure. But no motion meant death was near.

Returning to the track, continue west past Bay Farm and up through a pine plantation north then east along the rough, pot-holed beech-hedged lane. Past a white cottage is a minor crossing (677542). The road north descends past the steading at Corrachie to the A832 a mile and a half west of Avoch. Keep on over the crossing east to a T-junction amid the fields. Turn right, south. The road curves east past Drum to the Y-junction. Return as you came, past Castleton back to Avoch. So to our last Black Isle visit: Kilmuir, under Ord Hill (**51**).

71. Kilmuir *(Routes, Walks)*

Three miles west of Avoch above Munlochy Bay the A832 bypasses Munlochy, continuing three more miles to the A9 at Tore. At Munlochy turn south on the B9161 (signposted Kessock 5). At the south end of the village minor roads break west, both towards the A9, the second past Allangrange House (1760: 625515) and ruined St John's Chapel, a Mackenzie burial-ground allegedly founded by the Knights Templar.

The B9161 curves southeast over Littlemill Bridge (649527). From here a track to Munlochy Bay leads to Muilean an t-sail, site of an old saltwater mill. The road turns southwest past ruined Knockbain parish church (646522) to the A9. With woodland south of the road after the bridge soon, before Knockbain, the Drumsmittal-Kilmuir road forks left. Miss it, and there is a second turn soon after. This little road climbs a fine long avenue of old beech trees above moss-buried stone dykes. Leaving Bogallan Wood to a view of Ord Hill ahead, a sign on the right advertises the Black Isle Wildlife Country Park (01463-731656). Scant yards beyond, a road to the left (east) is signposted: Kilmuir 3.

Kilmuir is a hidden coastal hamlet under Ord Hill and the brow of a ridge leading to the Craigiehowe promontory above the mouth of Munlochy Bay. Past a first left turn to Mains of Drynie (see below), at a T-junction the right turn to Ord Hill soon leads to a left turn downhill to a wooded brae, then down to a steading above the firth. Left of the steading is the graveyard and ivy-clad ruin of St Mary's Church (676451). Probably 15th century, the first dedication here may have been to St Caiseag. What he'd have said about the bridge a mile away now named after him is anyone's guess, but the view southwest past Kessock to Inverness is pleasant.

From here a coastal walk runs northeast 1½ miles to Munlochy Bay and the cliff of Craigiehowe, a conglomerate outcrop with tree-clad slopes. This walk offers wide views, wild goats, varied bird-life and, near the shore, Craigiehowe Cave (685521), at its entrance a well once said to cure deafness.

The walk is there-and-back. Also well worth a visit for its splendid all-round views and delicate white lichen beds, high on the Craigiehowe ridge is Creag a'Chaisteal (Rock of the Fort: 669506), above Loch Lundie and east of Mains of Drynie (661505). From Kilmuir return as you came, right at the first junction, but then straight on at the second, north past Mains of Drynie along a dead-end road. Park as you can under the wooded ridge and walk on, not far, to No Parking notices where the road ends and tracks take off left, right, and straight ahead. Turn right. Just before a gated cattlegrid and a house, turn right on an obvious path up a lovely wooded slope, silver birch amid the heather. In five minutes this leads to the top, and the site of an Iron Age fort. The panorama is superb, the photograph here doing it scant justice.

To rejoin the Drumsmittal road to the A9 and Inverness, return south a mile, past the right turn to Mains of Drynie, and take the next right by a forestry plantation. At the Drumsmittal road turn left, over a crest to a splendid hill- and firth-framed view of Inverness, and so down the brae to the A9.

Or, rather than the right turn, continue straight, past the left turn to Kilmuir and the Ord Hill (**51**) car-park earlier visited, then right to a junction, and left down the brae to the A9.

Return over the Kessock Bridge for the last part of this tour - the land east of Inverness.

East of Inverness

Cawdor, Nairn, Culbin & the Findhorn

72.   Introduction: A Land of Castles *(Description)*

East of Inverness the tiny county of Nairn, since 1975 part of what is now Highland Council, is boundaried to the north by the Moray Firth and to the south by bleak moors. From Kessock the coast curves northeast to Blackness and Fort George; beyond, from Whiteness Head, an extensive region of sand-dunes and bars curves past the town of Nairn itself via the fascinating Culbin Sands to Findhorn Bay. Inland a fertile plain, widening towards and beyond Nairn (16 miles northeast of Inverness), soon gives way to the moors that stretch to the Cairngorms. These, in places forested, but largely empty, are intersected by three rivers running southwest to northeast - the Nairn, Findhorn and Spey; the latter beyond the scope of this tour.

East of the A9, Clava (**8**) and Kilravock (**77**), Strathnairn broadens out into a plain, the little river winding peacefully past Cawdor (**79**) on its way to Nairn and the sea. By contrast the Findhorn, lacking any fertile strath at all, boils violently through a series of gorges to the Laich of Moray by Forres (**92**) before its final run into Findhorn Bay.

A single two-lane main road, the A96, runs east from Inverness through Nairn and Forres towards Elgin and Aberdeen. Overcrowded and frustrating, it can be avoided. Much preferable as an eastward route is the B9006/9091, rising from Inverness over Culloden Muir, thence via Strathnairn bypassing Croy *en route* to Nairn. From it minor roads run through the bare uplands southeast of Cawdor. Bisected by the Nairn-Grantown A939, these back roads are boundaried (for the purposes of this book) to east and south by the Findhorn. From Forres to Dulsie (**96**), the Findhorn's east bank is followed first by the Forres-Grantown A940 then, from above Logie House (006507: **93**), by the B9007 through Ferness and past Lochindorb to Carrbridge, where this tour effectively ends.

73.   Smithton, Culloden & Balloch *(Route, Walk)*

From the roundabout below the A9 east of Inverness the A96 departs past Stoneyfield to the first turn (702462) south to Smithton, Culloden and Balloch, Inverness dormitories all rapidly growing on the broad slope above the firth. Currently, extensive changes to the road system hereabouts are under way but, as things stand, this right turn leads to a T-junction (traffic lights). Swinging uphill past Smithton to join the B9006 to Culloden Moor (**7**), the right turn from these lights soon passes the Inverness Forest District Office and Murray Road, opposite which a track into Culloden Forest leads to a car-park. This serves a waymarked circular 2-mile walk through mixed woodland, along it the family mausoleum of Forbes of Culloden; the 'Lord President's Seat' (referring to

Duncan Forbes: see below); and St Mary's Well - Tobar Mhairi, a cloutie well also known as the Well of Youth, Tobar na h'oige (723453). Legend claims that on the first Sunday in May its waters, often bright orange, turn to wine - obviously the day to visit!

Another way to this well is downhill from the B9006 via Blackpark Farm (726458).

Return north to Culloden (village) and right, past Culloden House (721465, now a hotel), a Georgian mansion built (1772-1783) probably by John Adam. In a former house on this site, owned by Duncan Forbes, Lord President of the Court of Session (see **32**), Prince Charlie spent a night before the Battle of Culloden, the exhausted men he was about to betray asleep outside in the parks. The battlefield (**7**) a mile away is reached from here by continuing east to Balloch, where a right turn leads south, climbing to the B9006. Here a right turn west soon reaches the museum and visitor centre. But as we've already visited both Culloden and Clava, from Balloch the next stop is a grim response to the '45 - Fort George.

74.   Balloch to Fort George: the Petty Seer *(Route, History)*

After the '45 the British government was determined to crush Highland dissent. To this end a new fortress, more elaborate than any before, was built on a spit of land a scant six miles from the battlefield. Today, Fort George remains in active service.

From Balloch, continue east to the A9, then a mile to the B9039. Though signposted to Inverness Airport and Ardersier, the road is not conspicuous, so be ready for the turn north. After a half-mile Castle Stuart looms ahead. Built 1625 by James Stewart, 3rd Earl of Moray (see **90**), this impressive five-storey towerhouse is best seen outlined against sea and sky beyond Alturlie Point. Restored, with accommodation available (01463-790745), it lies in Petty Parish - once in the care of the Rev. John Morrison, alias the Petty Seer.

Famed as a 'man of great sagacity, much humour and fervent piety', Morrison became minister here during the hard times after the '45 when many were in despair. Yet he inspired people: 'After his settlement in Petty his church was day after day literally crammed to the door with crowds hungering for the Bread of Life...' He never claimed to be a seer, but others claimed it of him; his deeds and words being famed long before A B Maclennan (contributor to Mackenzie's *Prophecies of the Brahan Seer*: **57**) recorded them in 1894. Many of his apparent foretellings may be due to his shrewdness. Thus, like other seers, he foresaw the Clearances. Yet, in a time of 15 well-off tenants in the parish, he predicted a time when: '...there will only be three smokes in [Petty]'. By the late

19th-century this was so: the only 'smokes' in Petty were at Kerrowaird, Morayston and Balmachree. In the same prophecy he added: 'After a time, however, the lands will again be divided, and the parish of Petty become as populous as it is at this day.' Which, also, has come true.

The road (another old military road) continues northeast over farmland past Dalcross Airport towards Ardersier, Fort George visible due north; Chanonry Ness immediately west over the narrows of the firth.

Ardersier was once two separate fisher communities, Stuarton (founded by the Stewart Earls of Moray) and Campbelltown (founded by the Campbell Earls of Cawdor). Now a neat if sprawling village, northeast of it atop the 100ft.-high raised beach is Cromal Mount, a huge motehill earthwork (782555), the vanished timber fort atop it once commanding the ferry-crossing of the old King's Highway from Nairn to Chanonry of Ross.

Just beyond to the north, Blackness is dominated by Fort George...

75. The Grimness of Fort George (*Tour, History*)

To see how seriously the Georgian establishment took the threat of further Jacobite rebellion after the '45, you need only visit this vast fortress. Built by General William Skinner between 1748-1769, still perfectly preserved, its maze-like, cyclopean outer walls enclose 42 acres: an area three-quarters of a mile deep by 300 yards wide. With five bastions, it is also protected by vast ditches, with flood-sluices to admit sea-water. Internally occupied by parallel rows of three-storey barrack blocks, it remains in active service - maybe in case Robbie the Pict and his ilk decide on a new armed uprising?

Built at a cost of £180,000 (then a fortune), the fort was never attacked or needed. It was a white elephant from the day it was planned. After Waterloo in 1815 Napoleon was to be imprisoned here, but St Helena (equally remote, at least to London politicians) was preferred. A scheme to use it as a prison came to nothing yet, while Fort Augustus became a Benedictine Abbey, and Fort William the depot of the North British Railway, Fort George somehow survived as a barracks, from 1881 to 1961 garrisoned by the Seaforth Highlanders. Opened to the public as an Ancient Monument in 1964, in 1967 it was again garrisoned, this time by the Royal Highland Fusiliers. It remains Scotland's only 'Ancient Monument' still functioning as originally intended, though to what end is anyone's guess.

Yet this history of military upkeep has its benefits. Here, frozen in stone, is a well-preserved demonstration of post-'45 Hanoverian military architecture and paranoia. Pay the Historic Scotland guardians their due, then enter the inner citadel with its museum and reconstructed barracks-quarters (waxwork figures and audio-descriptions). Next, climb one of six broad, grassy stone ramps to the zig-zag outer perimeter wall overlooking the firth and Black Isle slopes. Seagulls squall as you walk the thick-built, hard-cemented outer wall; the view northeast to the Sutor of Cromarty is sublime, the quaint stone-ball-headed perimeter sentry outlooks offer neat photo-angles, but this is no beauty-spot. This rampart of: 'The most considerable fortress and best situated in Great Britain', as Lt-Col James Wolfe put it in 1748, is awesome but grim. With massive 19th-century mortars and rifled Armstrong cannon confronting the firth at regular intervals from huge polygonal bastions (named after George II's various grandsons), these are defences to hold back more than a few ragged Highlanders.

Designed by John Adam of the family better-known for country houses and decorative mantelpieces, Fort George has a grim, stark style all its own, and cannot be a popular posting. Windswept and gaunt, it's a good site for dolphin-spotters, but the nearest pub is in Ardersier, the nearest Chinese takeaway in Nairn. Today the Army no longer punishes drunk sentries with 500 lashes or three months jail in an airless hole, but a spell of duty here cannot be fun. The soldier on guard at the wooden sentry-post by the drawbridged main gate was, when I visited, literally 'demob-happy'. Due to be discharged next day, he was enduring a final 24-hour stand of guard-duty. Yet, as the exhibitions of 18th-century barracks-life make clear, his time here had been luxury compared with the life led by the permanent garrison of 1,600 Seaforth Highlanders pent up in this bleak fort during the century or so after Culloden.

After this visit, essential for anyone interested in the history of these parts, return via the B9006 to Ardersier. South of the village the B9092 departs east over flat farmland past the Kebbuck Stone (826556) to join the A96 a mile short of Nairn. North of this road and Carse Wood is Ardersier Platform Construction Yard, somehow fittingly close to Fort George, with the beaches about both designated Danger Areas.

From Ardersier the B9006 continues south, over the A96 to a crossroads (805517) by Loch Flemington. Here it breaks right to Croy and Culloden. The continuing road, now the B9090, crosses the Croy-Nairn B9091 at Clephanton (817505) then, bridging the Nairn, swings northeast to Cawdor. Sometimes I think someone enjoys renumbering these roads to cause maximum confusion.

76.   Strathnairn: Culloden to Kilravock (*Route*)

From Inverness the B9006 is the key to the maze of lanes either side of the River Nairn and southeast over the moors to the Findhorn at Drynachan, Dulsie, Ardclach and Ferness.

The direct route to the castles at Kilravock and Cawdor, our next two visits, is straightforward. From Culloden continue nine miles northeast on the B9006/9091 past Croy (the road designation changes where the B9006 enters Croy) to the Clephanton crossroads (817506). The entry to Kilravock Castle is on the right immediately before the crossroads. For Cawdor Castle, turn right at Clephanton and follow the B9090 two miles east to a minor crossroads immediately after Cawdor village. Turn right to the castle car-park.

These routes miss a lot. There are more interesting, roundabout ways to go. First, via the north side of the Nairn, here is a possible route to Kilravock. After the visit to Kilravock, a back road route to Cawdor via Barevan is described.

From Culloden Muir (**7**) follow the B9006 northeast towards Croy past Cumberland's Stone (749452), the minor road to Clava, and the B851 Daviot turn-off. Crossing the railway at Newlands, continue two miles along the open slope to a left turn, opposite a farm track, to Cantraywood House (774474). Turn north through Cantraywood. After a mile an unusual arched gateway, as shown opposite, gives entry to Dalcross Castle (779483), an L-plan towerhouse built in 1621 by Simon Fraser, 8th Lord Lovat (**36**). With a north wing added in 1703 by the Mackintoshes, the building was restored in 1898. Also, on wooded high ground northeast of the castle is Dalcross Cairn (779484), another Clava-type ring cairn, while some 400 yards west of the gateway at Little Dalcross (775484) is the ruin of Dalcross Church ('Chapel' on the OS map), reached by continuing past a junction immediately beyond the castle and turning first left (the A96 is a mile further north down the brae).

Back at the junction fork left, east, rejoining the B9006 at a crossroads (782486) by the Free Church a mile south of Croy. Cross straight over, downhill past white-harled houses and the drive to Cantray House. Turning hard left above the Nairn the road passes The Square, Cantray (799482), now part of Cantraybridge Rural Skills College for handicapped people. With battlemented towers at the corners this large, impressive steading (until recently a fruit and poultry farm) is worth a look.

From here the road swings north back to the B9006; but more interesting is the right turn just east of the Square. This descends between stone dykes to a narrow bridge over the Nairn, past the entry to the College, then follows the riverbank past Mill of Cantray - all very walkable. Leaving the river, it climbs to a crossroads (806478) by Wester Galcantray. Here you can turn left to the B9090 and Cawdor three miles east, passing what some say was a Roman camp at Easter Galcantray, attractive Holme Rose (487484) gracing the north bank opposite, or continue straight on, south to Barevan (**78**).

Returning to the B9006, continue northeast a short mile to Croy. Here at the start of the bypass the B9006 breaks left through the village and north (fine views over the firth) to Loch Flemington, a name recalling Freskyn de Moravia, a Flemish knight invited into the region by David I (1124-53), his chief stronghold at Duffus near Elgin. He had a castle here too; amid the loch is Castle Island, perhaps artificial, its causeway sometimes submerged. To the east lies the Muir of the Clans, partly-drained bogland where a dug-out canoe and the oak piles of old crannogs were found a century ago.

The continuing B9091 bypasses Croy and soon reaches two sharp bends amid lush woodland above fields sloping down to the Nairn. Prepare for a right turn into Kilravock Castle driveway (815504) a few hundred yards west of the Clephanton crossroads.

77. Kilravock Castle (*Visit, History*)

A discreet sign by the driveway entrance advertises Kilravock (Kil*rawk*: 814494). Two miles from Cawdor Castle, well-concealed Kilravock is as impressive. Dominating the steep, wooded north bank of the Nairn, this massive square five-storeyed stone towerhouse is surmounted by a gabled garret with wall-top walk and bartisans. Built by Huchon Rose under licence from the Lord of the Isles to 'upmak a tour' (build a tower), it dates from 1460.

Huchon was not the first Rose (the name may also relate to the Celtic Earls of Ross) to live here. *C.*1190 a Norman knight of that name came north to marry and to settle in this beautiful place. The family prospered. Early in the 17th century the castle was extended. A four-storey domestic mansion with steep-pitched roofs was built, and linked to the keep by a square stair tower. A century later much of the interior was remodelled.

The Roses have remained in constant possession, though not always securely. Known in the 17th century as a Covenanting and 'godly' family, after the Restoration of Charles II and defeat of the Commonwealth they, along with Lord Brodie (**87**) and other lairds of Moray and Nairn, found themselves in trouble. A 1673 report to the Privy Council spoke of 'seditious meitinges and conventicles' in the area. Charles, 6th Earl of Moray (**90**), a staunch royalist and later a Jacobite, was ordered to suppress such illegal activity. Hugh, 14th baron of Kilravock, was persuaded by the spiritual zeal of his wife, Margaret Innes, both to resist government threats and fines, and to protect and give refuge to Covenanting preachers on the run from the Merry Monarch's not-so-merry men.

Kilravock's relics include two mementoes of Culloden - a punch bowl and a pair of leather thigh boots. It's said that before the battle Prince Charlie paid a visit and that Hugh Rose, though not a Jacobite, hospitably offered him punch from this bowl, then charmed the Pretender by playing him an Italian minuet on the violin. Next day, with Charlie gone, Rose received a second visitor - the Duke of Cumberland, celebrating his 25th birthday. 'You had my cousin here yesterday', remarked Cumberland, removing his boots. Accepting Rose's civil explanation, 'Stinkin' Billy' left without his boots. Maybe they didn't fit.

This is an odd tale. Later in defeat Prince Charlie became a drunk, while in victory the boots of Cumberland's men stamped all over the Highlands.

Kilravock and its lovely gardens and grounds are open to the public on Wednesday afternoons May to September or by appointment (tel: 01667-493258). You can climb the Tower, visit the museum, and walk the grounds; or take a guided tour then enjoy afternoon tea.

78.   To Cawdor via Clava and Barevan *(Route)*

From Clephanton the B9091 continues northeast through rolling farmland past a large earth-barrow (Hangman's Hill: 855519) to Nairn. This route (B9006/9091) is an excellent way to get from Inverness to Nairn without the stress of the A96. Also at Clephanton a left turn onto the B9090 leads (via a humpback bridge over the Nairn, with traffic lights) to Cawdor Castle, *en route* (827498) taking up the minor south bank road described below, from this end signposted to Galcantray, Dalroy and Craggie.

Now, the back road route to Cawdor via Clava and Barevan. Again on Culloden Muir (the last time!), by Cumberland's Stone turn south at the sign to Clava Cairns (**8**) and over the B851. As before, descend over the Nairn by Clava Lodge Hotel to a junction by Culloden rail viaduct, the cairns to the right. Continue straight, past a sign suggesting this as a scenic route to Cawdor Castle. The road breaks left under the viaduct and climbs to join (768445) the minor route on the south side of Strathnairn, near the start of the walk up Beinn Buidhe Mhor (**9**).

Here a left turn northeast leads six miles past Cantraydoune, Galcantray and Kilravock to the B9090 a mile west of Cawdor (**79**). This route, at first under the bare brows of the moors, follows the mostly-open slope above the Nairn. After two miles, by the road at Cantraydoune (789461) is a 12th-century motehill, site of a timber tower erected probably by Freskyn de Moravia, whom we met at Loch Flemington.

A mile and half beyond Cantraydoune and just past Wester Galcantray is the minor crossroads (806478) above Mill of Cantray. Turn right, south, towards Kirkton of Barevan (837472). The narrow road climbs steeply out of Strathnairn into dense dark Assich Forest. Leaving this dreich wood, it crosses a pretty humpbacked bridge over the Allt Dearg. On the hilltop to the north, hidden in the trees, is Dun Evan or Doune of Cawdor (828476), a ruined timber-laced stone fort with traces of vitrification. Amid a scrappy landscape the road soon passes the ruin of Barevan Church (837472: 14th century). Surrounded by lichen-stained tablestones, massive side walls inset with pointed Gothic windows are all that remain.

The site may be that of an earlier church dedicated to St Adamnan. Born in Donegal *c.*627, ninth Abbot of Iona, 'Wise Adam' wrote the biography of St

Columba in which Nessie (**27**) gets her first mention. Dying in 704, he left a bronze bell, now at Cawdor Castle.

By fine old stone dykes, the road continues to a junction: Cawdor 1³/₄, Dulsie 9. For the Falls of Achneim (**80**) and Dulsie (**96**), turn right. For Cawdor, turn left, north. This left turn crosses the Allt Dearg and briefly follows the 1754 military road by Cawdor Wood, then joins the B9090 just west of Cawdor village, a pretty off-road conservation area. Cawdor Tavern may invite you, while Cawdor Parish Church (844490: 1619) was built by Sir John Campbell of Cawdor after he survived a storm at sea near Islay.

For Cawdor Castle, at the crossroads on the B9090 east of the village, turn right (south) to the signposted car-park, where you may find you are not the only visitor.

79.   Cawdor Castle (*Visit, History, Walks*)

Thanks to Shakespeare, Cawdor is forever associated with Macbeth (**86**), though he died long before the original 13th-century 'moat stead' (timber fort) was built, probably at Old Cawdor, or Calder, about a mile north of the crossroads. Some speculate that the Thanes of Cawdor descended from Macbeth's younger brother, but the truth is unknown

The existing building was begun in 1372. It's said that William, 3rd Thane of Calder (later Cawdor), Constable of Nairn, was granted royal licence to build a new castle. But where? The tale is that in a dream he was told to load a donkey with gold and follow it until it lay down to rest. Five miles southwest of Nairn the beast duly lay down under a hawthorn tree. Here William built his tower-house. A tall tale? Carbon-dating of the dead hawthorn railed-off in the vaulted basement of the old tower gives - 1372.

This massive rectangular keep, with battlemented roof parapets, a sentry-walk, and open round corner turrets, may be the finest of its type in North Scotland. It dominates the entire complex of buildings later erected about it. Protected by a gully one side, a dry moat the other, and built round the keep, in its present form Cawdor Castle is largely 17th century. Yet the original drawbridge remains, as does the great iron yett (grilled gate) seized by William the 6th Thane in 1455 when (on royal orders) he razed remote Lochindorb Castle, once lair of the Wolf of Badenoch (**98**).

The castle was not long in Cawdor hands. John the 8th Thane died in 1498, leaving only a posthumous daughter, Muriel. The Earl of Argyll promptly sent the Campbells of Inverlivet to kidnap the child from Kilravock. Seven Campbells were slain during the assault, but the infant was seized and taken to the Campbell stronghold, Inveraray Castle in Argyll. To ensure recognition she was branded on the hip with a red-hot key, and had the top joint of the little finger of her left hand bitten off. When Argyll was warned that the child might die, he retorted that this would never happen so long as there was a red-headed lassie on the banks of Loch Awe. Forcibly married in 1510 to Argyll's younger son, Sir John Campbell, Muriel made the most of it, birthing the surviving line of the Campbells of Cawdor.

Displaying woven 17th century English and Flemish tapestries, portraits by Reynolds, Romney and others; and memorabilia like the muskets seized by John, 1st Lord Cawdor from the French army that landed at Fishguard in Wales in 1797 (the last-ever foreign invasion of the British mainland), Cawdor Castle (01667-404615) is daily open to the public from 1st May to the first Sunday in October. It's worth the visit, if you don't mind queues and crowds. There are three fine gardens, and nature trails in the broad woods above the castle - trails leading via the Cawdor Waterfall to the Falls of Achneim.

80.   Above Cawdor: The Falls of Achneim (*Walk*)

I was going to describe a circular moorland walk from Glengeoillie above Cawdor south along the east bank of the bare gorge cut by the Riereach Burn. Through barrens and grouse moor a track runs several miles past Clunes Reservoir before joining the minor road from Highland Boath (**81**) to Drynachan above the Carnoch Burn, a Findhorn tributary. Two miles south of Glengeoullie a second track breaks east over the moor towards Highland Boath. After a mile or so at a junction under the moor-top (Carn Maol: 324m), a third track heads north past Clunes Reservoir to the edge of the forestry above Cawdor, and so west back to the start.

But for three reasons this one is best left out. One, because of the grouse; two, because apart from the Riereach these moors are featureless; and, three, because the trails in Cawdor Wood are much more attractive - especially the walk from the Castle up past Cawdor Waterfall (839483) to the Falls of Achneim on the Riereach (857478).

Starting at Riereach Bridge, the falls themselves - a series of cascades - are less dramatic than the dizzily deep, narrow gorge (856476) carved out by the burn. Here, from a footbridge recently constructed by the Royal Engineers, you can gaze into head-reeling depths. Like a mini-Corrieshalloch amid fine woodland, this impressive ravine is no place to practice high-diving technique. Here and back from the Castle is about three miles through the wood but, as a road runs parallel to the gorge, you can also drive to it. There are two ways.

From the Castle car-park turn south (right) up the minor road by the eastern edge of Cawdor Wood, keeping right at both the junctions you meet. After

137

two miles south then south-west park by a forestry gate (857478), a firing range nearby and the warning DANGER DO NOT PASS THIS POINT WHEN RED FLAG IS FLYING. The path to the footbridge over the gorge starts from a gate a few yards back to the east, on the north side of the road.

Or, from the B9090 immediately west of Cawdor return south towards Barevan (**78**). At the T-junction (right turn to Barevan) continue on the road signposted: Dulsie 9. After a mile east through dense forestry the road descends over Riereach Bridge. On the east side of the bridge, with the No Through road to Glengeoullie on the right, follow the Dulsie road left and uphill a hundred yards or so to park by the forestry gate, as above.

From here it's seven miles south to spectacular Dulsie Bridge over the Findhorn, with Lochindorb and its ruined island castle a little further on. These, and other Findhorn visits, come after visits to Nairn, Auldearn, Brodie, Culbin and Forres - but this seems to be the right moment to tour Nairn's backlands, in a loop south towards Dulsie then north to Nairn.

81. The Nairn Backlands *(Route)*

Much of the land south of Nairn is spectacularly dreich. In parts, as with the vast moor about Lochindorb, the heathery barrens attain an awful beauty. You might as well be on the moon. Elsewhere, there is only bare dark moor or miles of sitka spruce interrupted by lonely steadings. Yet these barrens are never far from somewhere worth visiting.

Before we start, a brief account of the routes from Cawdor to Nairn and Auldearn, as we'll not be back this way, save to visit Rait Castle (**83**). Heading east from Cawdor, with rows of new bungalows on the southern slope at Piperhill, the B9090 passes Royal Brackla distillery, then continues through farmland up a mossy-dyked wooded avenue a mile to a junction. Here the B9090 turns north two miles over the river to Nairn. The continuing road, now the B9101, passes Geddes House and, a bit further on, the ruin of Rait Castle (894541). Crossing the Nairn-Grantown A939 it carries on two miles northeast to the haunted old village of Auldearn (**84**).

Now for the barrens. From Achneim take the Dulsie road east, right at the first fork (Dulsie Bridge 7½), over scrappy heath to a crossroads (872486). Turn right, south, towards Clunas/Dulsie over poor hill pasture and through forestry, past a large lonely house with giant model butterflies on its white-harled gable-end wall. Really! At 875465 a road on the right leads past Mains of Clunas and a treatment works to Clunas Reservoir: 1.6 miles of tedium. Continuing south (dense forestry, dreary pasture) the road reaches a junction (892452: Drynachan 4½ miles to the right, Dulsie 3¾ miles to the left). The Drynachan road past

Highland Boath (a bare gully) continues over the moor then descends to the Findhorn, and a pretty wooded riverbank road east to Dulsie. South of the river the barrens persist.

From the junction the Dulsie road enters then escapes more dense forest for brief wide views east to the Knock of Braemoray; views doomed by juvenile conifers planted as far ahead as the eye can see. But in another mile this route southeast (an old military road) passes the impressive but little-known Falls of Altnarie (**96**) *en route* to the fine old bridge (also **96**) over the Findhorn at Dulsie. From Cawdor this is the most direct route to these beauty-spots.

Just east of this thick forestry a left turn (916443) to Meikleburn soon re-enters the dark plantations then crosses a burn, signs by the lay-bys either side ordering No Overnight Parking. A bureaucrat's joke? Who'd stop here? This area is oppressive, dark and mournful, with few signs of ancient human habitation - no cairns, forts, or hut circles. There are no new retirement villas either, only old crofts and steadings with oddly-sinister names - Lynethobair, Midfleenas, Tomshogle, Slagachorrie - past which the backroads twist and turn for miles. A left then first right turn at the next two junctions north lead to Littlemill (914503), a hamlet by the Muckle Burn on the Nairn-Grantown A939 four miles south of Auldearn (**84**). East of the main road more back roads run north to Auldearn, or past Whitemire and Darnaway Castle (**90**) to the A96 west of the Findhorn and Forres (**92**).

From Littlemill a left turn onto the A939 leads north five miles, over the Cawdor-Auldearn B9101 to Nairn. For once I felt relieved to be back on a main road. The backlands are spooky. The moors are sour, the dark dense forests feel almost malevolent. Still, on a warm summer day it might look different and, true, I was deliberately seeking roads I'd never had reason to be on before, save as a means of getting somewhere else.

82.   'Nairn in Darkness and Light' *(Visit, History)*

Famously sunny and dry, this old royal burgh, originally Invernairn, was founded by 1214 at the point where the River Nairn (maybe *uisge na fearna*, 'water of the alder trees') meets the Moray Firth. Long a fishing and farming community, here Gaelic took over from English, so allowing James VI to boast of a town in his kingdom so large that folk one end of its main street couldn't understand those at the other.

'At Nairn we may fix the verge of the Highlands,' remarks Doctor Johnson in his *Journey to the Western Isles* (1775), 'for here I first saw peat fires and heard the Erse language.' He adds: 'If once it flourished, [it] is now in a state of miserable decay.' Forty years later Elizabeth Grant of Rothiemurchus agrees. In

Memoirs of a Highland Lady she describes this now-genteel seaside town as an 'odious fisher place', comfortless and dreary. The railway and the craze for sea-bathing changed all that. With a bathing machine on Nairn beach by 1793 'for the accomodation of persons who require the benefit of the salt bath', and a bath house installed on the links in 1821, the 1855 rail link to Inverness helped Nairn to become the 'Brighton of the North.' Advertising the bracing climate, London's Victorian physicians sent wealthy, fog-afflicted patients north to Nairn, Lossiemouth and other Moray Firth resorts for fresh air and 'after-cure' following spa treatment.

Nairn was transformed. Extensive rebuilding left only the original outline of the old medieval burgh, and after 1873 its new clients were also courted by an impressive indoor swimming pool, fed straight from the sea. A suite of private baths offering seaweed, pine, peat and other fashionable aqueous treatment followed. With many ex-military men and retired colonials settling permanently, the population rose from 2,672 in 1841 to 4,661 in 1911. Large villas were built as incomers sought not only salt water and ozone-rich air but to indulge their new-fangled passion for 'gowf', Nairn Golf Club being formed in 1887, for the upper crust only. In 1899 the Nairn Dunbar course was laid out for 'the artisan class'. Hosting the 1999 Walker Cup, the windy coastal Links are among Scotland's most popular.

In 1848 Nairn had more fishing boats (72) and fishermen (163) than Lossiemouth, but a century later its fisher community was gone. The Fishertoun retains its character, but the 1820 harbour (Telford again) now berths pleasure craft, not trawlers. The oil rig construction yard at Ardersier (**75**) provides employment, but Nairn's shops are increasingly sidelined by Inverness superstores. The one-way high street is sedate, with parking and trade commanded mostly by the supermarket next to the through-running, often traffic-jammed A96.

You can avoid the town via the back roads from Inverness to Auldearn. Yet Nairn is worth visiting for its beaches. With fine views over the Firth to the Black Isle their tidal rock-pools alone should delight anyone who enjoys playing at being Gulliver in Lilliput.

Lochloy Road (north off the A96 between river bridge and rail bridge) bears east past the Links towards Culbin Forest and Sands (**89**) - a coastal wilderness without parallel.

Nairn is poetically described in David Thomson's award-winning memoir: *Nairn in Darkness and Light* (1987). Born in India in 1914 to Scottish parents, until 1929 he spent his summer holidays at his grandmother's family home by Nairn - Newton, now a hotel. After many years as author and radio producer, he wrote this exquisite account of his early years in Nairn. Both spiritual autobiography and social history, its title betrays its main preoccupation: the delight of light great or small in a northern land of Presbyterian rigour and early winter darkness. He mentions the Newton stables in which, occasionally, 'somebody...shone the brass tethering rings so brightly that whenever we pushed a door open and looked into the dusky twilight we were welcomed by a small round gleam of light'.

William McGonagall, notoriously the 'worst poet in the world', also penned a paean to Nairn:

> *The town of Nairn is worth a visit, I do confess,*
> *And it's only about fifteen miles from Inverness.*

83. Nairn to Rait Castle (*History, Walk*)

Gloomy behind barbed wire amid spiky scrub on the north edge of Laiken Forest two miles south of Nairn, Rait Castle (894525) is unique. Gutted, roofless and rectangular (64x33ft.), its round southwest tower still intact, it looks more ecclesiastic than military, its wide mullioned second-floor windows Gothic-arched. Yet arrow-slit lower windows in walls six feet thick are defensible. Entry, at the east end of the south wall, was portcullis-protected.

It was built *c*.1300 by the de Rait family, supporters of the English during the Wars of Independence. Later held by Mackintoshes, it's told how in 1442 Mackintoshes, expelled from Rait by Comyns (the de Raits may have been Comyns) a century earlier yet still pressing their claim, were invited to feast at Rait. Warned by a Comyn lass who loved a Mackintosh, when Comyn dirks were drawn, the Mackintoshes were ready. Amid mayhem the lass tried to flee her blood-maddened father by leaping from an upper window, but he cut off her hands with a broadsword. Yet another Scottish love-story with the standard ending (unhappy).

Visible from the B9101 a mile west of the A939, you can drive to within half-a-mile of Rait Castle, then walk to it via Raitcastle Farm. Yet, to experience the transition from sea to hills, why not walk from Nairn?

Start from the A96 road bridge over the river. Follow the east bank park track south under the railway viaduct left past a footbridge, then bear right off the tarmac along the river, past a second (concrete-slabbed) footbridge. Past flat fields with the river now brisk, the narrow wooded up-and-down path meets the B9090 by a bridge and minor junction (877538).

Turn east (left) along the wood-fringed road a half-mile to a second junction. Turn right (south) through forestry past Raitloan Farm to the Cawdor-Auldearn B9101. A left turn (northeast) up the B9101 leads in 400 yards to a

farm-track on the right. This climbs past Raitcastle steading to the castle ruin. The upper part of the track may be cow-mired.

For a side-trip, from 877538 turn right 50 yards along the B9101 to a left turn to Burnside of Geddes and Geddes Churchyard (888528), a circular stone-dyked enclosure where old table-stones moulder under mature beech, new bungalows all about. Within crumbling rectangular walls atop the mound the Roses of Kilravock (**77**) are buried. With an old dedication to St Mary, this may have been the site of the old Hermit's Chapel. Geddes Market was once held in the churchyard on or about April 5th. Further south up the wooded slope of the Hill of Urchany is the ruin of Castle Finlay (888514), once a timber-laced stone fort. This is reached by a boggy footpath along the banks of the Geddes Burn.

From either Geddes Churchyard or Rait Castle return to the B9101 and past Raitloan through the forestry to the junction where, coming from Nairn, you joined the Raitloan road from what is now your left (884538). For a different route back, here keep straight on for a long, forest-fringed road-slog. At last the road bends left then straightens. At a gate by the next right bend, cross flat pasture to the riverside path and the second (concrete) footbridge earlier bypassed. Cross it, continue straight to cut across the riverbend, and so back into Nairn via the path on the river's left bank, choosing your own point of exit into the town.

84. Auldearn: Gateway to the Past? (*Visit, Tour*)

Two miles east of Nairn and now bypassed by the A96, the village of Auldearn is quiet again. At its west end, where the Cawdor B9101 arrives, the Covenanter Inn serves visitors and Nairn businessfolk, yet the chief sensation is of a place bypassed not only by the main road but, despite its modern bungalows, by the present. Here you may get a sense of time-slip. Auldearn is maybe *too* quiet, given the historic events that put it on the map. A terrible battle here in 1645 was followed in 1662 by a notorious witchcraft trial. Over a millenium earlier, the first Scottish kirk dedicated to St Columba was built here. Earlier still, neolithic farmers erected cairns and standing stones now mostly lost in nettle-choked sites.

The rural area to the south links with the region southeast of Cawdor already explored (**81**). The back roads north of the Muckle Burn and west of Darnaway (**90**) can be walked, but getting off-road isn't easy. This densely forested and fenced-off region of understated privacy discourages over-familiarity.

From Auldearn (we return soon) the Lethen road departs south past the battlefield (see below). After two miles, at a Y-junction by Easter Arr (933528), bear right along the straight minor road south-west past forestry to Achavelgin by the Muckle Burn (914509: a half-mile north of the A939 and Littlemill). Turn east past Braeside a mile and over the burn by a ford (934511), then left (northeast) up a road half-invaded by rampant *rhododendron ponticum*. This lovely hidden stretch south of Lethen House ends where the road again crosses the burn (this time by bridge) at Lethen, leaving the private woodlands to climb an open slope northeast to an open rural crossroads amid high fields with wide views. Here, by a bus-stop, is what the OS map (using that Gothic lettering) calls a Cairn (953536). Behind a tumbledown stone dyke an circle of small, half-buried stones lies hidden in dense undergrowth.

To return to Auldearn, take the next left fork northwest past Blackhills, past what the map calls (first) a Motte and (second) a Cairn & Stone Row. Seeking the motte, I found a quarry. The cairn and stone row, in a scrappy road-side wood, was a dump featuring a dead bicycle. As for the stone circle marked at the east edge of Auldearn itself, it may exist, but double-carport bungalows crowd its site.

Auldearn itself has plenty to offer, starting with the Boath Doocot (National Trust) on Castle Hill above the bypass. From the 12th-century royal castle of Old Eren (thus *Auldearn*) here William the Lion (1165-1214) issued his second charter to Inverness burgesses. The castle itself was destroyed in the 1180s by the treachery of its Constable, Gillecolm of Maddestie. Centuries later James Graham, Marquis of Montrose, raised the royal standard and on 9 May 1645 defeated the numerically-superior Covenanting army. The National Trust plaque and diagram at the doocot above the battlefield shows how the Royalist troops (half hidden behind Castle Hill) swooped on and slaughtered their opponents. This version has it that Montrose won by tactical bluff. More likely he was surprised and won the day due to the ferocious courage of his army, in it Irishmen, Highlanders, and Gordons from Aberdeenshire and Banff. No quarter was given: over 2000 Covenant men were slaughtered or cut down in flight and left to bleed to death in local ditches. Four months later Montrose's luck ran out, his army being routed at Philiphaugh. He was hanged in Edinburgh in May 1650 (**3,32**).

As for the 1757 kirk, harled plain grey with its grey slate roof. its site on a circular mound suggests (like so much else here) pre-Christian rites long before Columba got his first Scottish dedication here. And nearby, part of the village's waymarked heritage tour, a plaque mentions Auldearn's most notorious daughter - the self-confessed witch, Isobel Gowdie.

85. Isobel Gowdie & the Witches of Auldearn (*History*)

In 1593 the bizarre Edinburgh trial of the 'Witches of Berwick' and of Francis Stewart, 5th Earl of Bothwell, took place. Bothwell and the 'witches' were accused of trying to assassinate King James VI by raising magical storms, sailing to sea in a sieve, and burning wax images of His Majesty. James, the author of a book on witchcraft, took a keen personal interest in extracting confessions. Bothwell lived. The 'witches' did not. After horrible torture most of them were burned at the stake.

Did Isobel Gowdie meet the same fate? It seems likely. Little more than a child when the Battle of Auldearn left so many men dead in local ditches, by 1662 she was married to a farmer, a much older man. Still childless, she was not denounced by cuckold husband, zealous presbyter, or suspicious neighbour whose milk kept going sour. Uniquely, she denounced herself. Publicly claiming carnal relations with Satan, alias 'Black Johnnie', 'a meikle, blak, roch man', for six weeks between 13 April and 27 May 1662 she poured out astounding confessions to Nairn's appalled kirk elders, her testimony supported by Janet Braidhead, another self-proclaimed witch.

Without torture (though she was examined for the devil's mark) she told how, one night on the moors in 1647, she'd met a 'man in grey' who, that same night, had baptised her as a witch in Auldearn Kirk. Joining a coven that met naked in midnight sabbats and held whipping parties, she'd learned how to turn herself into a cat or hare. Once as a hare she'd been chased by dogs, only just in time recovering human form. Eagerly she described how the coven had buried the body of an unchristened child in a farmer's dungheap to destroy his crops. She said they'd killed the sons of the Laird of Parkis by sticking pins into clay images which then they'd burned - and, as everyone knew, the Laird's sons *had* all died, one after another. They'd yoked toads to a tiny model plough drawn twice round a field to make thistles sprout, not corn, so that that their own land got richer as a result.

Isobel seems to have delighted in shocking her inquisitors. Was any of it real? It sounds like the outburst of someone desperate to confess (and/or boast about) involvement in an S&M group with occult pretensions. A similar modern claim might be explained by 'False Memory Syndrome'. One day she began spilling out her fantasies and so enjoyed the shock she caused that she couldn't stop. Madly embroidering whatever did or didn't go on under the godly surface of this stolid little community, the more shock she caused, the more *important* she felt. Folk were *listening* to her.

The consequences? Probably she didn't care, until too late. And what of the 1645 battle? Might not the sight of crying bodies bleeding to death have deranged her? Were folk less sensitive, less disturbed by brutal events, then than now? My guess is that the battle and Isobel Gowdie's confession of witchcraft are connected. How to believe what you're taught having witnessed such violent slaughter in the name of the God of Love? You might well decide that all you've been told is a terrible lie, and so take another path, and fall between two stools, as she seems to have done. Her fate is unrecorded, but probably, like Coinneach Odhar, one day she was taken to nearby Gallows Hillock. As for 'Black Johnnie', the local Casanova, history says nothing of him. It seems he got away with it, 'scot-free.'

Men often did. One who didn't was Macbeth.

86. Meeting the *Real* Macbeth (*History, Speculation*)

About half-a-mile east of Auldearn just north of the A96 is a mounded field which once I was told was the 'Blasted Heath', where three witches allegedly met an ambitious thane. Not much further on, a mile west of Brodie and also north of the road by the regional boundary, is 'Macbeth's Hillock'.

Little in Shakespeare's 'Scottish tragedy' (few actors dare name it due to the curse on it) relates to the real King of Scots, ruler from 1040 to 1057. The *real* Macbeth (Maelbaetha or mac-Bethad, 'Son of Life') probably never met three witches, was not a tyrant or wife-ridden usurper, had little to do with Cawdor (**79**), and died at Lumphanan in Mar, not Dunsinane. Yet he may have been fooled by an advancing wood, a Scots ploy used in an earlier defeat of the Norse at Portknockie in Banffshire, and perhaps slew Duncan, if not where Shakespeare suggests.

Even so, the Bard of Avon drew not only on his imagination but on the *Chronicles* of Scots 'historian' Ralph Holinshed, inheritor of a tradition influenced by the 227-year-long rule of a dynasty birthed by Macbeth's nemesis, Malcolm Canmore ('Great Head' or, as some have it, 'Bighead'). The Canmores had good reason to hate and malign Macbeth. Descended from the slain Duncan, they were long plagued by his people, the unruly men of Moray. Most likely 'that dead butcher and his fiend-like queen' were nothing of the sort.

Macbeth was the son of Findlaech mac Ruaidri, Mormaer ('Great Steward') of Moray, a land then stretching from the Spey to the Outer Isles. Slain by the sons of his brother Maelbrigte in 1020, in the *Annals of Ulster* Findlaech is named *ri Alban*, meaning *a* (not *the*) king in Scotland. The House of Moray was highly-placed, and in constant conflict with the southern House of Atholl. Born in 1005 near Spynie, or maybe at Dingwall (**60**) Macbeth lived most of his life in Moray, even after his coronation. Records of Celtic monks of the old College of Roseisle call him their friend and neighbour. By birth he was Thane (*ri*) of Ross, becoming Thane of Moray by marriage to Lady Gruoch, daughter of Boedhe, a son of King Kenneth IV (995-1003). Another tradition has it that, after killing Duncan, he married Duncan's widow, 'Dame Grwok'. As to Duncan's death and Macbeth's succession, accounts vary, but a 'history' may be constructed as follows:

The Norse earls of Orkney had held the *borg* of Torfness (Burghead) for 200 years, digging 'torf' (peat) out of nearby bogs for export to Norway. Here on 14 August 1040 the Scots under 'the pure and wise' Duncan engaged Earl Thorfinn the Mighty. Of the House of Atholl and High King since 1034, that year Duncan had already been badly defeated attacking Durham. Moreover,

Thorfinn had just defeated him at Deerness: Duncan was already in flight on reaching Burghead. The chronicler Marianus Scotus says Macbeth was his general. More likely, given their later friendly relations, Macbeth and Thorfinn were allies. Duncan was Macbeth's cousin, but so was Thorfinn. Macbeth and the men of Moray had no reason to support this unpopular, incompetent High King. One tradition has it that in fact the battle was fought between Duncan and Macbeth, the former attempting invasion of Moray from the sea.

With the battle lost, Duncan fled, to be slain *a suis occisus est* ('by his own people') at Pitgaveny near Loch Spynie, or in a shed above nearby Hopeman. Did Macbeth deal the killing blow? Quite possibly. Marianus Scotus says so. Certainly Duncan's three sons fled the kingdom after Macbeth's victory. More important, the 'usurper' ruled so successfully that for a decade and a half there is little 'history' to record, save that, by the year 1050, Scotland was so peaceful that Macbeth was able to make a pilgrimage to Rome. Hardly a case of 'uneasy lies the head'. Yet in 1054 Malcolm Canmore invaded with an English army and defeated him at Dunsinane. Three years later a second invasion led to his death at Lumphanan.

Macbeth, the last Scots king buried at Iona, was the last great champion of Moray as a kingdom in its own right. Is this is why he was so maligned later? Just as Shakespeare also assassinated the character of Richard III to legitimise Tudor claims, so Canmore chroniclers misrepresented a man who was probably one of Scotland's better kings.

87. Brodie Castle *(Visit, Walk)*

Open daily Easter-30 September and October weekends Brodie Castle (979578: tel. 01309-641371) occupies wooded parkland north of the A96 six miles east of Nairn and four miles west of Forres. The simplest way to get there is via the signposted road breaking north off the A96 immediately east (Forres side) of Brodie village, also on the A96

Built on land given to the Brodies by Malcolm IV in 1160, this elegant lime-harled Z-plan towerhouse was owned by them until the National Trust acquired it. A charter from the reign of Alexander III refers to Malcolm Brodie as Thane and royal tenant of Brodie and Dyke, but of early Brodies little is known save for the 12th laird, Alexander, who in November 1550 was 'put to the horn' (outlawed). He had refused to stand trial for the armed waylaying near Forres of his neighbour, Alexander Cumming of Altyre. Outlawry failed to cramp his style: high on the gable of the south-west tower of the existing building a carved stone bears the date 1567 - the oldest part of the castle you see before you now. All other family records prior to 1645 were lost that year when, during the Civil War and on the orders of the Marquis of Montrose, the house was 'byrnt and plunderit' by Sir Lewis Gordon.

With 18th- and 19th-century additions, the castle with its conical turrets and coats of arms on the outer walls is approached down a beech avenue (the route to the car-park is more roundabout). Containing French furniture, and porcelain and paintings from England, Europe and China, its most notable internal feature is in the rectangular block added after the damage inflicted in 1645 - the spacious 'Chamber of Dais', or drawing-room, built by the 15th laird, another Alexander. Designed to be 'all glorious within' and embellished with a richly-moulded plaster ceiling, some of its figure-motifs suggest Dutch or Danish origin.

Alexander, a staunch upholder of the Covenant, was among those who went to Breda in Holland in 1649 to negotiate Charles II's return to Scotland. Inspiration for the Drawing Room may have come from this visit. During the '45 another Alexander strongly supported the Hanoverian cause, yet died in debt due to the extravagant good works done by his wife, Mary Sleigh. In 1786 Brodie burned again and Lady Margaret Duff, daughter of the Earl of Fife, died of suffocation. Her son James having drowned, the next laird was her grandson William, who added the eastern end in the then-fashionable 'Gothick' style, full of airy, well-lit rooms.

With an adventure playground, a picnic area, car-park and shop, and gardens noted for their daffodils, Brodie is well worth a visit and walkabout. From the castle you can head along the West Avenue, past copper beech and lime over a minor road to the artificial pond beyond. From a hide on the south side you can spot heron and coot. Returning up West Avenue, bear right before the castle and and along a path to Brodie village. By the railway level crossing turn left (northeast) along the minor road to the main entrance, then up the drive past Rodney's Stone (985576), a 9th century Pictish symbol stone (**66**).

The road leads through the village of Dyke, its church notable for a triple-decker pulpit, then to Kintessack and the vast coastal Culbin Forest, once a continually-shifting desert of sand-dunes concealing the legendary 'Buried Barony'.

88.   The Culbin Sandstorm of 1694 *(History)*

In 1694 Alexander Kinnaird, Laird of Culbin, should have been a happy man. It's said he owned 3600 acres of fertile land containing 16 farms, their tenants paying on average £200 Scots per annum in rent, plus 40 bolls of wheat, bere, oats and oatmeal. The climate was kind, the soil fertile, and the Findhorn so rich in salmon there was a glut of it. Then in two nights of storm every farm but one was buried in sand, the mansion house vanished, and the Findhorn was forced north to a new outlet in what is now Findhorn Bay. That's the tale. Yet the catastrophe was no surprise. The unstable Moray coast, much of it loose sand or shingle, has stranded beaches from Ardersier past Nairn to the Old Bar. For years fierce winter storms had driven sand inland. In 1663 the Laird of Brodie wrote in his diary how the town of Nairn '...was in danger to be quite lost by the sand and the water', and from 1676 on Culbin's fields were annually buried in up to two feet of sand.

Thus in autumn 1694 came the terrible storm, so sudden a ploughman deserted his plough amid the furrow; reapers of late barley dropped their sickles and fled. All night long the sand drifted, piling so high that in the dawn, when the gale died, Culbin folk had to break out of the backs of their houses to escape. In shock, they drove their cattle away. Amid a lull some came back for their goods, but then the storm returned. Blocked, the Findhorn burst north, engulfing the old village. Everything was buried...even the mansion house.

In 1698, three years after his failed appeal to Parliament to revoke debts caused by the sandstorm, Kinnaird sold the ruined estate to Duff of Drummuir. Broken, he died four years later, soon followed by his wife. Their son, an infant in 1694, died childless in 1743. So the Kinnaird line died out. Of the estate, only Earnhill Farm survived. The sands took everything else. A century or so later the shifting dunes revealed part of the old mansion. One man, calling down the exposed chimney, fell back in horror, claiming to have heard a hoarse voice and a ghostly laugh. Perhaps he believed the local tale that Kinnaird, punished by the Sands for making his tenants work on Sundays, was still locked down there, playing cards with Satan, unable to escape until Judgement Day.

Other ruins also occasionally appeared. Their stone was taken to build the dykes of new farms. The fruit trees of vanished orchards now and then blossomed when the shifting sands released them. It is said smugglers who buried brandy casks in the Culbin sands could never find them again.

Is the tale true? Yes and no. Kinnaird owned 1350 acres, not 3600 (the area of the Culbin Sands). There were six farms, not 16 - 16, the 1693 rental makes clear, means the number of tenants. The value of their rent is also exaggerated, also the wealth of the land. Due to poor weather, seven times between 1691 and 1700 the Scottish harvest failed. Famine and ruin were rife. And with the sand blowing for over 30 years, how by 1694 could Kinnaird have enjoyed 'highly cultivated fields with heavy corn' and 'extensive pastures with numerous crops'? And he had other problems. Both his grandfather and father had died in debt. With the estate in crown hands, by 1682 no more loans could be raised. When Kinnaird inherited in 1691 he couldn't pay his creditors. Worse, as a Jacobite, in 1689 he was listed as a 'rebel'. The sandstorm was simply the last straw, his appeal to Parliament encouraging the legend of the 'Buried Barony'. Unlike other landlords ruined and forced to sell up, Kinnaird is remembered, if only for making his tenants work on Sundays, and for playing cards with Satan.

Yet the sands remained, a vast desert until in 1839 Grant of Kincorth tried planting it, first with bent, then brushwood, then with young trees. His success led to imitation, so that during the Great War vast harvests of fir were reaped. Then fire destroyed much of the new forest. In May 1920 a violent westerly blew the newly-released sand in torrents. Old valleys became hills; hills were laid low; trees were buried. In 1921 the Forestry Commission took over 2,000 acres. The attempt to hold the sand by planting marram grass failed. Next, brushwood was tried, more successfully. Ultimately the FC planted 7500 acres, mostly of Scots and Corsican Pine. This forest prospers.

Britain's largest sand dune system, Culbin's once-barren desert is now a varied forest hosting 550 flowering plant species, many at their northern or southern limit, and over 130 species of lichen. Beyond it, a vast tidal lagoon and intertidal margins of mud-flat, machair and mussel-beds are hidden from the sea by the marram-topped dunes of The Bar, its miles-long beach stretching north

towards the Black Isle.

89. Culbin: Forest & Sands *(Walks)*

Culbin demands respect. The forest and its tracks form a maze in which it's easy to get lost. You can explore this vast area and the beach and sand-bar beyond it for days without fully seeing how it all interconnects, even though many of the tracks radiating from Wellhill and Cloddymoss are waymarked, with information plaques at points of interest. The OS map and a compass are essential, as are good boots - many of the tracks are bumpy or sandy. And as the minimum hike north to the sea and back is a good four miles, a piece to eat is a good idea. It also helps to mark your route in case you get tired or lost and need to back-track.

The Forest Enterprise leaflet with its outline map of the tracks and sites of interest is very useful. Call 01343-820223.

There are two main car-parks and entry-points - Cloddymoss (982600) nearer Nairn, and Wellhill (996614) by Kintessack, nearer Forres. A third car-park and the start of a trail is at Kingsteps (912573) at the forest's western edge. All three can be reached from Nairn by turning north off the A96 onto Lochloy Road, between river-bridge and railway bridge on the east side of town. From Forres, the turn-off (to Kintessack) is immediately west of the A96 bridge over the Findhorn. Stay right, first a mile east, then north past Moy House, then left to Kintessack at the Binsness-Kincorth junction. Just east of the hamlet, turn north to Wellhill Farm. Follow the road 200 yards into the forest to the car-park. Access via minor roads past Brodie Castle and Dyke is also straightforward.

Wellhill offers greater variety of access, so the walks I describe start there. However the Mavistown sand dunes (940600), some 50 feet high with flanks 1200 feet long, are best reached from Kingsteps or Cloddymoss, where an Educational Centre caters for school parties. Cloddymoss also offers the short-est route north to the intertidal flats of the Gut, part of an RSPB reserve, and to the Bar beyond it.

From Wellhill four main tracks depart, three from beyond the pole-gate to the north; the fourth into the wood to the east. Many variations are possible, but here I describe three walks, or routes:

(1) East then north round the edge of the forest via Binsness and Findhorn Bay; then west past Buckie Loch to the tidal lagoon by Duck Island and the Gut's inter-tidal mudflats;

(2) The straight path north to the sea, connecting with (1) then return routes or coastal routes west towards Nairn;

(3) A forest circuit west towards Cloddymoss, then north (options various), and back east past Duck Pond.

(1) Start east. The pleasant, open track curls along the forest edge two miles towards Binsness and Findhorn Bay, then turns north into deep forest. This northward turn leads, via various junctions (not all on the OS map) to several interesting sites. The Glade (017632: these and following references approxi-mate) is an area of Lagoonal sediment amid tall Douglas Fir. The Buried Tree

(018634) illustrates sand-movement since the forest began to grow, its partial excavation showing how deep others are buried. Lady Culbin (015644), one of the largest dune-systems and now stabilised by Scots Pine, is almost 100 feet high in parts. Shingle ridges further east (993634) support over 130 species of lichen. To find these sites obtain the outline map mentioned above.

If not seeking these out, leave the forest where the track swings north. Past a cottage, cut right to a track by Findhorn Bay's marshy tidal pools. Follow the shore east past Binsness House, then north past Findhorn village, mere yards over the seaward neck of the bay. Look out for seals lazing on the spit beyond it. Continue west two miles past Buckie Loch (largely dry, with fine fields of wild iris, and grotesque fungi on its silver birches) to the narrow-necked, broad tidal lagoon east of the Gut. Here, at a gap in the outer bars, may be where the Findhorn met the sea before 1694. Mussel-beds and mud-flats gleam, staked by poles erected to discourage German flying-boats during World War II. Tidal streams trickle out of the flat, anemone-rich machair past the old bothy on the grassy hillock of Duck Island (983638) on the east side of the lagoon. There are fine views over the Firth beyond Nigg to the northwest hills. You may see yachts sailing in. It is idyllic. Yet here the tide rapidly abandons then reclaims the flats, so don't get caught.

From here take one of the return routes to Wellhill as described below.

This is a fine, varied walk, but on days of strong westerly winds is best done clockwise, unless you like trudging into a gale of fine sand. Either that, or take to the forest where breaks in the low sandy cliffs occur.

(2) For the direct route north to the sea (and most popular, given the number of folk routinely on it), from Wellhill head straight past the gate to a large clearing and a staggered three-way track junction. Stay north on the middle track along the forest fringe, tending left to (tall pine both sides) a T-junction west of tad-pole-rich Gravel Pit Pond (994618). At this junction cross the east-west track and keep straight on, north into the forest, on the obvious broad sandy path (not on OS or outline map).

This is a delight. Weave up and down past old Scots Pine over dunes through a pygmy woodland of pine, silver birch and heath. Sphagnum mosses and delicate silvery grey-green lichens knit the sand with fey colour. The path crosses a second east-west track and continues to a third. Before crossing this third track, keeping north on the increasingly sandy path, stop. Note where you are. Leave a marker - you may return on the Forestry road from the west and will need to be sure of your right turn onto the homeward, southbound path.

Continue through a logged-out clearing up a steep dune crowned by a fringe of tall pines, many blown down. Beyond undulating dunes littered by logging debris and a final forest fringe gleams the lagoon, sea spilling in behind sandbars. Soon you're over the last main east-west track and by the wonderful lagoon. From here, turn east past Buckie Loch towards Findhorn (see above), return south to Wellhill; or head west, via the forest fringe and the Gut or outer beach towards Nairn.

The first and last of these walks involve distance, with miles of return involved. It's worth checking the tides and marking your route to ensure anxiety-free return.

Turning west, soon on the left is the start of a southbound track parallel to the path you just took. Intersecting the main east-west tracks and at one point climbing steeply up and over the Forest's highest point (29m), it returns to Wellhill reliably and without confusion.

If aiming for the Bar, you may be tempted to cut across the tidal flats to the marram-topped outer dunes. At low tide this is possible, but arduous. There are tidal ditches too wide to jump., and the gleaming muddy black mussel beds make for rough squelchy going. Taking the safer roundabout route, for a mile or so you hug the forest fringe and high-tide mark with its skeletons of tiny crabs. In time, over on the landward side of the dunes barring the sea, you see a small abandoned bothy. This is a good point to cut across. Also here, marked by a round gravel pond and a lone tree, a path into the wood leads south to a forestry track and a boring two mile slog through thick forestry to Cloddymoss.

The outer beach is wonderful. At low tide the sands seem to stretch almost to the Black Isle cliffs. To the west, they seem to stretch all the way to Nairn. Yet the mud and sand are everywhere bisected by tidal channels, so don't be tempted (unless you have a tide-table) to walk too far out. King Canute couldn't make it work, so it's unlikely that you can...

(3) A third route from Wellhill runs west. Immediately past the barrier turn left on a main track at the three-way junction. Fifty yards into the wood, turn left again (south) onto a pine-needled path. This meanders southwest towards the forest's edge and a track west to a T-junction at a logged-out area north of Kintessack. Turn right (north) 100 yards, then left (west) at a second junction, back into the forest. This is all waymarked. The track continues parallel to the forest's edge through an area devoted to 'species trials' (987606). Developed 1921-30 to learn which trees would grow best here, there are European (scruffy) and North Japanese Larch, Maritime (knotty and twisty), Western Yellow and Lodgepole Pine; and also the winners, Scots and Corsican Pine.

At the T-junction just after, turn right (north) 150 yards then left at another junction to a logged clearing - a giant, churned-up mess. At a third junction the left turn is signposted Cloddymoss 0.9m. Continue curving northwest past another Cloddymoss turn and through a young plantation. Briefly back amid mature wood swing right to a major crossing. The track ahead leads seaward; the right turn (yellow marker) heads east. Soon after re-entering mature forest, the track forks. Turn right then, under silver birch by a mossy bank to your left, climb this bank to discover Duck Pond (983615) - an old fire dam, now a wildlife habitat and lovely secret place to enjoy. Here in the forest depths blue and great tits nest; pipistrelle and long-eared bats may roost; Water Boatmen, Diving Beetles and Damselflies make themselves at home, and mallard duck breed; hence the name. This is a fine place to sit and relax. Beyond it the forking tracks converge to continue straight. Turn left at the next main crossing for the forest's highest point (see above) and the way to the lagoon. At the track junction after this, it's straight on for the Gravel Pit Pond (also above), left for the sandy path to the sea, or right to return 400 yards to Wellhill car-park.

Culbin is a wonderful place. For your sake and everyone else's respect it. There's quite enough ruin, pollution and litter elsewhere.

90. Darnaway & the Earls of Moray *(History)*

East of Brodie minor roads south off the A96 traverse Darnaway Forest past Darnaway Castle (994551: originally Tarnua), long the seat of the Earls of Moray and focus of a bloody history.

The first road (988574) a half-mile east of Brodie opposite a signposted turn to Brodie Castle soon joins the second. This leaves the A96 a mile further east (998577), signposted: Darnaway 2. It runs through attractive woods past the wrought iron north gates of Darnaway Castle Estate, over a crossing to a junction. Turn left (Conicavel 2; Whitemire and Redstone also indicated) over two crossroads. Mixed woodland gives way to fields, the massive front of Darnaway Castle now visible a half-mile to your left (east). Not open, the castle can be visited by appointment. Ring Moray Estates Office in Forres (01309-672213) for information.

Behind the battlemented facade of the present pile (early 19th century) is Randolph's Hall. Later created first Earl of Moray by Robert the Bruce, early in 1314 Thomas Randolph scaled the rock of Edinburgh Castle to rout the English garrison, then at Bannockburn routed much of Edward's army from 'Randolph's Field'. Established at Darnaway, he was attacked by the Cummings, evicted from the Findhorn's west bank to make way for him. But he was ready. Amid the ensuing slaughter only their chief, Alistair Cumming escaped (it is said) by leaping the Findhorn at a point still known as Randolph's Leap (**93**). Yet Randolph was more than a brawler. As Bruce's envoy to the Pope he argued the case for Scottish independence. He also concluded the treaty with France that cemented the Auld Alliance, so that until the start of the 20th century all Scots had an automatic right to French citizenship.

When in 1329 Bruce died, Randolph became guardian of the realm, himself dying in 1332. Both his two sons having died in battle, his daughter made her name as 'Black Agnes of Dunbar' by her six-month defence of Dunbar Castle in 1337. 'She indeed laughed at the English', claims the 15th century Book of Pluscarden, 'and would, in the sight of all, wipe with a most beautiful cloth the spot where the stone from the engine hit the Castle Wall.'

King James III (1460-88) briefly lived here and with Thomas Cochrane, Earl of Mar, built the old castle. In 1562 Mary Queen of Scots graced a tournament on the Meads of St John by the Findhorn, east of the castle, this after her half-brother James Stewart (natural son of James V and Lady Margaret Erskine) had defeated George Gordon, 4th Earl of Huntly. Stripped of the Earldom of Moray in 1550, Huntly had opposed Mary after her return from France in 1561. Hunted down after the battle at Corrichie Burn near Aberdeen, the Catholic Gordon died of apoplexy, and the Protestant Stewart became Earl of Moray. So began a bloodfeud between the two families, even as the intrigues of Bothwell, Darnley and Mary herself led in 1567 to her abdication and the coronation of her son, the infant James VI. Appointed the first of Scotland's four Regents, supported by England and upholding Protestantism, in January 1570 Moray was assassinated at Linlithgow by Hamilton of Bothwellhaugh. His infant son, also James, became 2nd Earl, known to history as 'the Bonnie Earl of Moray'. His life was energetic but brief. The feud with the Gordons escalated. Amid dispute over Spey fishing rights and ownership of Spynie near Elgin, tit-for-tat killings got out of hand. George Gordon the 6th Earl was a favourite of King James, whose Queen, Anne of Denmark, openly favoured Moray. Was James in on the plot? On 7 February 1592 Gordon's armed band surprised Moray at Donibristle Castle on the Fife coast. The indefensible 'castle' was fired. Moray fled to hide among the rocks, but two Gordon lairds found him, and:

'...Gordon of Bucky gave him a wound in the face: Moray, half expiring, said, 'You hae spilt a better face than your awin.' Upon this, Bucky pointing his dagger at Huntly's breast, swore, 'You shall be as deep as I;' and forced him to pierce the poor defenceless body.'

To Randolph's Hall early in the 20th century at last came home the gory portrait of the dead man, his bloody wounds depicted. His mother, Lady Doune, had it painted to stir up popular indignation. Even so (the 'Bonnie Earl' had been well-loved), Huntly got away with it: seven years later James VI made him a marquis. Later the murdered Earl's son married Lady Ann Gordon, daughter of his father's killer; a marriage promoted by James VI to end the feud. Unsurprisingly, the new Earl avoided politics. As for the gory portrait, it lay in a chest at Donibristle for centuries. All that survived of the 'Bonnie Earl' was a reproachful ballad:

> *Ye hielands and ye lawlands,*
>
> *O where hae ye been?*
>
> *They hae slain the Earl o' Moray*
>
> *And lain him on the green.*

The violence continued. In 1631 Clan Chartan invaded Moray, looting and pillaging. The peaceful Earl was ordered to exterminate the clan, leaving none alive except 'priests, women and bairns', the latter to be expelled to Scandinavia. His hesitation ended when the clan besieged Darnaway, plundering Dyke before escaping back to the wilds. Pursuing them, Moray took three hundred prisoners, executing many on the spot. William Macintosh, brother of the escaping chieftain, was hanged and quartered at Forres, his head spiked on a cross at Dyke, and his body shared between Elgin, Forres, Auldearn and Inverness. Such spectacles provided both public warning and popular entertainment. The blood was real, not reel-to-reel.

After the Civil War, when Randolph's Hall housed Cromwellian troops, Darnaway at last knew peace. Builder of the present pile, the 'Tree Planter', Francis Earl of Moray (1737-1810) planted a mere 12 million trees, including the great oak forest. His successors continued this policy, and in 1841 some 41 miles of recreational walks were laid out in Darnaway Forest.

Of these, open to the public are two fine circular walks above the Findhorn gorges, by Dunearn Burn on the west bank, and a mile further north at Sluie on the east bank.

91. Dunearn Burn at Conicavel (*Walk*)

Spectacular, with wider views than the Sluie or Randolph's Leap walks (**93**), the Dunearn Burn walk comes in two lengths, $1^{1}/_{2}$ or $2^{1}/_{2}$ miles, much of it along the very lip of the gorge.

From Darnaway, continue south through the neat little village of Conicavel to a sign: Dunearn Burn Walk 1 mile. Continue through woodland to a left turn into a car-park. The waymarked walk (green shorter, red longer) starts past tall pines into beechwood, then climbs a mossy bank high above the burn. Leaving the wood, a short detour leads to panoramic views east over Sluie and Forres to Findhorn Bay. The river gorge below is still hidden, but a mile southwest above

and across the river is a prominent white house: Logie House (also **93**).

The path descends cut steps, the river roaring louder. A sign amid silver birch warns: STEEP CLIFFS KEEP TO PATH. Suddenly the path reaches a spectacular railed viewpoint high above the junction of burn and river. Black waters boil over rocks far below: dense forest the far side of the ravine accentuates the giddy depth as the path continues south above the gorge, the drop so steep you can almost touch the tops of trees rooted below. Scary, but dangerous points are railed: there is no risk. Soon the path forks. The red route follows the edge another half-mile opposite Logie House to join an estate road then loop back to the car-park. Leaving the gorge, the shorter green route joins the road further north. Either way, the return up the track's final stretch offers stunning views over billowing woodland waves of russet and green across the gorge. A last turn through a tall stately grove and you're back at the car-park.

The road continues south through craggily wooded land before (now back in Highland Region) descending to a junction by the Findhorn. The left fork over the river via a fine old stone bridge climbs to the B9007 Carrbridge road south of Relugas and Randolph's Leap (**93**). The right fork continues southwest past Coulmony to the A939 (958473) just north of a turn southwest past Ardclach (**95**) to Glen Altnarie and Dulsie Bridge (**96**).

Before exploring these beauty-spots, we backtrack north, first to Forres, then via Sluie and Randolph's Leap down the east bank of the Findhorn.

157

92. Forres & Cluny Hill (*History, Walk*)

Beautifully sited, architecturally rich, historically resonant, and (vital nowadays) fully bypassed by the A96, Forres is among the region's most attractive burghs. With Grant Park's award-winning floral sculptures under the wooded folds of Cluny Hill, its streets and wynds testify to a long history. Possibly the *Varris* on Ptolemy's map, a royal residence by the ninth century (the castle stood at the west end of the High Street), it occupies a fertile flood-plain a mile east of the River Findhorn's final meander into Findhorn Bay just over a mile to the north.

Climb to Nelson's Tower atop Cluny Hill and look north through the trees. Beyond town and bypass (and railway) lie the Bay's gleaming flats, closing in to a seaward neck where Culbin Forest and Findhorn village almost meet. Yacht-sails flock against the Firth and the hills beyond. The Findhorn Foundation's caravan gardens hug the east shore, an enclave of 'New Age' ecology and therapies incongruously cheek-by-jowl with the sky-splitting thunder of Nimrod surveillance aircraft lumbering up from the adjacent Kinloss military air-base.

Closer, on the northeast edge of Forres by the bypass, now encased within an unlovely tall glass-and-steel cabinet to protect it from road-pollution, stands Sueno's Stone (047596), described earlier (**66**). Maybe the cage is necessary, yet the evocative power of this fine monument is reduced by the sterile modern enclosure.

The main body of the town lies below to the west, beyond the park. The High Street, dominated by crowstep gables and the bizarre 1838 Gothic reconstruction of the medieval Tolbooth, remains traffic-bound despite the bypass. Service families, visitors to the Findhorn Foundation, and retired southern settlers create an aura of prosperity. The town houses, hotels and villas hugging Cluny Hill's wooded western slope along the Rafford road are not dilapidated.

The easiest way up to Nelson's Tower (erected in 1806 to honour the admiral who didn't know how to use a telescope, now a museum) is to cross Grant Park and start up the woodland tracks winding round Cluny Hill. The intersections are too many to describe here, but keep left and up and you'll get there soon enough. When done with the view, don't abandon Cluny Hill. Explore its twists and turns. Quiet avenues of Douglas Fir and other elegant trees curve above grassy glades. In time, on the south-west side, you reach one of the creaking wrought-iron gates of Cluny Hill cemetery, full of peaceful walks amid the memorials and lovingly-shaped shrubberies. Amid so tranquil an oasis it's hard to recall that Forres was long at the heart of the witch-madness. The case of Isobel Gowdie (**85**) is best-known, but there are others.

When *c.*AD960 King Duff fell inexplicably ill on arriving at Forres from

Scone, witchcraft was blamed. Three Forres women, dragged to the top of Cluny Hill, were forced into barrels set inside with sharp spikes. With the lids nailed down the barrels were rolled down the hill. Three boulders were set up to mark the points where they came to rest. Of these 'Witches Stones', one is by Victoria Road, and a second near the railings in Grant Park. These and other violent events helped persuade Shakespeare to site the witchcraft scenes opening his Scottish tragedy (**86**) in and about Forres. For much other ancient villainy went on here - the murder in Forres in AD908 of King Donald; the slaying of his son King Malcolm nearby, maybe at Blervie Castle above Rafford; and then again, believe it or not, the murder of King Duff, again in Forres Castle. Moray has always known violence, human or elemental.

Of the latter variety, the 1694 Culbin sandstorm (**88**) and the 'Muckle Spate' (Great Flood) of 1829 (**94**), remain memorable. Chronicled by Sir Thomas Dick Lauder of Relugas above Randolph's Leap, the Spate was awesome, especially at Randolph's Leap.

93.   The Findhorn: Sluie Gorge & Randolph's Leap (*Walks*)

About a mile north of Dunearn Burn (**91**) on the opposite bank of the Findhorn, one of the best walks by this river tracks the woods above the gorge at Sluie. From Forres, take the A940 Grantown road south four miles past the Knockomie Hotel and the pretty little Loch of Blairs. At a small roadside sign, 'Sluie Walk' (014525), turn right by the lodge into the car-park under the trees. Of two tracks converging just below the lodge, take the lower one bearing right (west) towards the river, not visible from this point. Start downhill. With wood to the left and pasture to the right, bear left to a steading. The long low building here, now a ruin, once housed five salmon fishermen and their families.

The direct way to the gorge is to keep left (east) of and above the steading into the wood. Yet also worth a look is the stretch of river north of the gorge, with placid shingle-banks under the ruddy, tree-crowned cliff. Turn right through the steading to a forestry gate and keep right above the wooded river-bank along the edge of the pasture. Where the Findhorn bends sharp right, almost back on itself, there is easy access to the riverside.

Under the forestry gate a track, no longer the 'official' route, climbs steep left through the beechwood. Suddenly, without warning, just before meeting the path from the steading, is a sight to take the breath away. Far below, dark waters swirl between steep banks sprouting stunted but tenacious silver birch. The well-made path, with rustic benches at the best viewpoints, follows the lip of the gorge through a deep cool forest of larch and Scots Pine. Douglas Fir, planted *c.*1870, tower overhead, creating a cathedral atmosphere. There is no danger. But take care if you have children with you, or dogs, or if heights make you dizzy.

After nearly a mile the arrowed track reaches a clearing and turns sharp left, climbing away from the gorge back into the wood. Continue along the gorge, and you reach a gate with the warning request: PLEASE GO NO FUR- THER. One look at the steep, wooded bank ahead suggests that this is good advice. Following the forest track northeast, ignore a left turn and continue 400 yards to a T-junction. Bear right. The track leads into a clearing past a derelict croft. Here it swings hard left and (now parallel to the A940, up a bank through the trees) back to the car-park past more decaying ruins in the field to the left.

The distance is about three miles. There's no hard climbing involved and the path is fine all the way. Even so, wear good boots, and avoid the edge if you don't like heights!

For Randolph's Leap (001495), continue south on the B940 a long mile to the junction with the B9007 to Carrbridge. Follow this road downhill past the open drive on the right to Logie House and Steading (006505: 01309-611378). With tearoom, a gallery of local arts and crafts, and working craftshops, Logie Steading is open to visitors May to October (not Mondays). Continuing, cross the bridge over the Divie. Park higher up the wooded brae opposite the sign to Randolph's Leap. Follow steps down into lush beechwood to a viewpoint above rocky spurs below. Bare yards apart, they form a narrow gate through which the river foams into the gorge. This is Randolph's (or Cumming's: see **90**) Leap. Somehow Alistair Cumming made the jump from the far side to this. Nothing

like spears at your backside to turn you into a champion long-jumper.

Follow the narrow, twisting woodland path downstream, the river foaming over huge boulders below. With the dizziest sections of this path guard-railed, you come to a rocky spur below which Findhorn and Divie meet in a vast dark pool, an idyllic spot where salmon leap. From it, a steep path climbs the wooded east bank of the Divie back to the B9007.

Don't miss this wonderful place. And one more thing. Either end of the gorge you'll find two marker stones, each under an iron grille. The first, deep in the wood some 50 feet above the river where it enters the gorge between the rocky spurs of Randolph's Leap, is worn, its inscription hard to read. The inscription on the second, 50 feet above the confluence of the rivers, is legible. On it is carved: 'The Findhorn and Divie met here in flood, August 3rd & 4th 1829'.

94.   Thomas Dick Lauder & the Muckle Spate of 1829 (*History*)

On Saturday the 1st of August 1829, after months of unnatural heat, sudden downpours and weird atmospheric effects, a huge black pillar of cloud appeared over the Moray Firth. Joining sea to sky it whirled inland. Early on Sunday morning, it broke on the Monadhliaths. For three days and nights rain poured. Swollen rivers inundated the Laich of Moray. Bridges on the Findhorn, Lossie, Spey and Deveron collapsed. The ruin was immense.

The extent of the disaster was recorded by Sir Thomas Dick Lauder, an aristocratic eccentric from Lothian who by marriage had come to live at Relugas, 10 miles south of Forres and above Randolph's Leap. Thin, restless, voluble, devoted to the wild Relugas gardens, Lauder had published romances like 'The Wolfe of Badenoch', but had never found his true *metier*. Cushioned by wealth, he had remained aloof from local life.

Then the deluge began. The Findhorn and Divie rose with awesome speed. Late on August 3rd, after 36 hours of rain, Lauder was roused from dinner to find the Divie up over the strawberry beds. The waters were surging: 'with a strange and alarming flux and reflux, dashing over the ground 10 or 15 yards at a time'. Tall trees, undercut on the banks, leaned dangerously. Worst was the noise: '...a distinct combination of two kinds of sound: one, a uniformly continued roar, the other like rapidly repeated discharges of many cannons at once'. Lauder's description continues: 'Above all this was heard the fiend-like shriek of the wind, yelling as if the demon of desolation had been riding upon its blast...'.

Describing stripped leaves whirling by as trees like terrified beasts groaned before breaking, he adds: 'There was...a peculiar and indescribable lurid, or rather bronze-like hue, that pervaded the whole face of nature, as if poison had been abroad in the air.'

Next day the Findhorn was up 50 feet. By the marker-stone above Randolph's Leap the Relugas butler caught a salmon in his umbrella. Aghast, Lauder watched his gardens vanish as tall ancient trees plunged into the flood. 'Never', he wrote later, 'did the unsubstantiality of all earthly things come so perfectly home to my conviction.'

Outraged yet energised, he undertook to record the wider ruin. For months he travelled every flood-struck river and burn from source to sea - a journey of some 600 miles. He gathered eye-witness reports, then wrote a masterpiece of investigative journalism (1830). No longer in print, it should be, but local libraries still stock copies.

The chaos caused by the Spey was bad enough. Even more awesome was the Findhorn's inundation of the Plain of Forres.

Some 80 miles from source to sea, the Findhorn carries less volume than the Spey, but this volume is pent up in narrow gorges, as at Dulsie, Relugas, and Sluie, while the flood-plain is broader than that of the Spey. So a huge head of water burst over a vast area. Surging through the narrow neck at the Red Craig of Coulternose near Mundole, the torrent swept away the three-arched Bridge of Findhorn, then drowned over 20 square miles under up to five feet of water. From Mundole two miles west of Forres to Findhorn village four miles to the northeast the land was consumed. Forres folk retreated up Cluny Hill as the area north of Moy (Culbin Forest side of the A96) was cut off. 'Nothing could be more strange than to behold a sea of water from whatever window of the house one looked', a witness reported.

A Dr. Brands, looking over the Broom of Moy, could see only a few roofs peeping from the flood. Steadings, farms, beasts and houses were destroyed. Many folk drowned, but more were saved by boatmen risking their lives to reach the stranded. And even amid the catastrophe there was humour. One rescuer, a Sergeant Grant, was offered a second dram to warm him. 'Na, I thank ye, Sir,' he said, eyeing it askance. 'I like it ower weel; an' if I tak it I may forget mysel', an' God kens we need to ha'e a' our wits aboot us the day. But an we get a' the poor fouk safe, I'se no say but I'se get fou.' And some things never change. A man called Monro complained to Lauder: 'Was it na' hard that after a' that we had done, thay idle, weel held-up loons, the Preventives (*Excisemen*) gat a' the praise i' the newspapers, while we poor fisher bodies were never mentioned at a', although the lazy lubbers never pat their noses oot ower the door the hale day.'

Stand above the confluence of Findhorn and Divie to get some idea of the enormity of the torrent that drowned the plain of Forres. As for Lauder, he was so heartbroken by the ruin of his estate that he returned to Edinburgh and never came north again.

95.   From Ardclach to the Altnarie Falls (*Route, Walk, Waterfall*)

We're not done with the Findhorn. Upstream there's Ardclach and Dulsie, also the Falls on the Altnarie Burn near Dulsie. To reach Ardclach with its unusual bell-tower and old kirk by a wide riverbend, from Relugas continue south on the B9007 past Airdrie Mill to Ferness. Turn sharp right north onto the A939 and descend through the wood over the river. Passing a gated track following the west bank south towards Ardclach, climb the brae to the junction with the Ardclach-Dulsie road (960471) and turn left.

Or, a half-mile south of and above Relugas, fork right (992487) and descend over the river to meet the road from Conicavel. As described (**91**), turn left past Coulmony. At the A939, turn left then rapidly right.

Now on the the minor Dulsie road, after a mile turn left (south) by a swampy pool, dead trees jutting from it. From the farmhouse ahead to the right you can (as a sign indicates) get the bell tower key. A half-mile on above the riverbend a private road breaks left under the bell tower on its steep mound above. Park here, by a memorial stone erected (1961) by the Leprosy Mission to the memory of the Rev. Donald Mitchell (b.1792), son of the Ardclach parish minister and Scotland's first missionary to India.

A brief, steep stepped climb leads to the white-harled, rough-slated bell tower with its wide views (955454). The monogram MGB carved over the fire-place refers to its builder, Alexander Brodie of Lethen, and his wife Margaret Grant. An ardent covenanter several times attacked by royalists, Brodie needed this watch tower, which he erected in 1655.

The road zigzags steeply down to the old kirk on its brief flat riverside pas-turage. The mossy kirkyard is still in use but not the kirk, with boarded windows and a sign warning DANGEROUS ROOF NO ADMISSION. Both sides of the river are the ruined stone pillars of a vanished bridge. The banks are too steep for a riverside ramble so, if you'd rather walk to get here, park by the A939 bridge over the river, follow the track above its west bank, climb a path through silver birch to fields at the top of a steep bank, and follow the fenceline south a half-mile past a white cottage, the bell tower visible on its mound above.

From Ardclach continue five miles southwest, keeping left at each junc-tion, to Dulsie Bridge. First, seek out the Altnarie Falls (931435). These, not so easy to find, lie hidden in birch and pinewood just south of the road from Ardclach a few hundred yards before it joins the old military road (**81**) a mile north of Dulsie. The Altnarie (*Allt na Airidh*) runs under the road bare yards before the junction. The woodland path to the falls has vanished, and care is needed. The slope is steep and you come upon them suddenly, from the side. Cascading 80 feet down to a deep, wooded glen opposite a dilapidated view-house with a fine silver fir beside it, these falls were highly regarded in Victorian times. From the foot of the burn where it joins the Findhorn, I'm told a fisherman's path leads south to Dulsie Bridge, *en route* offering a fine view of Glenferness House (1837), built high above the river in the Greek style.

96.   Dulsie Bridge: the Findhorn and Tributaries *(Visit, Walk)*

'What on earth can exceed in beauty the landscape comprising the old bridge of Dulsie', wrote Charles St John, 'spanning with its lofty arch the deep dark pool, shut in by grey and fantastic rocks, surmounted by the greatest of greenswards, with clumps of ancient weeping birches, backed by the dark pine-trees.'

A single span (subsidiary arch on the north side) over the granite river-gorge, Dulsie Bridge was built in 1764 to carry the military road from Perth to Fort George. With parking on the south side, a swing gate leads to a viewpoint upriver. You're asked not to throw stones (anglers below), and an information board tells how the 1829 flood waters rose 40 feet to within three feet of the key-stone of the main arch; also that Dulsie (*Dulfhasaidh*) means 'meadow of the stance'. Meaning what? An ancient battle?

The region upriver is impressive. Waterfalls on the Leonach and Rhilean tributaries presage their confluence under steep bare moorland scarps (919395). North-running, their combined stream courses a lovely secluded glen of fey silver birch to join the Findhorn in a grand wide wooded glen (921406) a mile southwest of Dulsie. However, a notice on the gate of the track to Dulsie Cottage just south of the bridge prohibits 'unauthorised persons'. By it, another warns that 'Your dog could be shot if found amongst sheep' - and there *are* a lot of sheep about.

Continuing south on the road past the entry to Dunearn Farm, on the right is a wooded slope, atop it an old fort (thus *dun-earn*, 'river-fort'). Past Dunearn the road climbs to a sharp bend (936405). Here a track departs southwest over rough pasture to the rabbit-rich ruin of Lynemore steading (925399). A half-mile southeast of the Leonach-Rhilean confluence under a fine fall on the Leonach, the moorland track continues south above the Leonach, soon passing impressive cascades plunging from the high bare moor through shattered rock.

Soon the Leonach can be crossed without getting your feet wet. A trek north over the bare land leads to the shallow treeless glen of the Rhilean Burn. This too can be crossed dryshod, leading up over more bare moor (fine views every way), to the Findhorn at Banchor. Here a steep, wooded descent leads to a footbridge (913405) over the river, beyond it a track breaking left a half-mile to the Drynachan-Dulsie back-road. This completes the circuit via a longish mile or so back via Dulsie Bridge to the Lynemore track above Dunearn steading. The footbridge is private, and not necessarily open.

The road south from Dulsie Bridge soon intersects the B9007 (947403) at a minor crossroads. The moorland track continuing east past the bare low brow of the Hill of Aitnoch reaches the A939 due north of Lochindorb. But here we turn right on the B9007 into the bare wilderness north of Carrbridge. After three miles, watch for a tiny road on the left (950350).

Signposted to Lochindorb, this is our penultimate visit. It involves hiring a boat and rowing to a ruined castle with a dreich reputation..

97.   Lochindorb Castle: Rowing to Meet the Wolf *(Island Castle Visit)*

Unless you like rowing into wind, choose a calm day for this visit. Other than the route described above, Lochindorb is reached by driving south from Nairn (A939) or Forres (A940). Soon after these roads meet at Dava, amid bare land (004383) by a phone-box but little else, a minor road breaks west two miles over heather moor to a bleak glacial trench where the Moray-Nairn (and thus Grampian-Highland) boundary runs through this shallow, allegedly kelpie-haunted 'Loch of the Little Fishes'.

The beauty here is that of desolation. There are few trees. Pine and fir screen the Lodge on the southeast side, a Mohican fringe of forestry crowns rocky Craig Tiribeg (486m) to the east, great old ash trees sprout amid the ruin of the 13th-century castle on its maybe-artificial isle 300 yards off the east shore. Other than Lodge and Castle the only sign of human habitation, ancient or modern, is the rust-red roof of the byre at Terriemore Farm, deserted amid scant pasturage under the dark low Hill of Aitnoch to the north.

Yet the castle's solid outer curtain walls still fire the imagination - thus Maurice Walsh's romantic novel, 'The Key Above the Door' and, a century earlier, Thomas Dick Lauder's 'The Wolfe of Badenoch' (1827). Built by the Comyns, occupied by Edward I in 1303 and later by the Wolf of Badenoch, in 1455 it was razed by the Thane of Cawdor **(79)**.

From the A940 the road passes the castle before, by a forest fringe, a right turn leads down a rough drive to Lochindorb Lodge (355970). Or, from the B9007, you reach this turn to the Lodge before passing the castle. Having already rung (01309-651270) to book the boat, now all you have to do now is row 1200 yards north to the castle.

'The depth goes from about fifty feet to just two or three', the estate under-keeper may warn you, pointing out choppy white-capped black water. 'You'll probably ground and have to push off at least twice.' And you may also find, as a friend and I did one brisk May day, that a stiff breeze holds you back. It took us 45 minutes to round the isle and dock at a tiny inlet on the north side, under a wide gap torn through the twenty-foot-high wall.

Inside, the original Comyn buildings are gone, leaving an uneven grassy

quadrangle. On the east side huge ash trees sprout between an inner wall and its outer neighbour. By the water-gate (its iron yett removed to Cawdor in 1455) the stonework is pitted, as if by hostile fire. A 1993 archaeological survey found five stone balls in the loch 25-30 metres offshore, probably slung by a trebuchet (siege-engine) used by Sir Andrew Murray during his 1335 assault. A submerged ridge this east side suggesting a causeway to the shore is natural, yet the isle was built up or developed to support the walls. Masonry drowned off the north side may be from a harbour, or the walls of an earlier fortress pillaged to build the 13th-century castle.

Oddly, for a place so haunting from the shore, it held no morbid presence. Yet it was a May afternoon, white clouds scurrying above. I'd not want to visit on a wild November night with the banshee in the blast...nor meet the Wolf of Badenoch in a bad mood.

98. The Wolf of Badenoch *(History)*

Upper Strathspey is easily flooded, and so *Badenoch*, 'the drowned place'. And by 1390, with Scotland 'nocht governit' and in chaos, Alexander Stewart, fourth son of King Robert II, had become notorious as the 'Wolf of Badenoch', lordly predator of the north.

Born *c*.1343 to Robert's first wife Elizabeth, this ruthless man seized titles, property and power as he could. He had every opportunity. His father had been a golden youth yet, when crowned in 1371 aged 54, slack-witted Robert had 'bleared' red eyes, and was widely reckoned as past it. Granting 'our dearest son...our whole lands of Badennach...with the castle of Lochyndorbe...', by 1374 he'd made Alexander Earl of Buchan, King's lieutenant from 'Moray to the Pentland Frith [sic], and within the whole county of Inverness'. So the Wolf did as he pleased. Made Earl of Ross in 1383 by his marriage to Euphemia, Countess of Ross (**67**), he soon abandoned her for a mistress, Mariott Athyn, who bore his five sons.

In 1384 admitting his incompetence, Robert incompetently gave power to John, Earl of Carrick. Though kicked silly by a horse in 1388, in 1390 John became king, calling himself Robert III, so invoking the name of the Bruce, denying the ill luck of the name 'John', and sidestepping the Balliol claim by calling himself neither John I nor John II. Derided as 'John Faranyeir' ('Yesterday's John'), he told his wife Annabella Drummond he desired burial in a dunghill under the epitaph: 'Here lies the worst of kings and the most miserable of men.' Declared unfit to rule even before his coronation, his brother Robert Earl of Fife became Governor of the Realm. The royal finances and laws of the realm soon collapsed into vicious farce, as epitomised by the Wolf's anarchic adventures.

These led from dispute with Bishop Burr of Moray over Alexander's claim to Church lands by Kingussie. When in February 1390 Burr proposed switching protection payments from Alexander to the Sheriff of Inverness, the Wolf was outraged. 'Hand over the land!' he demanded. Burr replied by excommunicating him for abandoning his wife.

Thus provoked, in May and June of 1390 with his 'wild, wikkid heilandmen' the Wolf roared forth from Lochindorb to torch church properties in Forres, then Pluscarden Abbey and Elgin Cathedral (the 'Lanthorn of the North'). Mostly he attacked only the church, not the common folk, many of whom viewed churchmen as even worse than the Wolf. Thoroughly cowed and in hiding at Spynie Palace near Elgin, Burr wrote Robert III a pathetic letter of complaint. In time the Wolf did formal penance - a matter of words - and when he died was royally buried at Dunkeld Cathedral.

The lesson? Crime pays, if you're of royal birth and live in medieval Scotland.

99.   Carrbridge: The Dulnain to Inverlaidnan *(Walk)*

East of Lochindorb the A940 leads south over the moor to Grantown-on-Spey, established by the 'Good Sir James', founder of Milton and Lewiston (**24**). West of Lochindorb, the B9007 runs south through the awful barrens to the A938 two miles east of Carrbridge, start of our last, circular walk - west above the River Dulnain past Sluggan to Inverlaidnan, than back via the south bank.

Leaving the B9007 to turn west to Carrbridge you're now in Badenoch. This is another land. Everything looks and feels different on the wooded run-in to Carrbridge past numerous tourist accomodations. By a big hotel at the entry to the village a left turn (B9153) onto the main street crosses the Dulnain close to the steeply humpbacked span that gives Carrbridge its name - see opposite. Costing £100 when built in 1717, this high arch lost its parapets during 1829's Muckle Spate (**94**). Just beyond it is the Landmark Visitor Centre (01463-841613) with its treetop walks, restaurant, gift-shop, and so on.

The walk begins a half-mile west of the village. Continue on the A938 almost to the 30-mile limit. By a minor road on the left signposted Dalrachney 1^1/$_2$, park in the layby. Start along the Dalrachney road above rough riverside pasture and a footbridge (the return route) past advertised hostels. Under a bridge carrying the railway this track leads up to the A9, the only distraction on the walk. Fortunately, the view either way is clear.

Cross the A9 with care. Opposite is a surfaced road (gate removed) to Lynphail. This passes a steading then bends north over a burn. A wooden foot-bridge leads to a clear green track west through rough pasture, north of the river. Climbing the edge of a heather moor where dead trees above make spooky shapes, the track approaches forestry. The crossing over a burn leads to a high stile over a deer-fence. The heathery, sandy track now climbs steadily through thick forestry. From a shallow top it declines through more open woodland, bare Monadhliath hilltops now visible to the west.

At a fork, leave the main track (right) and cut left down the forested slope towards the river, visible below through the trees. Past a deer-fence the muddy track reaches a ruin just north of the derelict Sluggan Bridge (869221), a single stone arch almost as fine as the Carr Bridge itself. Gated off, this was once part of yet another Wade military road (**15**).

From here the main track breaks northwest into forestry. Instead, follow the riverbank west of the bridge over rough pasture under juniper bushes and crags on the east side of the river. Where the river bends, climb the open heather slope into a lovely wooded area above the shingled, sparsely-wooded flood-plain. Find your own way (the going is easy) along this high bank with its regenerating nat-ural woodland and grassy slopes to a boggy gully across your path. Here turn south to a fenceline then, under electricity pylons by a ditch, pick your way on through a wooden gate past a ruin to the track by Inverlaidnan (862215).

Take this track south over a burn and the broad flood-plain to a wooden bridge over the Dulnain, sandy wooded scarps on the south side. By the water is a good place to stop and eat or spend some time contemplating nature and life.

Soon (865210) this track meets a minor road west from Carrbridge to Dalnahaitnach. Turn left, north, back towards Carrbridge. A moorland track to the left a few yards up may entice but, after a few yards, I returned to the road.

With wide views west from the heather heath, after a mile it enters forestry. Here, via a deer-fence and stile, the old Wade military track southeast from Sluggan Bridge may be followed south for most of a mile, before another track turns northeast, back to the road.

Past Féith Mhor Country House and a high-stiled junction with the return track from the Wade road forestry loop, this road runs east through high fresh open land. With the A9 visible ahead, a gypsy-style caravan home in the last woodland leads past a large sawmill to the Carrbridge 30-mile limit.

Under the A9 and past the turn-off right to the railway station, on the left Urquhart's Brae leads, via a pebbly path, downhill right past a white-harled house and on between fences under a wood to the Ellan footbridge - built by the Gurkhas in 1992 - over the Dulnain river.

On the north bank, turn left up a path some 20 yards to a stile over a barbed-wire fence. Climb the bank and wriggle under (or tear your trousers crossing) another barbed-wire fence, and so return, right, a few hundred yards back to where you parked.

And that's it. Journey's end.

100. Round-up *(Epitaph)*

The purpose of this final chapter is simply to get to 100, right? What can I say?
From this last walk you can return in two short miles to the A9, and so back past
Tomatin and Moy, and all the places visited at the start of this tour, to Inverness.
End in beginning.

Or you might take a different direction altogether. You might go east to
Grantown then up Speyside to Moray one side and Banff the other, two wholly
different territories, with Buchan to the east, all as described in another tour. Or
from Grantown you might head east via Tomintoul over the Lecht to Braemar.
You might head south past Aviemore and up over the Drumochter Pass into
Perthshire, then west past Schiehallion, the lovely 'Fairy Hill of the
Caledonians', into another land altogether. There are so many ways to go, and
so many places in Scotland to explore.

It's strange, to end one journey knowing it's only the start of another.
Stranger still, nowhere have we been much more than 30 miles from Inverness,
yet we've travelled centuries.

I hope you've enjoyed it. I have. *Slainte.* Goodbye for now.

The Inner Moray Firth from Chanonry Point

Glossary of common place-name prefixes and suffixes

Key to abbreviations: B = Brythonic/Brittonic; E = English (OE = Old English); G = Gaelic; L = Latin; N = (old) Norse; S = Scots

Aber	Brittonic/Welsh	'meeting of waters'; i.e., 'estuary' (see *inver*) or 'confluence'.
Ach	Gaelic *achadh*	'field'
All	Early Irish *all*	'rock'
Allt	Gaelic *allt*	'stream'
Ard	Gaelic *aird*	'height', 'high place', 'promontory'
Auchter	Gaelic *uachdair*	'upper part of', 'high ground'
Bal	Gaelic *baile* *(L., ballium)*	'town', 'village', 'enclosure'
Barr	Gaelic *barr*	'crest', 'height', 'top of'
Beg	Gaelic *beag*	'small', 'little'
Ben	Gaelic *beinn*	'mountain', 'horn'
Blair	Gaelic *blar*	'battlefield', 'cleared ground'
By, Bie	Norse *byr*	'farm', 'hamlet'
Cam	Gaelic *camas*	'bay', 'bend', 'crooked'
Cardine	Brittonic *cardden*	'copse, 'thicket'
Corrie	Gaelic *coire*	'hollow', cup-shaped depression
Dale	English *dale; (dalr:N; dol:B; dail:G)*	'valley', 'field', 'haugh'
Dour	Gaelic *dobhar; (dwr:B)*	'water'
Drum	Gaelic *druim*	'back', 'spine', 'ridge'
Dun	Gaelic *dun*	'fortress', 'castle', 'hill', 'mound'
Erin	Gaelic *Eireann*	'of Ireland'
Ey	Norse *Ey*	'island'
Firth	Norse *fjordr (art;G)*	'sea-estuary'
Fo	Gaelic	'under'
Fort	English	'fort'
Gart	*gardr (N); garth (B); garradh (G); garden (E)*	'garden', 'enclosure', 'yard'
Glas	Gaelic; Brittonic	'grey' or 'green' (G); or 'water' (B)
Glen	Gaelic *gleann*	Scots Highland usage only
Hope	Norse *hop*	'bay', 'refuge', 'valley'
Inch	Gaelic *innis*	'island', 'meadows by a river', 'field'
Inver	Gaelic *inbhir* (see *aber*)	'river estuary'; communities later

		built there: Inverness etc.
Kil	Gaelic *ceall, cill*	'monastic cell', 'church'; but all 'kil' prefixes may vary in meaning
Kin	Gaelic *ceann*	'head'
Kirk	Scots *(kil:G; kirkju:N)*	'church'
Knock	Gaelic *cnoc*	'round hillock'
Kyle	Gaelic *caol*	'slender', 'thin, 'sea-strait'
Lanark	Brittonic *llanerch*	'glade', 'clearing'
Linn	Gaelic *linn;* Brit. *llyn*	(1) 'pool', (2) 'lake'
Loch	Gaelic *loch*	'loch', also sometimes 'black'
Long	Gaelic *long*	'ship' (Eng. *long* = Scots *lang*)
May	Gaelic *magh; moigh*	'field', 'plain'
Monadh	Gaelic *monadh*	'moorland', 'flat-topped ridge'
More	Gaelic *mor*	'great', 'big'
Ness	(1) *naes (OE);* (2) *nes (N)*	'point', 'headland' (L. *nasus*, 'nose')
Ochil	Brittonic *uchel*	'high'
Pit	Continental Celtic *petia*	'part', 'share', 'piece' (?)
Rath	Gaelic *rath*	'fort'
Shee	Gaelic *sithe, sidhe*	'fairies', 'fairy hills'
Shieling	Norse *skali*	'hut' (usually on high pasture)
Ster	Norse *bolstadr*	'farm', 'stead', 'steading'
Tigh	Gaelic *tigh*	'house'
Tobar	Gaelic *tobar*	'well', 'source'
Tom	Gaelic *tom*	'conical hillock'
Ton	English *ton*	'homestead'
Tor	Brittonic (Cornish) *tor*	'hill'
Tref	Brittonic *tref*	'settlement', 'village', 'homestead'
Tulloch	Gaelic *tulach*	'eminence', 'ridge', 'knoll'
Way	Norse *vagr,* also *voe*	'bay'
Wick	(1) Norse *vik*	'bay', 'creek'
	(2) Anglo-Saxon *wic*	'settlement', 'camp', 'farm'

Bibliography

Some of the books and other publications I have plundered or which you may find useful in following up topics mentioned in this itinerary are as follows (some out of print or hard to find):

Anon., *Miscellanea Scotica*, John Willis & Co., Glasgow 1820 (texts on second sight: see **53**)

Bord, Janet & Colin, *Alien Animals*, Panther Books, London 1985
- *Mysterious Britain*, Paladin, London 1974
- *Sacred Waters*, Paladin, London 1986

Clayton, Peter, *Guide to the Archaeological Sites of Britain*, B T Batsford, London 1985

Dorward, David, *Scotland's Place-Names*, William Blackwood, Edinburgh 1979

Ives, Edward D, *The Bonny Earl of Murray: the Man, the Murder, the Ballad*, Tuckwell Press Ltd., East Linton 1997

Jackson, Kenneth, *The Symbol Stones of Scotland*, Orkney Press, Kirkwall 1984

Jarvie, Gordon (ed.), *Scottish Folk and Fairy Tales*, Penguin, London 1997

Lenman, Bruce, *The Jacobite Clans of the Great Glen: 1650-1784*, Scottish Cultural Press, Aberdeen 1995 (1984)

Lockhart, J G, *Curses, Lucks & Talismans*, Geoffrey Bles, London 1938

Lynch, Michael, *Scotland: A New History*, Pimlico, London 1992

Mackie, J D, *A History of Scotland*, Penguin Books, London 1964

Maclean, Loraine, *Discovering Inverness-shire*, John Donald, Edinburgh 1988

Mackenzie, Alexander, *The Prophecies of the Brahan Seer*, Constable, London 1977 (1877)

Meldrum, Edward, *From the Nairn to Loch Ness*, Highland Herald, Inverness 1973
- *From Loch Ness to the Aird*, Highland Herald, Inverness 1978
- *The Black Isle*, John G Eccles Printers Ltd., Inverness 1979

Newton, Norman. *The Life and Times of Inverness*, John Donald, Edinburgh 1996

Prebble, John, *Culloden*, Penguin, London 1967
- *The Highland Clearances*, Penguin, London 1969

Ritchie, Anna, *Picts*, HMSO, London 1989

Sellar, W D H (ed.), *Moray: Province and People*, Scottish Society for Northern Studies, Edinburgh 1993

Simpson, Eric, *Discovering Banff Moray and Nairn*, John Donald, Edinburgh 1992

Spence, Lewis, *Magic Arts in Celtic Britain*, Aquarian Press, London 1970 (1946)

Sutherland, Elizabeth, *Ravens and Black Rain,* Corgi, London 1987

Towill, Edwin Sprott, *The Saints of Scotland*, Saint Andrew Press, Edinburgh 1983

Wightman, Andy, *Who Owns Scotland*, Canongate Books, Edinburgh 1996

Willis, Douglas, *Discovering the Black Isle*, John Donald 1989

For information on obtaining Forest Enterprise pamphlets detailing forest walks phone (Fort Augustus) 01320-366322; (Inverness) 01463-791575; or call at Forest Enterprise, 21 Church Street, Inverness - near the Tourist Information Centre at Castle Wynd (01463-234353).